The Silk Road

RECENT TITLES IN

OXFORD STUDIES IN CULTURE AND POLITICS
Clifford Bob and James M. Jasper, General Editors

The Silk Road

Connecting Histories and Futures

TIM WINTER

OXFORD

UNIVERSITY PRESS

OXFORD
UNIVERSITY PRESS

Oxford University Press is a department of the University of Oxford. It furthers
the University's objective of excellence in research, scholarship, and education
by publishing worldwide. Oxford is a registered trade mark of Oxford University
Press in the UK and certain other countries.

Published in the United States of America by Oxford University Press
198 Madison Avenue, New York, NY 10016, United States of America.

Library of Congress Cataloging-in-Publication Data
Names: Winter, Tim, 1971– author.
Title: The Silk Road : connecting histories and futures / Tim Winter.
Other titles: Connecting histories and futures
Description: New York, NY : Oxford University Press, [2022] |
Series: Oxford studies in culture and politics | Includes bibliographical references and index.
Identifiers: LCCN 2021044585 (print) | LCCN 2021044586 (ebook) |
ISBN 9780197605066 (pb) | ISBN 9780197605059 (hb) | ISBN 9780197605080 (epub)
Subjects: LCSH: Silk Road—Civilization. | Asia, Central—Relations. |
China—Relations. | Geopolitics—Asia, Central—History. | Yi dai yi lu (Initiative : China)
Classification: LCC DS329.4 .W56 2022 (print) | LCC DS329.4 (ebook) |
DDC 958—dc23/eng/20211027
LC record available at https://lccn.loc.gov/2021044585
LC ebook record available at https://lccn.loc.gov/2021044586

DOI: 10.1093/oso/9780197605059.001.0001

1 3 5 7 9 8 6 4 2

Paperback printed by Marquis, Canada
Hardback printed by Bridgeport National Bindery, Inc., United States of America

Contents

PART FOUR. GEOPOLITICS

PART FIVE. CONCLUSION

Illustrations

Preface

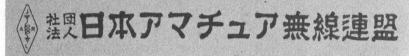

QTH：〒630 奈良市水門町 100 番地シルクロード博春日野会場内

8J3SLK OPENED FOR SILK ROAD EXPO '88, NARA
The Occidental and Oriental cultures met and flourished in the
Japanese Capital City of Nara in the 8th Century. The Asian Highway
along which they were carried was called the "SILK ROAD." Please
come and join us in "SILK ROAD EXPO '88, NARA" and discover
Romance and Wisdom in the ancient arts exhibited and event shows
presented by the Silk-Road countries. You can also enjoy Friendship
with members of JARL by 8J3SLK (open April 24 - October 23).

社団法人日本アマチュア無線連盟

Figure 0.1 Excerpt from press pass issued for Nara Silk Road Exposition, 1988.
Credit Line: Photo by Author.

The above image comes from a media pass to the 1988 *The Grand Exhibition of Silk Road Civilizations* held in the city of Nara. Drawn from the archives of Silk Road memorabilia, the pass tells us something about an important juncture in "Silk Road" history. The exhibition took place at a moment when international interest in the concept was gathering momentum. Its organizers were evidently aware that the term should be treated with care and caution and thus judiciously added quotation marks to qualify its usage. In what might seem to be an insignificant gesture, scare quotes signal to a reader the need to hold up a term for inspection. They attempt to withhold familiarity and its propensity to conceal any semantic ambiguities and inaccuracies that may be lurking below.

In the three decades since the exhibition, the term has increasingly naturalized such that grammatical qualifiers are seemingly no longer required. Indeed, despite widespread recognition that the Silk Road is a nineteenth-century invention, we have not seen a sustained debate about its merits and problems as a framework for understanding complex historical events spanning continents and centuries. Likewise, all too often Silk Road discourses present regions, cultures, and peoples in contrived and romanticized ways, and yet the concept has rarely been subject to the types of scrutiny familiar to postcolonial scholarship.

My intention with this book, then, is to ask the reader to re-insert those inverted commas, albeit metaphorically. As a small convention of punctuation that carries significant analytical weight, they suggest the need to retain a certain disposition of analysis and questioning. My aim is to make the Silk Road at once both strange and more familiar, to both unsettle an idea that is too readily taken for granted and, simultaneously, argue for greater analytical precision in how it is used and discussed. The book calls attention to the importance of critically interrogating the means by which, and to what ends, the term is put into circulation. As I have endeavored to show, the Silk Road has become far more than merely a narrative of history. Today it is about envisaging and building futures on a grand scale. By implication, many more chapters will still need to be written, as usage of the term continues to proliferate.

In no way, then, does the book proclaim to be definitive, not least in accounting for the ways in which Silk Road discourses evolved and stabilized over the course of the twentieth century in different contexts. Future publications will furnish greater detail about its popularization in China, Italy, and Iran or across different domains of policy. My own PhDs will show why Silk Road discourses lie at the heart of new forms of cultural infrastructure across Asia, the illicit trafficking of objects recovered from the seabed, and forms of digital power that involve setting global standards and new norms of digital governance. The chapters that follow are thus offered in part as primers for a more expansive mode of interdisciplinary enquiry. To that end, the concluding chapter includes reflections on some potential pathways for a field of Silk Road studies.

I extend my thanks and gratitude to the team at Oxford University Press and in particular to Koperundevi Pugazhenthi, Emily Mackenzie Benitez, and James Cook for their help in shepherding the text through reviews and production. Special thanks go to James Jasper for his persistence and generosity in seeing the book through. Writing on China today exposes you to politicized peer reviews, and in that regard, I very much appreciate the time spent by those who offered generous and critically productive reviews of the manuscript at different points. I would also like to thank those who have offered feedback on drafts along the way. The book is one of the endeavors made possible by a Future Fellowship awarded by the Australian Research

Council (FT170100084). Thanks and love go to my mum for understanding it's a work that carries on. Once again, extra special thanks go to Toyah Horman for her patience, resilience, and assistance. It's been a long and bumpy road, but I hope the oases we have discovered along the way have made it all worthwhile. Throughout the book, the citation of East Asian names follows the convention of family name first, except for those who predominantly publish in the West.

Parts of the book were written during lockdowns and border closers. Both the Silk Road and ideas about internationalism seemed to be part of a world that was disappearing from view in the turbulent and confusing times of a pandemic. Writing at a time defined by immense suffering and disconnection seemed, in equal measure, to both contribute to and hold at bay the gloom of meaningless activity. Like most, it is a book marked by personal upheaval. But lost in connectivity, I discovered true connection. That one grain of sand, from across the desert.

The Silk Road

The Morning Bulletin, Rockhampton, Australia
Saturday, 15 May 1943[1]

Almost as much romance attached in ancient days to the caravan routes as to the driblets of trade and tidings from distant lands and of different people which flowed along them. As caravans wind through Biblical history, so did the routes pass from inhabited regions into the wild uninhabited wastes and so by the merest threads of paths to other worlds. Only luxury goods could bear the cost of such transport, and so the desert and mountain robber added more than a spice of danger to the undertaking and went as richly caparisoned as any merchant.

Not all of those caravan routes have been closed by man's conquest of the air. Until recently caravans dived from Abyssinia into the heart of Africa, returning months later with ivory and oasis products. The caravan routes between Tripoli and Central Africa are now dotted with aerodromes for the accommodation of Allied bombers on their way north to the re-conquest of Europe, while Allied engineers are poring over maps and blue prints of the old Silk Road which has for many centuries connected China and Russia.

To early western eyes the Silk Road appeared literally to be the golden window of the east. Travellers—no more truthful then than now—saw to it that their adventures along this romantic route lost nothing in the telling, though silk required no tale-spinner to ensure it a welcome. It was one of the most highly prized products of distant China to reach Rome, and its fame spread to the road along which it was carried. Marco Polo passed along it in 1272 on his way to proud Cathay, and military motor caravans are now carrying war material which passes from Krasnovodsk on the Caspian Sea, by rail to Bukhara, Taskent and Alma Ata on the Turkman—Siberian railway, thence 600 miles by good road to Urumchi, thence 1000 miles by the Silk Road to Lanchow and so to Chungking. So it is that Sinkiang, or Chinese Turkestan, has come into highly strategic importance.

The mountains and deserts and the fiercely reclusive people have long been the main characteristics of Sinkiang and Tibet, and nobody bothered much about them until the Japanese invasion of Burma in April, 1942, closed the Burma Road, and so severed China's last considerable link with the outside world. That event sent roadmakers and surveyors into the fastnesses of Tibet to look into the matter of developing some of the old caravan routes between there and China. They seem not to have had much success, but those who worked from the tongue of plateau in eastern Assam may have had better fortune. Sadiya which is the capital of this remote corner is only 700 air miles from Chungking, is connected with the Indian railway system, and is in comfortable proximity to a fairly good supply. The country between Chungking and Sadiya is mostly on end, but that is not likely to trouble carrier planes which are mustering on the Assam plateau.

Expecting for such transport developments as may be proceeding under the dark cloak of military secrecy, it would appear that Sinkiang still provides the best back door through which China may have access with the west, and that because it is traversed by the ancient Silk Road along which for so many centuries have passed caravans of hundreds of beasts carrying the treasures of China to an ever-eager western world. Generations of nomadic Tartars, Mongols and Siberians dwellers of Sinkiang valleys and uplands have watched, since long before the Christian era, while strings of camels and mules, led by an unladen ass for luck, wound their way westward along the way that was little more than a hoof pad. The Silk Road is throbbing now where for centuries it drowsed, the honk of motor horns has replaced the tinkle of caravan bells, the stream of death dealing machines from Soviet factories is now flowing east at 30 miles per hour, where gossamer silk for Roman beauties drifted West at 20 miles per day. The delicate fibre of luxury has become a steel ribbon of security for China, whose civilisation is older than the Silk Road, against the forces of barbarism which would destroy her.

1

Introduction

Imagine the Silk Road.

My guess is that you're picturing a line of camels striding across the desert, perhaps silhouetted between a sweeping sand dune and setting sun. Alternatively, might it be a bustling market scene where carpets, jewelry, exotic animals, or bundles of silk are being bought and sold? Perhaps that manuscript, the ceramic bowl, or seated Buddha that you saw at the museum comes to mind? Or that documentary host, waving her arms in front of a turquoise mosque, excitedly depicting the "epic history" of trade routes connecting Rome and Xi'an and the new high-speed rail lines that China is building across Central Asia? It seems as though we have all grown up with a vague idea of what the Silk Road was: a northern and southern route or was it a whole network of roads straddling Europe and Asia? But if the Silk Road has become ubiquitous, a history familiar to all, why would Susan Whitfield—an author who has published extensively on the topic over several decades—open her 2019 volume with the somewhat curious assertion that "there was no 'Silk Road'" and that it is a "modern label in widespread use only since the late 20th century and used since then to refer to trade and interaction across Afro-Eurasia from roughly 200 BCE to 1400 CE"?[1]

While recent research suggests that the term was coined by the German geographer Carl Ritter in 1838, it is widely attributed to Ferdinand von Richthofen, a geologist and baron, who, on returning from a surveying trip to China in the early 1870s, referred to a road of silk (*Seidenstraße*) to describe trade routes heading westward from China during the Han Empire (206 BCE–220 CE).[2] In the late nineteenth century, scholars across Europe were only beginning to piece together the complexities of Asia's history, and by combining Chinese and European sources, Richthofen captured a tiny fragment of a much larger story of premodern trade, exchange, and regional empires. In his 1877 book *China*, he described two routes running either side of the Taklamakan Desert and evidence of precious commodities such as silk reaching the markets of the Roman Empire.[3] Given this, we might ask, then, by which criteria is the Silk Road said to have lasted until 1400? Or why is it

The Silk Road. Tim Winter, Oxford University Press. © Oxford University Press 2022.
DOI: 10.1093/oso/9780197605059.003.0001

that scholars in India regard it not as a story of trade between East and West but as the history of Buddhism spreading northward to China? And if it is a story of land routes, what exactly is the Maritime Silk Road, and why did it gain popularity at the end of the Cold War?

In answering such questions, this book challenges the idea that the Silk Road is a "modern label" that has been merely attached to history, stuck on to identify events and places that were connected through various means. Instead, I show how it *produces* history in certain ways. China's Belt and Road Initiative—framed as the "revival" of the Silk Roads for the twenty-first century—has led to a dramatic increase in interest in the concept and the idea of geographies of connection "old" and "new." The vast majority of articles and books that talk about the Silk Road in historical terms do so in normative ways, uncritically invoking it to frame accounts about the spread of religions, ideas, or language or the story of commodities traded over great distances. For a term that is widely cited in both academia and popular culture, few step back to challenge its validity or ask questions about the politics of its aura. This book heads in such directions, revealing how and why the Silk Road has become so popular around the world and why that matters.

In contrast to other books, this one interrogates the concept itself in two distinct ways: first, by critically reflecting on its merits and problems as a narrative of history; and second, by offering a biography of the term that traces how it has evolved and circulated in the past century and a half as a domain of scholarship, popular culture, government and international policy, branding and marketing as well as a tool for future-making, diplomacy, peace, and cultural governance.

Questions of History

To set the scene for discussing this fabled idea, in this opening chapter I first want to consider the tricky question of the Silk Road's status as a depiction of history. We might begin by asking what it illuminates and represents from the past and whether it is a useful concept for the historian, professional or otherwise, or whether we are best moving to the other end of the spectrum and viewing it as a phantasmatic invention, a creation of nostalgia for a world that never existed. To approach this question, we first need to consider some of the factors that influence how events from the past come to be collated, interpreted, described, and sanctioned as history. In the field of historiography, much has been written about the rise of narrative. It seems common sense to suggest that events are narrated, but closer inspection reveals the complex, and often unlikely, processes by which narratives emerge and retain their currency over time. Narratives about the past stabilize at particular moments and often form at the intersections between popular culture, political events, material worlds, and expert commentary. All too often it is the present that influences how the past is interpreted. The events of 9/11 offer a case in point. In 2008, the UCLA academic Anthony Pagden published *Worlds at War*. The book traced a "deep history" of a freedom-loving, law-abiding, and civilized West, embattled with an East depicted as having cultural and political proclivities toward enslavement and tyranny. Such Eastern "characteristics," he argued, were said to predate the birth of Islam, and by offering a deep history of East and West stretching back 2500 years, Pagden contrived the battle between the Greek city-states and Persians in 480 BCE into a story of freedom versus tyranny. Establishing these misleading prototypical categories involved omitting details about the capturing of slaves by the Greeks during their conquests and their own subsequent enslavement by Rome. Clearly, Pagden's account was intended to align with the narrative of the moment. In so doing, he connected 9/11 to popular culture depictions of the Battle of Thermopylae. Portrayed as an "against all odds" defense of Western civilization, the battle, along with Sparta, have been source material for numerous films, computer games, historical novels, and television series. The 2007 film *300*, for example, pushed the tropes and clichés of East versus West to the point of provoking accusations of racism and Iranophobia. The movie drew its narrative from the 1998 comic book series written by Frank Miller, which, in turn, was inspired by the 1962 film *The 300 Spartans*.

Such an example is a reminder that narratives of history not only shift in accordance with the hopes and anxieties, values and events of the present, but also rework and reassemble the past in ways that give comfort, promise to reclaim order from chaos and fragmentation, and help legitimize the actions of those who seek to shape the present and thus the future in certain ways. Through the work of Eric Hobsbawm and others, we now better appreciate how "history" can act as the handmaiden to the political project of forging collective identities. Hobsbawm reminds us that the nation is an artifact of modernity, "a very recent newcomer in human history, and the product of particular, and inevitably localized or regional, historical conjunctures."[4] But as nations sought to cement their "place" in history and in the modern world, they searched for foundational pasts, forging narratives that proclaimed continuity, cultural, ethnic, religious, or territorial—a history to be proud of and one that must be defended when placed under threat. This has created widely held misconceptions that nations stretch back into history and hold pasts that merely require the historian to discover and recover. Hobsbawm and others have shown us the fallacy of such a world view, revealing how pasts come to be reconstructed and traditions invented as part of the social engineering of nationalism in the constitution of nations. As he reminds us, "nations do not make states and nationalisms but the other way round."[5] And here, material worlds and arcs of continuity matter. Stories come to be built around them.[6]

Such insights have a bearing on how we need to think about the Silk Road. This book traces its emergence as a geocultural narrative of the past built around the themes of mobility, connection, and exchange. It will be argued that it has become an important narrative for and of internationalism. Today the Silk Road is known around the world as a depiction of trade routes between the East and the West, of religious exchanges across Asia, and of the diffusion of languages, technologies, and ideas. As we will see, distinct visual and material cultures have emerged and consolidated around these, and the book illustrates why its popularity stems in part from its elasticity and capacity to absorb different regions and themes. I also address the question of why, and at what point, its geographies and timelines proliferate by examining how scholars working across countries and disciplines toil, debate, and congregate over Silk Road pasts, adding new themes, locations, and forms of connection. Crucially, however, it will also become apparent that Richtofen's original use of the term has been transformed by and through popular culture and by various institutional policies across multiple countries. The Silk Road is thus a quintessentially modern concept, one that projects the concerns, anxieties, and ambitions of the contemporary onto the past.

It will be argued that over time those key narrative motifs of mobility, connection, and exchange have come to be infused with ideas of peace, harmony, mutual respect, and the sense that a better world emerges from the interaction and exchange of cultures. The Silk Road roots these ideals in a deeper past, giving substance to a world view that has been threatened by the nationalism and conflict of modern times. In the same way that nations and nationalist movements have sought legitimacy through history, the Silk Road has provided internationalism with its own deep past, an antiquity that is constructed and reconstructed around the ideals of cosmopolitanism, tolerance, and intercultural dialogue. Drawing on different forms of material culture, it weaves together events separated by millennia and places divided by continents into a singular, beguiling account of the past. The evidence of a "circulatory system of Eurasian development [spanning] over 2000 years," as Andre Gunder Frank puts it, is irrefutable.[7] But the Silk Road exemplifies how narrative can triumph over geography and history.[8] It has its iconic heroes, those who are celebrated as grand adventurers and embody the ethos of cosmopolitanism. Accordingly, a number of the chapters take up Silk Road internationalism as a response to the destructive consequences of modern nationalism and the political and cultural instabilities in the international system since World War II. This is not to say, of course, that Silk Road discourses are free of nationalistic agendas. Indeed, in accounting for such entanglements, the book also looks at the concept's development and expansion through the lens of geopolitical and imperial ambition.

The romantic appeal of a long-lost road of trade, of luxurious goods, of adventures across desert sands also means the Silk Road remains an ever-popular framing for tourism, restaurants, and cookbooks, as well as an array of musical, dance, and theatrical performances. In the West it evokes all the mysteries and fantasies of an exotic Orient: images of great civilizations that stretch across expanses of time and land and of rich, colorful cultures shaped by mountain, desert, and vast open plain. By pulling these different threads together, the book argues that the Silk Road has now become one of the key geocultural and geostrategic concepts of the twenty-first century. China's vast Belt and Road Initiative (BRI) has further accelerated its usage in international trade, diplomacy, infrastructure development, and statecraft and as a narrative framing for countless media, museum, publishing, tourism, heritage, and other cultural sector projects.

In this Silk Road, Belt and Road nexus created by China, we are witnessing the commingling of a geocultural imaginary of antiquity—which privileges ideas of transoceanic and transcontinental exchange, harmony, and open-borders and does so with a distinct disposition toward romanticism—with what is arguably the most ambitious foreign policy ever undertaken by a single country. The full implications of this are yet to be properly grasped. Emphasizing commingling over mingling signals the fundamental intermixing of Silk Road pasts with Belt and Road futures. In the process, both are being remade. This raises issues and questions that fall between the cracks of academic disciplines. The Silk Road has now migrated out from Archaeology, Asian Studies and History into International Relations, Political Geography, Religious Studies, Public Health, and Urban Studies, to name a few. Such developments raise important questions about how to interrogate and locate the Silk Roads, conceptually and empirically. Given that China views the Silk Roads as both "shared heritage" and "shared destiny," we need to ask what their "revival" by Asia's ascendant power tells us about global futures. COVID-19 greatly accelerated and amplified China's ambitions for its Health Silk Road platform. And the reduction of people and goods across international borders in the wake of COVID-19 leant additional weight to the development of a Digital Silk Road infrastructure. Such themes are taken up in the final chapter, which explores the Silk Roads in relation to cultural internationalism and China's world-ordering ambitions.

The Long Road to Global Fame

The Silk Road began to enter the public consciousness in Europe and North America in the 1930s. Sven Hedin, a former student of Richthofen, was one of the more accessible writers of this cohort of scholar-explorers, and his 1938 book, titled *The Silk Road*, was widely read across Europe. Around this time, Marco Polo was also becoming a figure of popular culture, in large part through a Hollywood film industry fascinated by both grand adventure and the Orient. A brief but golden moment of twentieth-century transcontinental adventure—during which motor vehicle expeditions sponsored by André Citroën, Buick, or Esso crossed Asia—involved romantically depicting trips as "retracing" the steps of the thirteenth-century traveler and his "route along the Silk Road." Indeed, Marco Polo became its quintessential journeyman, and as authors of the 1930s inflated the significance of their own exploits through reference to *The Travels*, Polo stretched the Silk Road story in the popular imagination through to the thirteenth century and down through the Levant region of the Middle East.

By the early 1990s, the Silk Road had come a long way from Richthofen's original depiction of trade routes between Han dynasty China and the Roman Empire. The profound changes of the post-Cold War period were generating new questions about historical precedence and whether levels of connectivity were fundamentally new or an iteration of patterns that stretched back centuries. Late twentieth-century globalization needed its own history and thus acted as a catalyst, driving interest and debate among scholars across a number of countries about premodern forms of connection and the validity of global or world history as frameworks for analysis. As

Lynn Hunt notes, globalization offered "a new purpose for history: under-standing our place in an increasingly interconnected world."[9] Pursuing such ideas required overturning some key assumptions of modern historiography, namely the privileging of the nation-state as the architecture within which past events were interpreted. Over the course of the twentieth century, var-ious subfields of history had come to be oriented around a series of norms and assumptions captured by the term methodological nationalism. Debates about empire, development, progress, sovereignty, identity, rule of law, and democracy have all pivoted around such a paradigm. In tracing this pro-cess, Diego Olstein notes that historical thinking has often been constrained by the borders of language and modern politics. He argues, however, that the 1990s was a distinct turning point in the attention paid to geographi-cally more expansive accounts of history, citing theories of civilizational and world systems, together with world and global histories, as among the areas that gained momentum during this period. Although each has endeavored to construct its own distinctions for understanding the past, in broad terms these fields foregrounded ideas about interconnection and the emergence of networks and systems at the regional or planetary scale.[10]

It was within this context that interest in the Silk Road thrived. But here we also need to turn to the seismic changes of that period. The ideological divides of the Cold War created clear distinctions between a capitalist West and com-munist East, each with their spheres of influence. Few areas of the world were left unaffected by the collapse of the Soviet Union, and as walls and curtains were consigned to history, the political maps of Europe and Asia needed to be redrawn—a set of transitions that demanded new ways of thinking about the East and the West. These geocultural categories have a deep legacy, and their continual use belies the different associations and hierarchies they invoke. As Alexander Maxwell reminds us, the "cultural fault lines between Islam and Christianity, Orthodoxy and Catholicism, socialism and capitalism, NATO and the Warsaw Pact, the European Union and the former Communist bloc" are among the ways in which these terms have constructed realities histori-cally.[11] The competing ideologies of the Cold War cleaved Europe into two, with Austria and Germany among those countries discursively positioned as the bulwarks between the East and the West. Depending on a commentator's location, sides were viewed as old and new, free or entrapped. But in the 1990s, was it really the end of history, as Francis Fukuyama claimed, and if so, were these geocultural categories still required in a world where capitalism recognized no barriers?[12] Globalization, it was argued, was bringing us all together, such that analysts trumpeted the metaphors of the "global village" and a "flat world" to explain what they saw as a planet of seamless connectivity and opportunity. New technologies, most notably the Internet, were also compressing, even erasing, traditional notions of time and space.[13] Some saw this as a new era of civilizational dialogue and looked to the Silk Road as an analogy from the past upon which internationalist futures could be built. At such a moment, the Silk Road appeared to provide the evidence of how East and West could be "bridged" through harmony, friendship, and peace.

If East-West relations were no longer to be defined by a grand ideological schism, new alliances were required, and the power vacuums created by the collapse of the Soviet Union needed to be filled. Such transformations meant Central Asia was once again a region of geopolitical significance. Rich in natural resources yet precariously nestled in between Eurasia's preeminent powers—Russia and China—Central Asia faced an uncertain future. As we will see in greater detail later, various observers in the West identified the strategic importance of the region to international affairs and proposed "New Silk Road" strategies. Religion, most notably fundamentalist Islam, came to be seen as a geopolitical threat, meaning that Afghanistan, Pakistan, and a number of their neighboring countries were once again on the radar of think tanks and politicians in Washington and elsewhere. But as Chapter 9 illustrates, governments in East Asia and Europe had their own reasons for engaging with a region in transition, with trade and energy security of primary concern to diplomats and departments of foreign affairs. Over the course of the 1990s, the "opening up" of Central Asia also heralded a new age of Silk Road tourism. The region was one of the last frontiers of the international travel industry, and its remote locations could be marketed as a destination of luxurious adventure, with itineraries incorporating camel rides, exclusive heritage hotels, and "exotic" cultures, supposedly untouched by modernity.

Such processes and connections are traced in the book in order to reveal how, where, when, and why the Silk Road has formed as a geocultural narrative that privileges certain subjects over others, reduces complex events into particular motifs, and constructs space as routes and networks, and the flows of a select group of cultural forms, material and non-material. In understanding its usage in foreign policy, diplomacy, and museology I seek to emphasize the political work its metaphorical qualities are doing. And in examining the Silk Road as a depiction of Eurasian and Afro-Asian history, I want to consider the implications of authors, curators, and filmmakers passing over events such as war, famine, piracy, invasion, or the darker sides of empire. We will see that the geographies and timelines of the Silk Road alter depending on authorship, such that Iranian, Chinese, Indian, Italian, or Japanese depictions have distinct differences yet are conjoined by the motifs of connectivity and exchange. In effect, the concept has gained notoriety as a highly stylized depiction of premodern Eurasia, one that is framed around ideas of free and unrestricted trade, tolerant and open religions engaged in harmonious dialogue, and the flow of ideas, technologies, and commodities along corridors of commerce. By narrating Eurasian history through the motifs of market towns, inland or coastal, and long-distance explorers, imaginings of benign neoliberalism and cosmopolitan virtue seem to be suspended in an aesthetic harmony. Silk Road objects are interpreted in ways that tell the story of movement and carriage, transmission and flows. And in what has become an iconic visual culture—camel caravans crossing desert and mountain or Arabian dhows laden with porcelain—lie tales of adventure and the traversing of frontiers, both physical and cultural. All of this has implications for the production of history and foreign policy, as we shall see.

In recent decades, a second, maritime route has gained currency, upending previous accounts that proclaimed this fabled land-based network "declined" once sea trade gained ascendency in the fifteenth century. The incorporation of oceanic routes has stretched the geographies of the Silk Road to Africa and given much greater attention to Afro-Asian historical connections. This addition was primarily triggered by a decade-long initiative led by UNESCO at the end of the Cold War, Silk Roads: Roads of Dialogue, which brought together dozens of countries to celebrate a broad gamut of East-West, intra-Asian, and maritime-based histories. Today, then, it is common to see documentaries and museums depict sweeping transcontinental arcs that connect Athens with Nara, Oman with Venice via a maritime cartography of "stops." Such representations invariably erase the complexities of oceanic history in relation to waxing and waning empires, piracy, migration, or the spread of religions, to cite a few examples. And yet in popular Silk Road historiography published by prestigious university presses in the West today, the story often continues to focus on land-based routes and market towns. It is a geocultural imaginary, I would suggest, that remains infused by an orientalist exotica: the "romance" and "mysteries" of a remote Central Asia sustained by images of tiled mosques set against cobalt blue skies and those iconic camels. Best-selling books by Valerie Hansen, Frances Wood, Susan Whitfield, and others thus depict the Silk Road through the manuscripts and artworks unearthed in the remote caves of Dunhuang in the late nineteenth century, coupled with accounts of the caravanserai of Persia and the role of Chang'an (Xi'an) in China as its "cosmopolitan terminus."[14] In her 2015 book *Life along the Silk Road*, Whitfield invokes the narrative device of the archetypal voyager—pilgrim, soldier, merchant, courtesan, and horseman—to tell a grand story of mobility and carriage.[15] Two years later, Hansen argued for a new history of overland connectivity to be written, one built around texts and maps.[16] Interestingly, however, by 2019 the geographies and events of Whitfield's Silk Road had begun to expand, with a final chapter dedicated to "seas and skies."

Further confusion comes from such accounts now sitting alongside other Silk Road depictions that have broadened outward to include many other events, themes, and regions. It is now common for Silk Road historians to open their account with the observation that it was not merely one road, or primarily about the trading of silk, and that readers are to bear in mind that there were many routes along which cultures and religions interacted and shared ideas about technology, agriculture, and viticulture. Such observations have thus led to an ambiguity in terminology and a constant slippage between the Silk Road as singular or plural. The latter is now more common, a trend that has further gathered momentum as a maritime route gains currency. The singular remains a valid means for signaling the concept, with an additional "s" signifying the designation of multiple routes and a recognition that interpretations of the term have continued to evolve. The chapters that follow adopt this distinction. But as we will see, such a qualification is in fact only the starting point for unpacking the misunderstandings, loose assertions, and controversies that surround the term.

For instance, today there are competing claims over when the Silk Road supposedly "opened," to which regions it reached, and at what point trade and exchange reached its "height." Whitfield's designation of a third-century BCE beginning contrasts with the claim now commonly made in China that Zhang Qian's diplomatic trips westward "opened" the road in 138 BCE. Equally, others cite trade routes between India and China from earlier centuries or look to trade and migration southward from Siberia to push the chronology back even further. The inclusion of the maritime domain also complicates any idea of historical end points. Some argue for the arrival of Europeans into the Indian Ocean as the natural cut-off point. Others include the era of steamships.[17] Peter Frankopan seems to adopt an even more arbitrary time frame, including the Soviet Union and two world wars as part of his international bestseller, *The Silk Roads: A New History of the World*.[18]

More significant than the debate over dates and start and end points however, is the question of the actual validity of the concept. As a narrative of history, it has come to occupy a unique cultural position in contemporary society. It is neither national nor global history, neither a history of a land or a people or even a region. Advocates of the term argue it is the key to salvaging an unknown history of regional connections that in many cases left little record or evidence and that has been overshadowed by historiographies built around the nation-state.[19] Those scholars who adopt the Silk Road to orient their work value it as a lens for opening up a rich history of cultural connectivity and its capacity to shed light on the complex and poorly understood trade networks that defined the earliest phases of globalization. It does this by helping to foreground the ways in which ideas, technologies, religions, languages, and a vast array of cultural products migrated among populations and across regions. We still know little about the cultural and environmental histories of nomadic groups residing in the Eurasian Steppe or the various ways in which maritime and land-based trade networks intersected in Asia. With so much world history of the twentieth century suffering the biases of Eurocentrism, the Silk Road constitutes a platform for highlighting much neglected histories of Afro-Asian and intra-Asian connectivity. There are others, however, who adopt a more critical perspective, highlighting its thematic and empirical biases and the troubling ways it reduces complex, fragmented events into a single overarching, romanticized narrative. As authors such as Millward, Waugh, Rezakhani, and Thorsten all note, the Silk Road circulates as a romanticized, stylized depiction of history, steering attention away from episodes of plague, war, empire, piracy, prostitution, and such like in favor of more benign themes of harmony and friendship, exchange and cultural enrichment.[20] Rezakhani thus suggests:

> not only that the concept of a continuous, purpose-driven road or even "routes" is counterproductive in the study of world history but also that it has no basis in historical reality or records. Doing away with the whole concept of the "Silk Road" might do us, at least as historians, a world of good and actually let us study what in reality was going on in the region.[21]

Given the approach here is historiographical and biographical, the chapters that follow trace how these ideas and discourses of history have formed and entered circulation across different contexts over time. It is erroneous to approach the Silk Road as an idea established among the corridors of academia, which then became increasingly popular over time. Instead, the chapters here recount its formation as a series of intersections and confluences across countries and across various domains of culture and society. Engaging with histories of tourism, literature, travel writing, museology, film, and such like reveals the nostalgic and aesthetic qualities that define Silk Road imaginaries, imagery, and materialities. The book also shows how such qualities both lead to and emerge out of its co-opting by institutions, including governments, in different parts of the world.

Thinking Geoculturally

To pull these different strands and arguments together, the book conceptualizes the Silk Road as a geoculture. Ulf Hannerz reminds us that we are disposed to think geoculturally. Geocultural forms circulate in everyday life and in popular culture, and a broad array of institutions rely on geocultural concepts to function and construct the realities they aim to build. While ideas about geoculture have been explored across a number of scholarly disciplines, relative to those concepts to which it is akin, namely culture or geopolitics, geocultural thinking remains underdeveloped. At its simplest level, invoking the "geo" seeks to build a more robust understanding of how space and culture are mutually constituted. How are we to think about the geographical arrangements of culture across boundaries, how it is constituted through networks, flows, and coalitions, or how we might think about culture in topographical or topological ways? Pursuing such lines of enquiry also helps to open up new ways of thinking about those arrangements and assemblages that are more readily thought about as political categories. The nation-state, and the international system within which it sits and gives form to self and other, are among the examples that might be cited here. It also helps us to think more critically about those geocultural forms that circulate in more circumspect ways, such as East and West, civilization, or organized religion. Hannerz refers to these and other examples as geocultural scenarios in order to account for the ways in which they are both spatial and temporal imaginaries. The reasons why "people and their practices and ideas arrange themselves, or get arranged, over territories and maps" invariably involves reconstructing the past in the present to envisage and proclaim certain futures.[22] Again, we might think of Hobsbawm's argument concerning the paraphernalia of boundary-marking, othering, and myth-making that form in the nurturing of collective pasts and futures.

There is thus significant analytical value in understanding how geocultural forms emerge and take shape. Depending on the context, this might mean attending to the transnational processes by which ideas circulate via a "web of social relationships, . . .which again stimulate further cultural production."[23] Such processes can involve the generation of ideas by experts that circulate and gain ascendency within echo-chambers and across networks, to more popular narratives and representations that take hold in the public imagination. Isaac Kamola and Merje Kuus have pursued the former, examining the role of experts in shaping ideas about globalization and the European Union respectively.[24] But, of course, the Cold War, Europe, or West also circulate as geocultural forms through symbols, narratives, and physical goods. Together, these both help to construct and transcend borders, define and delineate territories. As we shall see, the Silk Road affords geocultural thinking for institutions working across a variety of sectors. By implication, this is far more than a mere question of imagery and symbols, as Immanuel Wallerstein demonstrated in his contemplations of the geoculture that formed part of the historical processes of state formation and the emergent global capitalist system.

To account for the complex and often contradictory interplay between nationalism and internationalism, which co-formed alongside modern capitalism, Wallerstein co-authored with Peter Phillips in 1991 to argue that ideological and economic struggle took place within the profound cultural and philosophical changes of the seventeenth and eighteenth centuries. European success depended in part on Enlightenment ideas that were proclaimed to be applicable to all "thinking subjects, all nations, all epochs and all cultures."[25] Undergirding the world system, then, was a fundamental tension between a commitment to the universal—as manifest in the fields of science, law, and politics—and the valuing of the localized particular. As postcolonial scholarship has laid bare, Europe's ascendency also involved the studying, codifying, and governing of other cultures and societies through the universalist lenses of progress and modernity, coupled with the ethos of a civilizing mission rooted in particular world views about religion, race, and barbarity. For Wallerstein then, the geoculture of the world system involved the gradual aggregation of European, come Western, values, epistemologies, and ideals, which, through their export to other regions, emerged as key pillars in the core, periphery dynamics of trade and empire. In the short book *European*

Universalism: The Rhetoric of Power, he took this line of thinking through to the 1950s and the formation of development and democracy as geocultural forms that reproduced this regime of values to secure influence in an era of decolonization and Cold War alliance-building.[26] Of course, in their critiques of world systems theory, Gurminder Bhambra, Walter Mignolo, and others have pointed to the co-production of this geoculture and the ways it was contested and appropriated by those outside Europe.[27]

In considering the Silk Road in geocultural terms, there are two points to note here. First is an emphasis on how geocultural forms are produced in multiple ways, and thus the importance of analytically embracing how this occurs across public and popular discourses, institutional and expert practices, and via different material worlds. Second is the role such processes play in the construction of world orders. Geocultural forms are not merely reflections of particular realities but actively constitute their production. Like the first, this second point runs through the book, starting with nineteenth-century debates about civilization and pan-Asianism, through to twenty-first-century geopolitics and the role of cultural internationalism vis à vis possible world order shifts in the wake of COVID-19.

To explore these different themes and the various pathways the Silk Road has followed in the past century and a half, the book is divided into five parts. This structure not only reveals the key ingredients that come together in concocting Silk Road imaginaries, but it also helps the reader to better understand the different pathways the term has followed. As we have already seen, the Silk Road is a narrative of history, albeit a problematic one. Part One traces the events and processes through which these framings of antiquity emerged. It focuses on the explorer scholars that visited Central Asia in the decades running up to World War I and argues that interpretations of the region's history were in part shaped by the geopolitical circumstances of the period. Today, the Silk Road is commonly depicted as an apolitical history of transmission and dialogue between East and West, Asia and Europe, but we learn in the three chapters here that below the surface lie ideas about the geographical reach of civilizations and claims about the "roots" of modern European and Asian societies. To address the bias toward European scholars in the many accounts of this period, Chapter 4 focuses on Japan. This provides a foundation for understanding how the Silk Road comes to be shaped in the second half of the twentieth century as its popularity in Japan grows, a dynamic that influences international discourses at the end of the Cold War. In effect then, Part One identifies the core narrative themes for interpreting Eurasian history, which stabilize in the late nineteenth, early twentieth centuries. The focus here then is Central Asia, including regions in what is today northwest China. But as the second half of the book shows, themes of mobility and exchange are then transposed onto other regions and to the seas and oceans that surround the Eurasian landmass.

Part Two turns to consider another Silk Road, that of adventure and travel. It begins by tracing the concept's entry into the popular imagination in the 1930s and the forms of cultural production that give rise to a more ethnographic Silk Road centered around depictions of grand adventure and cross-cultural encounters. Politics and conflicts, as well as shifting borders and technologies of mobility, have defined the routes of modern Silk Road adventures. But as the two chapters in this section demonstrate, a historical framing of boundless regions and cultures in dialogue converges with the motifs common to modern travel cultures, resulting in regions and events separated by centuries being dissolved into a seamless geocultural Silk Road. Depictions of "traveling the Silk Road" told in film, image, and text thus fold the past and the present back on one another. To explain this, I point to the ways in which the Silk Road comes to circulate in the popular imagination via a symbolic economy of "retraced" pasts, where modern travelers continually proclaim to follow those iconic sojourners of previous centuries, namely Marco Polo. Through this analysis we see how an ethnographic, come tourist, gaze has contributed to the romance and aura that surround the Silk Road today, a gaze that reproduces the aesthetic tropes of Asia as a land of "exotic" cultures living much like they did in "Marco Polo's time."

The two chapters that make up Part Three address the Silk Road's emergence as a vehicle for diplomacy and cultural internationalism. Here, then, the discussion returns to Japan, and by focusing on the decades following World War II we see Japanese scholars use premodern histories of cultural transmission and connectivity as a platform for engaging with a UNESCO initiative designed to promote tolerance and mutual understanding. These scholars engage with, but critique, Ferdinand von Richthofen's notion of the Silk Road. Some years later, the term becomes part of the branding for the first Olympic Games held in Asia, the 1964 Tokyo Olympics. Focusing on such events and diplomatic projects with China and the Soviet Union, the first chapter explains how the Silk Road emerges as a vehicle for repairing Japan's postwar reputation. It also traces the rise of "Silk Road fever" in Japan through to the late 1980s, led by those committed to internationalizing the country's sense of collective identity. The second chapter in this section explains the dramatic rise in interest in the Silk Road around the world at the end of the Cold War. Part Two accounts for the role of tourism in Central Asia in this process, but the discussion here focuses on UNESCO's Silk Roads: Roads of Dialogue project. This pathbreaking, multilateral initiative opens up the geographies and timelines of the Silk Road narrative. It is here that we see the idea of the Maritime Silk Road begin to gain currency, as do Buddhist and Islamic routes. The 1990s also saw momentum gather around museum exhibitions. But in distinct contrast to UNESCO's expansive vision, Silk Road museology pulls the story back to Central Asia, based on the artifacts and photographs stored in archives and vaults since the early 1900s. The chapter concludes with an overview of the projects and discourses of cooperation that make up China's Silk Road "revival" in the twenty-first century under the Belt and Road Initiative. The focus here is on the cultural dimensions of Belt and Road in order to leave the more substantive discussion of the Silk Road as a discourse of foreign policy for Part Four.

In the fourth section, then, I turn to the terrain of geopolitics. Since the 1990s we have seen a number of governments take up the Silk Road to orient their foreign policies for Central Asia. To understand what's at stake here, the opening chapter of Part Four returns to some key metaphorical concepts that have shaped geopolitical analysis in the past century or so, notably Heartland and Rimland. It will be argued that such terms have not merely reflected the realities of a particular period but have actively contributed to their formulation. This provides the basis for considering what norms, values, and ideas are being advanced through the "Silk Roads of the twenty-first century." Running through Part Four, then, is an analysis of how certain narratives about geography and history inform geopolitical analysis and the foreign policies of governments. By invoking a language of Silk Road connectivity— past, present, and future—Belt and Road is the latest iteration of this.

Part Five concludes by returning to questions and issues raised in this introductory chapter, namely the role and value of the Silk Road as a narrative of history and as a framework for cultivating forms of cultural internationalism in the twenty-first century. The discussion integrates various themes raised in the book and speaks to the future of the Silk Road in relation to China's seeming long-term investment in the term. The chapter asks whether Eurocentric histories of premodern pasts are now going to be overlaid with Sinocentric depictions. I also reflect on China's geopolitical and geo-economic ambitions relative to its commitment to Silk Road internationalism. Together then, these two themes attempt to signal likely ways the Silk Roads will hold significance in the future and why this demands a more sustained conversation about how they should be discussed and studied by scholars.

The first four parts begin with an introduction. These are written as navigational devices and can thus be read together or revisited as necessary. They are also designed to signpost the key analytical pivots made over the course of the book and explain why the Silk Road, in all its ambiguities and confusions, continues to captivate and draw interest around the world.

PART ONE

CONNECTING CULTURES

Formulating the Silk Roads as a narrative of history has been a true international collaboration that has spanned many decades. In all its evocative imagery of crossing deserts, mountains, and even continents, the Silk Road has become a past shared by many rather than one that is owned by a single country. Part One traces the processes and events that led to such unique readings of history and the themes that would form the backbone of the Silk Road concept once it gained recognition in the years either side of World War II.

To give context to this, Chapter 2 opens by outlining some connections that were forged in nineteenth-century Europe between the nation, material culture, and those more amorphous ideas of civilization and East and West. This brief overview highlights the geopolitical contexts through which the histories of regions such as the "Near East" formed via archaeology, philology, and antiquarian studies. This sets the scene for understanding Ferdinand von Richthofen's trip to Central Asia, an area that, by contrast, Europeans knew little about. Central Asia was remote, in large areas sparsely populated, and home to groups notoriously resistant to European control. The circumstances of his trip meant that he combined surveys for a possible rail route to Europe with his broader interests in geography and history. As Chapter 2 explains, Richthofen combined sources obtained during his travels with those from Europe to sketch out small fragments of a much larger history of premodern trade, exchange, and regional empires. Understandably, given these limited resources, his account was vague and built around a series of suppositions.

One of the key aims of the book is to challenge the widely held misconception that Richthofen's use of the Silk Road term in 1877 immediately gained currency and that it has remained a stable, coherent concept ever since. This starts to become apparent in Chapter 3, which focuses on the scholar explorers who traveled to Central Asia from Europe and Japan. The principal

characteristics of the Great Game—its vast landscapes, strategically important rail lines, and porous boundaries—served as the backdrop against which
connectivity, transmission, and entanglement emerged as the intellectual
keys for unlocking the region's past. Our key characters here, Aurel Stein,
Paul Pelliot, Ōtani Kozui, Sven Hedin and others were all operating at a moment when the apparatus of European colonialism was developed to its fullest extent. But unlike other regions in Africa and Asia, I argue that the work
of these men was not directly incorporated into colonial attempts to tie local
populations back into historical kingdoms in order to define territories and
build ethnocultural nationalisms. This discussion also reveals the geopolitical and infrastructure aspects of the Silk Road story and sets the scene for
the discussion of Part Four.

The nature of the Great Game meant multiple countries from outside
Central Asia—Britain, France, Germany, India, Japan, Russia, and Sweden—
were all invested in the region's history. As we will see, by the time World
War I breaks out, the key narratives of history and culture, religion and trade
are in place—intellectual and romantic foundations that would make the Silk
Road so compelling through the twentieth century. Over the course of the
book, it becomes evident that both world wars along with the Cold War fundamentally change East-West politics and the way in which ideas of history
and civilization for these two regions are discussed by intellectuals. Chapter 3
argues that World War I, along with the subsequent creation of the Soviet
Union and ongoing pursuit of national histories in the first half of the twentieth century, makes it impossible for any discourse around Eurasian connectivity and histories of harmonious relations to make headway. It is suggested
that these events closed down opportunities for researching such themes. In
the case of the Soviet Union, for example, the co-opting of archaeology and
ethnography in the designation of distinct cultures and peoples in the name
of modernization represents a major departure from the kinds of exploration
and historical research developed in the late nineteenth century.

One of the aims here is to move beyond the much celebrated explorers
and scholars of Europe. Chapter 4 therefore turns to Japan. It begins by
noting the debates about civilization and nation that emerged in the closing
decades of the nineteenth century. This provides context for a discussion of
Japanese scholarship that focused on premodern trade and forms of cultural and religious exchange across different parts of Asia. This chapter thus
creates the necessary foundations for understanding why and in what ways
the Silk Road emerges after World War II. We will learn that through Japan's

influence it becomes a platform for understanding histories of intra-Asian connectivity, notably the migration of Buddhism and other Asian religions. This occurs from the 1960s onward, as certain discourses of cultural and pan-Asian affinity orient Japanese Silk Road narratives within popular culture and contexts of diplomacy. Looking further ahead to Chapter 8, we will also see that Japan's take on the Silk Roads heavily influences UNESCO's 10-year multilateral program, Silk Roads: Roads of Dialogue, which was launched during the twilight years of the Cold War.

Together, then, the three chapters in this opening section trace the processes and events by which the Silk Road gains its key attributes as a narrative of history and geocultural pasts in the decades that span Richthofen's initial cartography and the term's road to popularization in the 1930s. The template is set by the fabled overland Silk Road, one that is eventually applied in equal measure to maritime histories. To anticipate this, early steps taken by scholars in Asia toward tracing maritime pasts are also briefly noted in Chapter 4. The discussion is limited to these developments, rather than giving a fuller exploration of the formation of maritime history in the West, since it becomes apparent in Part Three that they influence ideas about a Maritime Silk Road that first surface in the 1950s.

2

The Routes of Civilization

Searching for Antiquity

Over the past two centuries, so much of the past has come to be shackled
to the nation, a connection around which identities have been forged, the
norms of everyday life crafted, and the legitimacy of state rule justified. Back
in 1983, Hobsbawm and Ranger argued that "the invention of tradition"
reached its zenith in the closing decades of the nineteenth century.[1] But
while they looked to events and cultural practices developed in the seventeenth and eighteenth centuries as the repositories from which the collective
memories of the nineteenth were constructed, others have traced national
imaginaries back to antiquity. In the case of modern Greece, for example,
narratives of Athenian glory, embodied in architectural ruins and artworks,
provided what Hamilakis has referred to as a "monumental topography of
the nation."[2] The Acropolis and Temple of Hephaestus were among those
sites put into service as "the material and monumental frame that structured
human movement and action, and inspired and elicited awe, piety, and respect."[3] The demolition of monuments built after the so-called "golden age"
helped to form an idealized epic time, to cite Bakhtin's aphorism, such that
the Acropolis acted as "a reservoir of meanings," onto which multiple values,
myths, and ideologies could be ascribed in the making of a modern Greek
identity.[4] But as we also know, by the nineteenth century Greek antiquity
had also been reconstructed as a shared European past, thereby identified as
a foundation for Western civilization. Europe's self-assurance in modernity
and what it could deliver stemmed in large part from the revolutions of the
previous two centuries and the fundamental impact they had on ideas about
law, liberty, and the relationship of the individual to church and state.[5] These
transitions, some of which began with the Renaissance and Reformation,
fomented debates about the constituents, or essences, of Europeanness. In
the nineteenth century, archaeologists identified regions of Iraq and Syria
as cradles of civilization, and studies of Egypt and Mesopotamia pushed the
roots of Europe back to the dawn of writing.[6] But the classical cultures of

The Silk Road. Tim Winter, Oxford University Press. © Oxford University Press 2022.
DOI: 10.1093/oso/9780197605059.003.0002

Greece and Rome remained the origins of law, democracy, art, and so forth; the very qualities of civility, with archaeology and philology providing a direct lineage of aesthetics, technological prowess, and belief in the democratic ideal. In a teleological account of modernity, "the Ancient Greeks were the original fount of modern (i.e. Western) civilisation," to quote John Hobson, who has referred to this as the "Greek clause" in European historiography.[7]

In the age of empire and global trade, this narrative of history provided Europeans with a framework to proclaim moral and political superiority; a belief system buttressed by ideas of material, technological, and economic progress and an unbridled confidence that both nature and history could be mastered through science and technology.[8] Over the course of the nineteenth century, antiquarianism was transformed into the more scientific disciplines of archaeology, preservation, and the classificatory systems that formed within the university and museum. Crucially, such pursuits found their intellectual and political purpose within the context of empire, such that material remnants from the past—objects, buildings, artifacts, manuscripts, and inscriptions—became the "texts" through which cultures and lands outside Europe were studied, photographed, classified, hierarchically ordered, and exhibited. As fields such as archaeology harnessed the language of science for their legitimacy as knowledge domains, Europeans positioned themselves as expert, and thus rightful, guardians of the past of others. As a number of historians of archaeology have noted, scholars either willfully ignored, or unwittingly advanced, the broader ambitions of empire, settler colonialism, and nation-building. Benjamin Porter, for example, has demonstrated this in the coastal ports of Jaffa and Beirut and the regions surrounding the strategically important cities of Aleppo, Damascus, and Jerusalem.[9] Archaeological institutes allowed European countries to establish a presence in areas where rivals anticipated diminished Ottoman rule, such that excavations became a tool of military intelligence in the run up to World War I.[10] The archaeological work of the Palestine Exploration Fund (PEF) directly crossed over with Britain's military and political objectives. As Abu El Haj has shown in fascinating detail, the "excavation" of artifacts by the PEF also played a critical role in conjoining a people with a homeland and homeland with a people for those Zionists migrating from Europe to Palestine.[11] With the Old and New Testaments providing both the arc of time and geographical orientations of Holy Land scholarship, little attention was given to histories of Islam or connections across Asia outside India.[12] Justin Jacobs notes that

Throughout the nineteenth and early twentieth centuries, most Western archaeologists continued to evince the remarkable ability to cast their gaze out over mostly Muslim lands and see nothing but various incarnations of Greeks, Romans, and Jews. This gaze was further adopted by the first generation of Westernized Ottoman collectors and archaeologists to work along their side: the staff of the Imperial Ottoman Museum in Istanbul did not produce a single exhibit on Islamic artifacts until 1889, more than forty years after the founding of the museum.[13]

Indeed, across the Levant, European scholarship throughout this period primarily framed the past through Hellenistic and Roman connections and did so by using the accounts of Alexander the Great, Herodotus, Ptolemy, and more recent travelers to the region.[14] The construction of this transregional history did more than just privilege the cultural and military achievements of European civilization; it played a critical role in conjoining modern Europe and the "Near East" in ways that served the ideological and territorial goals of European colonialism. As Osterhammel reminds us, over the course of the nineteenth century intellectual cosmopolitanism lost out to the commercial, bureaucratic, and ideological imperatives of empire.[15]

Photography and cartography were among the technologies that transposed a Cartesian world view onto the non-European other, reinforcing humanistic fields of enquiry oriented by particular epistemologies of world history and hierarchically ordered cultures and civilizations. Through the work of Maya Jasanoff and others, we also have a much better sense of the links between empire and the collecting of artifacts through the eighteenth and nineteenth centuries.[16] In the case of India, Bernard Cohn, noted that "European effort[s] to unlock the secret of the Indian past called for more and more collecting, more and more systems of classification, more and more building of repositories."[17] Tony Bennett has called for such practices to be read as an exhibitionary complex wherein nineteenth-century European museums projected national and imperial power and ideas about citizenry, metropolitan or otherwise.[18] In their crafting of national imaginaries, these museums also gave form to ideas about Western and Eastern civilization. In the era of imperial rivalry, state-supported cultural institutions, buttressed by new forms of scholarship and historiography, thus mobilized geocultural histories to create unified narratives of past, present, and future. As Stefan Berger notes, the visitor to the British Museum "was left in no doubt when he sampled its global treasure trove that it was due to Britain's domination over

the world that all the treasures had ended up there . . . the museum was one
way of celebrating the achievements of empire."[19] More broadly, the intellectual political milieu within which ideas about civilization, both singular and
plural, that formed in Europe meant that certain qualities were ascribed to
those regions and cultures lying beyond its frontiers.[20] Ancient civilizations
in India, Iran, and Southeast Asia were admired and studied, but having
come to be framed in geocultural terms as the Oriental Other of a modern
West—a process that Edward Said famously argued reached its peak in the
1880s—their achievements were placed on a different moral and cultural
plain.[21]

Plotting for Continents

Viewing scholarship through a geopolitical lens also tells us much about the
ways in which this production of historical knowledge reflected the geographies of empire and exploration. As we have seen, the reasons that some
regions and countries received intense and sustained attention were complex and varied. Egyptomania and the craze for Pharaonic culture stands out
as a fascinating example of how certain aesthetics and ideas about antiquity
could permeate popular culture, genres of architecture, the arts, political
discourse, and so forth in the West through the late nineteenth, early twentieth centuries. And while the visitor to the British Museum today will encounter Egyptian artifacts as part of a collection of the "world's civilizations
and cultures," it is easy to forget how knowledge about different regions
and their "histories" was, and continues to be, assembled in highly uneven
and fragmented ways. Colonial structures, together with the intellectual
paradigms of European scholarship, meant that far less was known about the
regions pertinent to this discussion, namely Central Asia and China. Central
Asia was a long way from Europe, both physically and metaphysically, and
in the case of China, there were few, if any, reliable sources for Europeans to
draw on. Here then Claudius Ptolemy's *Geography* from the second century
offers an interesting example, which, as Geoffrey Gunn has shown at length,
has long remained a source of guidance for European scholars.[22] They include Ferdinand von Richthofen as he sat down in the 1870s to document
and add his contribution to "the history of geographic knowledge in the West
with regard to China and conversely, in China with regard to the West," as
Daniel Waugh puts it.[23]

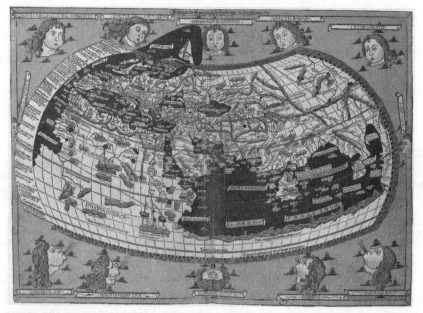

Figure 2.1 Ptolemy World Map as depicted by cartographer Nicolaus Germanus, 1482.
Credit Line: Public Domain.

Geography represented the most comprehensive map of the Greco-Roman world and would play a definitive role in establishing the convention of dividing the world, understood as a globe, into 360 degrees via the grid of lines that make up longitude and latitude (see Figure 2.1). On the back of its translation from Greek to Latin in the early fifteenth century, mapmakers produced graphical versions of the text, some of which circulated via new print technologies. For Ptolemy and the other cartographers of Alexandria, the Mediterranean was their cosmological center, around which they depicted the regions and civilizations of an Afro-Asian landmass.[24] Long-distance trade connections meant China was dubbed the land of silk, and with Ptolemy believing the Indian Ocean to be an enclosed world, he wrote "the inhabited part of our Earth is bounded on the east by the Unknown Land which lies along the region occupied by the easternmost nations of Asia Major, the Sinae and the nations of Serice."[25] The Copernican revolution undermined Ptolemy's notion of the celestial universe, and modern scholars have been divided over the degree to which *Geography* continued to impact intellectual thinking over the longer term.[26] In the Age of Discovery, his underestimation of the Earth's circumference caused problems for those sailing the high seas, and his overestimates of the eastward extent of Eurasia meant he misplaced China. But in understanding the latter, Renaissance Europe had little to go on. Prior to Portuguese ships putting down anchors along China's coastline, there were only the vague, and invariably embellished, accounts of Venetian merchants, most famously Marco Polo. More accurate estimates of distance would begin to appear in the late sixteenth century as Jesuit missionaries visited the region.[27] But even for those who traveled up through Central Asia in the nineteenth century, such as Richthofen, calculating distance between China and Europe remained a challenge.

With no means of accurately measuring distance relative to degrees, Ptolemy miscalculated the span of Asia as a landmass, and Richthofen set about correcting his errors (see Figure 2.2). Suzanne Marchand notes that Richthofen was the most experienced European traveler in China since Marco Polo and understood its capacity for development and industrialization.[28] Born in 1833, he became interested in geography and geology while on trips to the mountains of southern Europe. Marchand tracks the career choices that led him to China, indicating that his illustrious family name was a likely factor in him being invited to join a trade mission to the region in the early 1860s.[29] Deciding to stay on, he eventually left for the United States to avoid the turmoil of the Taiping Rebellion. There he found employment undertaking geological surveys in the lucrative mining sector. Drawn to the career possibilities China seemed to offer, he moved back in the late 1860s and surveyed different parts of the country over a four-year period. Sponsorship for such trips came from the Bank of California, which funded his first year, and the Anglo-American Shanghai Chamber of Commerce supported three additional years.[30] Once back in Germany, he completed the first volume of *China* as part of his travails to become professor at the University of Berlin in 1886. The publication appeared via five lavish volumes between 1877 and 1912, a project for which, as Marchand documents, he received financial support from the Kaiser and Prussian Academy of Sciences after some considerable effort.[31] As a geographer, Richthofen laid out his commitment to understanding both the physical landscape and histories of human settlement. He thus dedicated considerable attention to the theme of trade, including that of silk, and particularly those networks established during the Han dynasty (206 BCE–220 CE). It is here that he introduces the term *Seidenstraße* (Silk Road). Tamara Chin explains at length the factors that shaped his approach to cartography, noting that it integrated Chinese sources with those of European antiquity, namely Marinus of Tyre and Ptolemy, and Marco Polo's *The Travels*.[32] To distinguish between the different trade routes taken around the Taklamakan Desert, he used red ink to plot European sources and a blue line to depict a southern route used by Chinese traders (see Figure 2.3). Chin also notes "Sērica ... Richthofen argued, is etymologically derived from the Chinese term for silk, si, transliterated by Greek speakers as sēr. Those who traded their silk were called Sēres or 'bringers of silk.'"[33] To extend the connection to Europe, he reproduced the route west of Balkh, in present day Afghanistan, plotted by his German rival, Heinrich Kiepert. Richthofen's 1877 publications refer to both the singular *Seidenstraße* and its plural *Seidenstraßen*. In the following year, articles published in *Geographical Magazine* and *Popular Science Monthly* recounted a lecture he delivered on the topic in Berlin. There, readers were introduced to his theories of long-distance trade across Asia and the importance of a "Silk Trader's Route," referred to in the singular.[34]

Figure 2.2 Portrait of Ferdinand von Richthofen.
Credit Line: Public Domain.

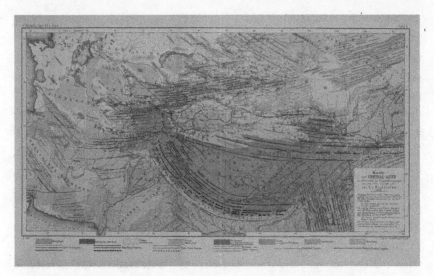

Figure 2.3 Ferdinand von Richthofen's map of Central Asian trade routes, 1877.
Credit Line: Public Domain.

Richthofen's publications included a number of speculative deductions and suppositions. Acknowledging that many of his sources were unreliable, he postulated about connections between Persia and India, how far west Chinese traders reached, what inferences might be drawn from the mention, or indeed spelling, of place names in different texts, and the possible references to the luxuries of silk made by the Greek historian Herodotus in the fifth century BCE and by the tenth century Persian poet Ferdusi. He also drew on the work of his contemporaries, including Henry Yule, the British geographer, whose accounts similarly relied on Ptolemy, Marinus, and Marco Polo. In 1871 Yule published a translation of Polo's *The Travels*, the impact of which we will learn more about in Chapter 5. But as Tamara Chin notes, Ricthofen's research was also oriented around the calculation of the shortest and most feasible rail corridors between Europe and Asia. The rapacious demand for coal in Europe created by modern warfare and industrialization had created a new breed of explorer with geological expertise. Britain's success in the Opium Wars prised China open to foreign exploration for coal and mineral deposits. With the first transcontinental railway completed in the United States in 1869, American corporations joined their European counterparts in pursuing the new economic possibilities China posed. It was within this context that Richthofen secured funding to survey the geology of

THE ROUTES OF CIVILIZATION   31

its central and western regions, with the aim of identifying coal and the most suitable rail routes for transporting such intensely heavy resources to Europe.

One of Richthofen's students, Sven Hedin, would eventually help to popularize the Silk Road term in the 1930s. But in the expedition reports both men produced in the late nineteenth century, their geological and geohistorical insights were tailored toward those interested in the political and commercial benefits of large-scale infrastructure investment. This was a region where Russian, British, and Qing officials were looking to expand their influence. To counter Britain's dominance in sea power, Russia had embarked on an ambitious railway program from the 1860s onward. By 1888, the first phase of the Trans-Caspian Railway was completed, connecting the east coast of the Caspian Sea with the city of Samarkand. A decade later, the line extended to Tashkent and Andijan in present-day Uzbekistan.[35] In 1891, work also began on the eastern end of a route that would eventually become the Trans-Siberian Railway. An extraordinarily ambitious project designed to connect Moscow with the strategic port city of Vladivostok in the east, the Trans-Siberian was constructed in sections over a span of nearly 20 years at great financial and human cost. Some decades later, W.E. Wheeler argued that the shipment of troops and hardware along these lines played a crucial role in securing economic and military control over vulnerable and frontier regions.[36] In other words, Russia's long-distance rail infrastructures proved vital in its quest to secure its position as Eurasia's preeminent land power.

Over the course of the nineteenth century, Tsarist rule had continued to expand eastward. Napoleon's invasion of Egypt in 1798, and the possibility of a Franco-Russian alliance expanding eastward toward Persia, created long-term insecurities in London about its prized possession, India.[37] Although the British enjoyed naval supremacy, "strategically unsatisfactory frontiers" on land, as Edward Ingram puts it, led to a strategy of transforming Persia, Turkey, and Afghanistan into buffer zones in an attempt to forestall Russian military advances.[38] Britain's attempts to maintain stable trade and diplomatic relations with the states lying along India's northwest frontier and retain Afghanistan as a client state failed, leading to defeat in the First Anglo-Afghan War of 1839–1842. Subsequent treaties and agreements ensured that the country was carved up between the two imperial rivals over the course of several decades. Further north, a region broadly equivalent to modern-day Kazakhstan had come under Russian rule, with military personnel and merchant traders continually acting to control the conditions of trade across the wider Central Asia region. But as local powers resisted forms of economic and political control, borders and boundaries remained vague and porous, and altered with each new declaration or incursion. Such events have become infamous in the annals of military and geopolitical history, in large part because of the romantic epithet assigned to this period, the Great Game. Widely read books by Peter Hopkirk and Karl Meyer and Shareen Brysac tell stories of espionage, battles, and the ambitions of capturing land and resources.[39] They also emphasize that for a vast region of expansive plains, deserts, and mountain ranges, knowledge about topography and the surveying of access routes was the linchpin of both military strategy and planning for long-distance rail.

I began the chapter by highlighting some of the formative processes by which history has been tied to the nation and those more amorphous ideas of civilization and East and West. This helps to give context to understanding where the Silk Road has sat as a form of historiography in the twentieth century. Across the world we have seen fields such as archaeology and history oriented around the nation-state, an entity that has sought to legitimize its authority by building historical "roots" and associated ideas about territory. As we will see in later chapters, it is not until the 1990s that histories of transregional, transcultural "routes" gain widespread attention as the zeitgeist shifts toward globalization and new ideas about connecting East and West. To clarify this point, one of the lines of argument running through Part One concerns the Great Game and its vast landscapes, strategically important rail lines, and porous boundaries. These are seen as the all-important backdrop against which the themes of connectivity, transmission, and entanglement could prevail in shaping a geocultural narrative of the past. Richthofen was only able to assemble a tiny fragment of a much larger history of premodern trade, exchange, and regional empires. Given the limited resources at his disposal, his attempt to construct a picture of premodern trade networks was understandably vague and constructed around a series of suppositions, as noted earlier. The sources he drew on spanned regions, languages, and centuries and suffered the reliability problems familiar to early mapmaking and the era preceding print. But his particular circumstances meant that his account of historical mobility, trade, and exchange came to be overlaid with a cartographic imperative to connect Asia to Europe via direct lines of rail. We will see in later chapters that Japanese scholars critique his notion of an East-West corridor for being too limited and negligent of the broader histories of connectivity in Asia, thereby proposing more thematically and geographically expansive definitions of the Silk Road.

To head in that direction, the two chapters that follow examine those explorer-scholars who unearthed further details about the multivalent, multidirectional flows and networks of a premodern world system stretching across the Eurasian landmass. As we will see, researchers and explorers from Britain, France, Germany, Japan, Russia, and Sweden all traveled to Central Asia during a period of intense imperial and national rivalry. But unlike the work in other regions in Asia or Africa, the work of these men was not directly incorporated into colonial attempts to tie local populations back into historical kingdoms in order to define territories and build ethnocultural nationalisms. Many of the regions of the Great Game were sparsely populated and home to groups notoriously resistant to European control. Unlike the fields of Egyptology or Southeast Asian archaeology, there were no great temples or mausoleums around which scholars could build narratives of premodern kingdoms and empires. I noted earlier that the artifacts and structures of antiquity in India, Greece, and Egypt were used to map ancient kingdoms onto the cartography of both modern nations as "imagined communities" and ideas about civilization as a cleavage between East and West. This helps to emphasize the important point that Central Asia was not subjected to the same cultural politics of imperialism or Biblical archaeology. But for these very reasons, European scholars showed much less interest in Richthofen's discoveries from China.[40] As we will see, interest in a history of transcontinental connectivity only began to grow once manuscripts and artworks traveled from Central Asia to Europe. But even then, the romance of trade and cultural transmission along a fabled Silk Road remained several decades away. Among the intellectual circles of the *fin de siècle*, discoveries showing Asia's influence on Europe or the extent of cultural transmission across different regions of Asia were often overshadowed by an excitement about the possible "reach" of Western civilization, evidenced in texts found in China showing possible Hellenic or Roman influences.

3

Frontiers of Antiquity

The Rush for Manuscripts

Over the course of the 1800s, Britain and Russia commissioned expeditions to what is today Afghanistan, Inner Mongolia, Tibet, and Xinjiang, exploring areas where few if any Western travelers had ever visited. The diaries and reports of spies and military personnel included descriptions of ancient ruins, monasteries, and lost cities. Invariably, such details were ignored as the mere color of adventurous travel. Nikolai Przhevalsky, for example, a self-taught botanist and zoologist who gained fame through four long military intelligence expeditions, documented finding monasteries and abandoned settlements in Tibet. Similarly, the Russian botanist Albert Regel recounted discovering the extensive ruins of the ancient Uyghur capital Karakhoja (Gaochang), and in that same year, 1879, a Hungarian expedition arrived at the caves of Dunhuang on the southern edge of the Taklamakan Desert.[1] In his acclaimed volume on the international race for archaeological remains, *Foreign Devils on the Silk Road*, Peter Hopkirk describes the strategy adopted by the British in the 1870s and 1880s of sending local Indian clerks on reconnaissance trips, thereby avoiding the risk of their own military personnel being captured or murdered. In many cases, clerks would supplement descriptions of Russian military camps with tales of abandoned cities and priceless treasures.[2] Although such stories filtered back to the metropolitan centers of Europe, they garnered little excitement among an archaeological world primarily concerned with the great civilizations of the Mediterranean, Egypt, and the Holy Lands.

This began to change with the acquisition of the Bower Manuscript in 1890, a text that opened the window to previously unimagined histories of civilizational contact and premodern mobility. Named after the British officer Hamilton Bower, who purchased it from a team of local treasure hunters in Kucha in present-day Xinjiang, the manuscript was considered to date back to the fourth or fifth century, and its seven parts provided the first evidence of contact across India, China, and Central Asia, as well as revealing

The Silk Road. Tim Winter, Oxford University Press. © Oxford University Press 2022.
DOI: 10.1093/oso/9780197605059.003.0003

the depth of the region's literary traditions and ideas about medicine. Those scholars and archaeologists in Europe curious about the diffusion of Buddhism and languages, and histories of cross-cultural interaction more broadly, eagerly read published translations and small teams from Britain, France, and Russia set off for Central Asia over the following decade. But crucially, as Justin Jacobs notes, curiosity about the region stemmed, in large part, from a desire to understand a Western civilizational history. He takes up the example of Alexander Cunningham, the famed British archaeologist, who focused on Buddhist ruins in the very north of India rather than Hindu and Muslim sites, for they offered potential connections back to the expedition of Alexander the Great. Moreover, Jacobs suggests that Alexander, along with theories of Gandharan art attuned to the Greco-Roman influences on Buddhist art, formed part of the intellectual framing for expeditions to the region:

> It was this particular Greek (or, to be more precise, Macedon) figure that would bring Western explorers and archaeologists into the northwestern frontier of the Qing Empire. Much like their predecessors in the Middle East, Mesoamerica, and India, men such as Stein, Le Coq, Grünwedel, and, to a lesser extent Pelliot were most interested in recovering the material remains of peoples whom they could somehow place within their preferred lineage of Western civilization. The fourth century BC conquests of Alexander the Great brought Greek culture, language, and administrative models to the lands and peoples of present-day India, Pakistan, and Afghanistan.[3]

As manuscripts, mural fragments, and other artifacts arrived at universities and museums in St Petersburg, additional expeditions were organized, with the Russian Academy of Sciences funding a trip to Eastern Turkestan in 1898. Led by the collector Dimitri Klementz, the team returned with reports and photographs of ruins near Turfan on the edge of the Gobi Desert.[4] The prospect of discovering lost cities also inspired Richthofen's student Sven Hedin to venture deep into the inhospitable terrain of the Taklamakan Desert in 1895. With little formal training in the humanities, Hedin proclaimed that the items he recovered from the region demonstrated Indian, Greek, Persian, and Gandharan influences.[5] Undertaking another expedition four years later, he visited Loulan, a garrison town located on the eastern side of the Taklamakan Desert, "discovering" its Buddhist stupas, statues, and carved reliefs. Negotiations over access to historical sites and the removal of artifacts reflected the political asymmetries of the period, with Qing officials anxious about the consequences of offending foreign missions, including those from Japan.[6]

To the south, British officials in Calcutta were also building a sizeable collection of Central Asian artifacts. The appointment of Lord Curzon as viceroy in 1898 further ensured their commitment to archaeological expeditions beyond India's frontiers. Frustrated at the Indian government's disregard for the material culture of the ancient past, Curzon appointed himself as Director of Antiquities and established the Archaeological Survey of India. In the story of Central Asian antiquity, his meeting with Aurel Stein in April 1899, at that time employed as principal of the Oriental College in Lahore, would prove to be a significant moment. A keen historian of the region, Stein was in search of expedition funding, and with Curzon's support yielding a grant some months later, he set off for Chinese Turkestan, an area that had become politically sensitive for the British to visit. A son of Budapest, Stein studied Persian and Sanskrit at university with postdoctoral appointments taking him to England. At the age of 25 he traveled to India, putting to good use the surveying and mapmaking skills acquired during a period of military service back in Hungary. But it was his passion for coins and texts acquired in the museums and university libraries of England and Central Europe that inspired his search for the objects of antiquity. Before his death in Kabul in 1943, Stein undertook four lengthy expeditions in Central Asia and a number of trips across the Middle East, including Iran. His maiden trip of 1900 began in Srinagar and he reached Kashgar some months later. There he entered a world afflicted by decades of political upheaval. On the back of defeating the Tajik ruler Yakub Beg in the 1870s, Peking had declared Xinjiang a province of the Qing dynasty since 1884. By the time Stein arrived in 1900, however, the level of Russian influence had grown considerably. The Boxer Rebellion had broken out and the Russian army was in the process of invading Manchuria. Nicholas Petrovsky, stationed in Kashgar since 1882 and by then acting in the capacity of consular to Peking, exerted his influence over the affairs of the region. Like Curzon, Petrovsky was keenly interested in history and languages, lending his support to Russia's growing archaeological programs.[7] The 1898 excursion led by Klementz unearthed the contents of 130 Buddhist cave temples some distance north of Kashgar in Turfan. As Stein ventured out on his trips from Kashgar, he avoided areas north of the Taklamakan under Russian control and instead headed south

Figure 3.1 Site of Niya, excavated by Aurel Stein in 1900, British Library.
Credit Line: The British Library Board, Falconer_2006b: 1048.

toward Khotan.[8] Today, the Stein Collection in the British Library includes more than 45,000 manuscripts and other materials in a number of languages, including Chinese, Khotanese, Kuchean, Mongolian, Sanskrit, Sogdian, Tangut, Tibetan, Turkic, and Uyghur. It also includes paintings on paper, textiles, and wood (see Figure 3.1).

In these various expeditions, we begin to see how scholarly research reflected the political frontiers and lines of control being drawn up across the region and what Jacobs refers to as "geopolitical pragmatism."[9] Figure 3.2 illustrates their geographical distribution, with Russian teams predominantly targeting the area north of the Taklamakan and the British using their route of access from India in the south and safe passage along the southern rim of the desert. Not surprisingly, roaming scholars were invariably viewed by local bureaucrats with suspicion, fearful that their surveying was in preparation for military action.[10] Indeed, there were good reasons for this, for as Kreutzmann points out, "the exploration of Chinese Central Asia needs to be discussed in the light of imperial interest of expanding the respective spheres of influence by the superpowers of the time."[11] With the British and Russians harboring similar suspicions toward each other,

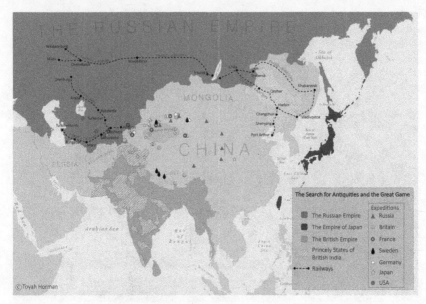

Figure 3.2 The search for antiquities and the Great Game.
Credit Line: Courtesy of Toyah Horman.

archaeology was fast becoming an arena of competition. But this meant that it also furnished opportunities for international cooperation and collaboration, even across the fault lines of imperial rivalry. Petrovsky granted permission for Stein to return home to Europe with his cargo of 12 boxes of artifacts and manuscripts via the Trans-Caspian Railway. But as Stein explored alone, teams from Russia and Germany set about planning joint expeditions.[12]

Outside Germany, the four trips to Chinese Turkestan that made up the Turfan Expeditions have received far less attention than those undertaken by Stein, Hedin, or Pelliot. Albert Grünwedel led the first in 1902, and under the leadership of Albert von Le Coq three additional trips ran through to 1914. Suzanne Marchand argues that the 16,115 kilograms of manuscripts, artworks, and artifacts that arrived back at the Prussian Academy of Sciences and Berlin Ethnographic Museum played a valuable role "in opening new perspectives on the Orient in an age of growing dissatisfaction with western culture."[13] Having trained as a linguist, Grünwedel worked as a museum curator, and as his interests broadened he forged relations with foreign scholars and collectors, including Dimitri Klementz, who visited Berlin en route to the International Congress of Orientalists in Rome. Grünwedel confirmed that the Buddhist frescoes Klementz acquired showed Indian and Iranian influences, and their conversation led to a proposed Russo-German collaboration.[14] Richthofen had long struggled to excite students about Central Asia, and in the 1890s the German state showed little interest in supporting archaeological expeditions. But with private and museum funds in hand, the first joint expedition returned from Turfan in 1903 with nearly 50 chests of artifacts, followed by a second trip a year later with an even larger shipment that included frescoes and wall carvings extracted by saws. Marchand rightfully observes that such drastic measures exemplified the "frenzied" nature of acquisition by the various teams trawling Central Asia at this time, a situation that differed significantly from the more scientific, careful excavations and surveys, which by then had become the order of the day in regions closer to Europe. As she states, "all of these teams were well aware that they were working in a subcolonial setting, where there were no antiquities laws or government oversight. Moreover, they were dealing not with Greek sculptures or biblical texts, but with little-understood manuscripts and aesthetically unappreciated art. It is no wonder that the tales of their feats read like adventure novels, in sharp contrast to the descriptions of the contemporary excavations at Olympia or even Pergamon, where there is no humor, no danger, and no luck."[15]

In the early 1900s, the Trans-Caspian Railway had reached as far as Tashkent, greatly easing passage into Central Asia. This dramatically increased both the speed of travel and the weight of cargo that could be carried back and forth. Additional archaeological trips undertaken before World War I helped Germany to maintain its reputation as a leading force in Oriental Studies. Germany and Russia had also developed a pact as to which areas each would study and excavate, but as Whitfield illustrates, this would subsequently break down with accusations that gentleman's agreements were not being honored.[16] By 1912, the Berlin Turfan collection had grown to more than 30,000 manuscript fragments, with scripts spanning 15 languages. This included 6000 Chinese, 8000 Sanskrit, and 4000 Tocharian fragments, all of which are now held at the Oriental Department of the Berlin State Library. The Berlin Brandenburg Academy of Sciences and Humanities holds Middle Iranian and Old Turkish texts. Under the guidance of Grünwedel and Le Coq, a number of German scholars produced "sensational publications," as Simone-Christiane Raschmann puts it, which demonstrated the region's complex processes of cultural transmission and linguistic diffusion.[17] These collaborations also helped the Russians to catch up with Britain in the prestige stakes and obtain expedition funding when their own government was reluctant to commit.[18]

Fin de siècle congresses in Rome, Paris, and Hamburg enabled scholars from across Europe and the United States to share ideas and findings. In Hamburg, the foundations for the Association Internationale pour l'Exploration Historique, Archéologique, Linguistique, et Ethnographique de l'Asie Centrale et de l'Extrême Orient were put in place, and with St Petersburg nominated for its headquarters, the British refused to join.[19] Archival work by Hansen, Wood, and others demonstrates how the different strands of research and international collaborations established during this period shed new light on the extent of connections between Europe and Asia stretching back millennia.[20] Selçuk Esenbel also notes that the insights gleaned from Central Asia helped to forge new understandings of world history in that the region offered "the exciting discovery of cosmopolitan encounters and plurality of national identities of an indigenous demography that incorporated the historical interconnections among nomads, traders, and settled peoples, independent of the neighboring Russian and Chinese empires . . . [it] . . . represented an extraordinary 'international' history of the descendants of the Greeks, Nestorian Christians, Sogdian merchants, Turkic and Mongol nomads, Uyghur kingdoms, Chinese travelers, and Indian pilgrims."[21] There were, however, disputes over how such long-distance entanglements should be conceptualized. For Albert von Le Coq, everything pointed back to Greece, with Hellenistic culture providing the roots for Indian, Iranian, and Chinese artistic expression. Paul Pelliot remained critical of such Eurocentric theories and stressed the need to understand the bidirectional forms of cultural transmission between the two regions.[22]

The pinnacle of this brief, but golden, era of archaeology and philology remains the visit by Aurel Stein to a network of grottoes a few miles outside Dunhuang in 1907. At its height, Dunhuang was the crossroads of two principal trade routes bordering the Taklamakan and served as an important stop on the north-south road connecting Mongolia with Tibet. A witness to Mongol invasions and Muslim conquests, the site was also a refuge for Buddhist monks for more than a thousand years between the fourth and fourteenth centuries. During this period, an estimated 45,000 murals were painted across a landscape comprising 500 or so grottoes. In the now infamous story, Stein discovered more than 50,000 manuscripts hidden behind a bricked-up cave entrance. The grottoes were under the careful watch of a local Taoist monk, Wang Yuanlu, and after some careful negotiation

Stein persuaded Wang to allow a small sample of items to be carted off to England. Meyer and Brysac describe Stein's haul of 12 cases in the following terms: "Paintings on silk, embroideries, sculptures, and, most importantly, more than a thousand ancient manuscripts written not only in Chinese but also in Tibetan, Tangut, Sanskrit, Turkish and a scattering of other, obscurer languages. The crown jewel was the world's oldest known printed book, dated May 11, 868, the Diamond Sutra, a popular spiritual text. All this, Stein proudly wrote to his friend P.S. Allen, cost the British taxpayer a mere 130 GBP, the sum he donated to Wang for the upkeep of the site."[23] Stein's hauls were divided into two, with plans for numerous objects to stay in India. In 1915, however, the Government of India requested the British Museum to manage the entire collection, and four years later the remaining items were shipped to London. Once there, items entered the museological world of cataloguing, curation, and conservation.

In the years that followed, Dunhuang was visited by teams from France, Japan, and Russia. Among the artifacts shipped to Paris by Paul Pelliot—the highly talented Sinologist employed by the École Française d'Extrême-Orient—were 50 pieces of sculpture. Hundreds of manuscripts were acquired for museums in St Petersburg by the acclaimed Russian orientalist Sergei Oldenburg. Stein returned to the region as part of a three-year expedition that began in 1913 and included an exploration of the Mongol Steppe, the Pamir Mountains, and Iran. The discoveries made at Dunhuang cemented the idea of Central Asia as an important center of civilizational exchange and cultural production. Stein was fascinated by the connections to India, but further interpretations of his finds using the writings of Marco Polo and Ptolemy provided evidence for an account of long-distance trade stretching from the Mediterranean to East Asia. Such analyses would become the bedrock of the fabled Silk Road, and in the years leading up to World War I they were beginning to pose important questions to long-held assumptions in Europe concerning the historical divisions between East and West.

Writing Grand Histories in the Aftermath of War and Revolution

World War I, together with the fall of the Ottoman Empire and the revolutions of 1917 in Russia, both transformed the political landscape of Europe and remapped the center-periphery relations of Eurasia. The unprecedented loss of life and scale of the conflict led intellectuals in Europe to question the cultural and spiritual foundations of both the West and the East and whether the notion of a Western civilization retained any meaningful value in the age of nation-states. In Germany, Oswald Spengler published *The Decline of the West* in 1918, proclaiming that the end of the Western world was coming. Spengler viewed history as a series of cultural organisms, which both evolved and declined. The final stage of culture was civilization, a point the West had by then reached. In Germany, Spengler provided a new architecture for world history, one that questioned the universalism of the European experience. Prasenjit Duara suggests that it also created a discourse of Eastern civilization, one that was "affirmed in the West before it was confirmed in Asia."[24] Beginning in the 1920s, his ideas permeated the English-speaking world through Arnold Toynbee, whose widely read writings grappled with the qualities and future of Western civilization.

Japan's defeat of Russia in 1905 rattled Europe, and throughout the 1910s tensions between Tokyo and Washington continued to grow, reaching the League of Nations in 1919, where the US government blocked Japan's requests for formal recognition of racial and national equality. The fate of the political discourse of East and West was further sealed through the formation of the Soviet Union in 1922. This set in motion changes that disconnected Central Asia from the West for much of the twentieth century. With significant phases of the Great Game coming to an end, the door began to close for scholars interested in the types of cultural and historical connections previously found in Central Asia. In the region itself the dynamics of historiography were also about to take a different turn. In the academic institutions of Tsarist Russia, archaeology had built a solid intellectual base. Its position relative to the imperial state, the monarchy, and the public was secured by regular congresses and the famed museums of St Petersburg and Moscow.[25] The rise of political Marxism, however, brought wholesale changes to the humanities and social sciences, transforming both what was studied and how it was interpreted. With a new generation of scholars entering the fields of archaeology and anthropology, by the 1920s previous typologies of culture and history were abandoned and discredited in favor of a Marxist conception of historical "stages" and their socio-economic formations.[26] To accommodate these intellectual shifts, archaeology was renamed "the history of material culture."[27] Moscow and St Petersburg (then Leningrad) remained centers of scholarship, and as the Soviet Union expanded over the course of the 1930s, they trained scholars for positions in the newly established National Academies of

Sciences of the republics in the Caucasus. As Pavel Dolukhanov explains, in the years leading up to World War II archaeology in Central Asia was largely undertaken by Russian archaeologists.[28] But the nature of the research they conducted altered once again in response to the turmoil of the period. Bulkin et al. describe "an especially rapid increase in knowledge of the ancient past" across Central Asia, the Caucasus, and Siberia as part of an effort to promote the cultural enhancement and national self-consciousness among groups living in these regions.[29]

Soviet ethnography followed a similar path. On the back of the formal constitution of the Soviet Union, the Bolsheviks increased efforts to implement a nationalities policy.[30] *Korenizatsiya*, or "putting down roots" as it is commonly translated, was conceived to fix the wrongs of the Russian Empire by creating a federal union defined by diversity and unity, an ethos encased in a Marxist ideology of modernization and developmental progress.[31] New policies on language, education, and the political representation of non-Russians also extended to prescribing categories of ethnicity and their associated territories. In her fascinating book *Empire of Nations*, Francine Hirsch focuses on three technologies of governance—the map, census, and museum—all of which formed part of a strategy of double assimilation, whereby diverse groups were categorized both into national populations and a wider Soviet society.[32] As Hirsch illustrates, ethnographers played a key role in guiding how such policies were implemented. Oksana Sarkisova also traces the processes by which this ideology was transposed into a series of state-funded documentaries. Initially given the title of *Kulturfilm*, a term borrowed from Germany, these films were designed to provide audiences—primarily metropolitan Russian—with a visual vocabulary for understanding the Soviet Union as a vast land of immense linguistic and cultural diversity, yet one that spans the Eurasian continent with a single ideology. Filmmakers set off on expeditions throughout the 1920s, frequently collaborating with ethnographers and cartographers. As Sarkisova explains, "*Kulturfilms* gave a tangible form and shape to imaginative concepts such as civilization and backwardness, and highlighted the entanglement of colonizing and modernizing attitudes in the Soviet context."[33] For Central Asia, this involved producing films both on the traditional practices of different cultural groups and the implementation of infrastructure projects, most notably the Turksib Railway. *Krysha Mira*, or *The Roof of the World*, made in 1927, involved a trip to the Pamir Mountains for what Sarkisova describes as a "taxidermic" representation of ethnic prototypes based on their nomadic or sedentary lifestyles.[34] By contrast, Viktor Turin's much celebrated 1929 film *Turksib* portrayed the transformational power of Soviet modernization projects, in this case a railway, and their ability to help the remote regions of Central Asia "leap straight into a brave, new, industrial world."[35]

Across the border in Xinjiang, ideas about the region's history and culture were also being reworked on the back of major political change. The previous discussion of European archaeology in Chinese Central Asia reached as far as the twilight years of the Qing dynasty, which collapsed in 1912. Throughout the period, foreign travelers and scholars enjoyed the privileges accrued from China's vastly weakened position relative to foreign powers. For those local bureaucrats who came into contact with foreign expeditions, their primary concern was the avoidance of diplomatic incidents. As Justin Jacobs points out, this trumped any concern for questioning, let alone policing, the removal of artifacts.[36] By the late 1920s, this situation had changed significantly. Both Stein and Hedin made return visits to Xinjiang shortly after Chiang Kai-shek declared Nanjing the capital of the Republic of China in 1927. In a fascinating account of what he refers to as the "domestic geopolitics" of their two trips, Jacobs describes how they came to be manipulated both by the Nanjing government and by the provincial governor of Xinjiang, Jin Shiren, under the guise of cultural sovereignty. In the face of heavy Soviet interference and unrest from local warlords, Nanjing attempted to retain control over its frontier province. In 1929, Sven Hedin traveled from Europe via the Trans-Siberian Railway, leading a team of five Swedes and two Chinese. Suspicious of their motivations, Jin declined them entry but relented under pressure from Nanjing, which in turn took instruction from powerful academics in Beijing.[37] Nanjing's support for the trip stemmed from a signed agreement that any artifacts found by the team would be deposited in a museum in Nanjing and that the expedition would retain two Chinese members. The trip spanned several years despite the suspicions of Jin. Supporting this Sino-Swedish collaboration served the national unity agenda of the Nationalist Party elite. But as Jacobs reveals, so too did shaming Stein's expedition, which set off a year later. Supported by the Fogg Museum of Harvard University, Stein made the strategic mistake of traveling to the region without Chinese partners.[38] The Chinese press thus cast him as a potential looter and threat to cultural sovereignty. His presence in the region also made the government in Nanjing suspect he was undertaking military surveys for the British in support of a possible move by Jin for greater autonomy. In the air of mistrust over Stein's motivations regarding the removal of artifacts, both Jin and Nanjing sought to retain their credibility in the media by publicly declaring their commitment to national unity. Stein left the following year with a cloud over his name, never to return to China.

Evidently, this episode signaled a major transition in the domestic politics of antiquity and how the cultural past of China's frontiers had become part of the discourse of nationalism and aspirations for revival.[39] Elsewhere, Jacobs has traced this process through to the 1940s with respect to the establishment of the wartime capital Chongqing.[40] He argues that the move gave new symbolic significance to Dunhuang, as the political and intellectual elite searched for a new spiritual heartland after an enforced retreat from the Japanese army. As Chinese scholars visited the caves for the first time, they were struck by their grandeur and began absorbing their artworks into ideas of a Han Chinese ancestry. Dunhuang's frescoes were reproduced as wartime museum displays, and by citing the renowned painter Zhang Daqain, Jacobs illustrates how deep histories of contact with Europe were framed for a public embattled by conflict with an imperial Japan:

> By closely scrutinizing the features of the people depicted in the Dunhuang frescoes and other Tang paintings, Zhang was able to conclude triumphantly that "the moustache and hair resemble those of western Europeans." The implication was that Tang Chinese "clothing and cultural trappings . . . had once spread all the way to western Europe," such was the strength of ancient China back in the day. Because the Dunhuang murals preserved intact the spirit of those vigorous and admirable Chinese who flourished during the Tang, the fine art connoisseurs who crowded Lanzhou and Chengdu's exhibition halls during 1943-1944 could gaze upon Zhang's lifelike copies and silently intuit the long-lost cure—the cosmopolitan Tang imperial spirit— for China's current malaise.[41]

Part Two revisits these decades leading up to World War II to illustrate how the Silk Road enters popular culture. Sven Hedin forms part of this story, notably his publications and films depicting his time in China. The Silk Road term had only rarely featured in the accounts of the scholar-explorers described in this chapter. Most notably, Albert Herrmann used it in a 1910 book publication that retained Richthofen's time frame of Han dynasty China but offered a more substantial account of the trade routes and possible East-West connections of the period. Through to the 1930s, then, the Silk Road remained a neologism.[42] As we shall see in Part Two, its popularization occurs through the romance of grand adventure. Sven Hedin's evocative writings reached much wider audiences than those of his counterparts. His 1936 work, *The Silk Road*, published initially in Swedish, with subsequent translations in German and English, contributed to the term entering the public imagination across Europe.[43] As Waugh notes, the book was an early example of a travelogue imbued with the "romantic aura" of Silk Road adventure.[44] Before we get to such developments, we first need to consider the constructions of Central Asian history that emerged from within Asia, and specifically Japan, and the different political trajectories they followed.

4

Japan as Asia?

In Asia and the Middle East, Silk Road imaginaries take on different
inflections, depending on the country. This becomes apparent in later
chapters as I highlight examples from China, India, and elsewhere. Recent
research is beginning to reveal the term's circulation across the region at different moments in the twentieth century, and future studies should add further detail to this picture. Here I focus on Japan for two reasons. First, it helps
to illustrate a broader pattern in Asia regarding how the Silk Road comes to
be a narrative of intra-Asian connectivity and not just about trade between
East and West. This foregrounds themes such as the movement of Buddhism
and other Asian religions, as well as histories of regional exchange and exploration. As we will see, this becomes significant from the 1960s onward as the
premise for advancing certain discourses of cultural affinity and pan-Asian
values within popular culture and contexts of diplomacy. Second, Japan
influences Silk Road discourses in important ways as the term gains popularity around the world at the end of the Cold War. UNESCO's 10-year multilateral program, Silk Roads: Roads of Dialogue was oriented around three
core routes—oasis, sea, and steppe—a structure that stems from initiatives
developed in Japan from the 1950s onward. To understand the roots of these
developments, and some of the core values and ideas that come to be ascribed
to the Silk Road in Asia, this chapter focuses on Japanese debates about civilization and those forms of scholarship from the early twentieth century that
focused on premodern forms of trade and cultural and religious exchange
across the region.

Japanese Civilization, Caught between East and West, Tradition and Modernity

If we shift the focus on late nineteenth-century debates about civilization
and the roots of history from Europe to Japan, a somewhat different picture
emerges. In simple terms, Japan's sense of historical identity in the modern

The Silk Road. Tim Winter, Oxford University Press. © Oxford University Press 2022.
DOI: 10.1093/oso/9780197605059.003.0004

era has followed two broad arcs. First, there is the perception that the country has a distinct, even unique, set of traditions distinguishing it from the West as well as its regional neighbors. Paralleling this is a commitment to understanding Japanese civilization as the product of entanglement and an infusion of values and ideas from the outside world. Although such debates can be traced back centuries, the early decades of the Meiji era—a phase of intense international exposure and engagement—are of most relevance here. Meiji intelligentsia understood the security threats posed by rapidly modernizing naval power in Europe and United States. By implication, embracing industrialization was of paramount importance, a situation that also required constructing a framework of national culture and civilization compatible with the changing times. As Arnason, Duara, Eisenstadt, and others have shown, new dualities of *uchi-soto* (inside and outside) were created in order to raise awareness of the ways in which Japanese society was indebted to the outside world.[1] Historically, this had taken place primarily through contact with the cultures of South and East Asia, and in particular China, as evidenced through language, calligraphy, painting, and, most significantly, Buddhism and Confucianism. As Duara explains, Japanese intellectuals of the Meiji era thus framed the country's past and future in terms of a "discourse of civilizations."[2]

The Iwakura Mission of 1871–1873 created the all-important political openings required for incorporating such ideas into the state. This extraordinary initiative involved a team of government ministers, ambassadors, and scholars visiting the United States and Europe over a two-year period to witness first-hand the scale of industrial development and the societal transformations it produced. But as Mark Ravina notes, through such trips Western modernity came to be equated with ideas of universalism and civilization, a notion of cultural, social, and technological progress from which Japan could learn and emulate.[3] The concept of *Bunmei Kaika*—civilization and enlightenment—thus became a debate about Japan's place in a fast-changing world, where ideas reflected both admiration and anxieties about rising military power in Europe, not least from Russia, and the determination to avoid the humiliation suffered by China. In 1875, the prominent author Fukuzawa Yukichi published the book *An Outline of a Theory of Civilization* (*Bunmeiron no Gairyaku*), which argued that Japanese development was best served through the acquisition of knowledge and the creation of a culture of higher learning. Holding Europe as the highest expression of civilization, Fukuzawa subsequently argued in a newspaper editorial that Japan was best served by joining the West and "escaping" Asia.[4] His writings were read by millions of Japanese, sparking intense debate about civility and the outward importance of civilized behavior, perceived as necessary for gaining respect from Western elites.[5] Fukuzawa's arguments for attaining equality with the West were taken up by those harboring ambitions of imperialism and the conquest of territories in the region. For others, however, *Bunmei Kaika* meant drawing Japan closer to Asia, and it is these men that are of particular importance to our story here. By the late 1880s, there were sharply divided opinions concerning the country's future trajectory. A new wave of nationalists were critical of Western culture and argued that Japan needed to find its own national essence. In contrast, those close to the emperor saw merit in using Confucian standards as the foundation for a rapidly modernizing society.[6]

It was a debate that helped to justify a role for museums, institutions where the Japanese state could demonstrate its commitment as the guardian of the cultural past and provider of a civic education. In his capacity as Japan's first prime minister, a role created as part of the centralization of the Meiji state in the 1870s, Itō Hirobumi recognized the need for patrons of the arts. Aware that European countries had developed new cultural institutions and curatorial practices, Itō insightfully saw the importance of appropriately exhibiting art and culture as one of the markers of a modern civilized society. To that end, he recruited four experts: Ernest Fenollosa, Okakura Kakuzō, Kuki Ryūichi, and Sekino Tadashi, three of whom are vital characters in our story here. Over the coming decades, these men would provide a template for Japanese archaeology, architectural history, and museum practice that remains in place today. Crucially here, their efforts also gave credence to a historiography of Japan's material culture built around ideas of diffusion and phases of development defined through episodes of trans-Asian connection. Ernest Fenollosa was an American scholar trained in a number of humanities topics who arrived in Japan in 1878 to teach at the Tokyo Imperial University. He subsequently developed an interest in the country's religious heritage and extended his academic career through a position at the Tokyo Fine Arts School. In these roles, Fenollosa studied the sculptures and other treasures located in some of Japan's oldest temples in an effort to understand their cultural and spiritual origins. As Hyung Il Pai explains, his academic positions gave him access to the most important temples of Nara—the capital for much of the eighth century—despite protests from resident monks fearful that their artifacts would lose supernatural power through exposure to the modern researcher. Over time, Fenollosa developed theories of artistic progression and typologies of style and design via his teaching and writing. In 1886 he also undertook a "grand tour" of Europe and the United States, visiting an array of educational and cultural institutions to gather new ideas about the funding and management of art. Such trips provided the evidence needed to lobby for the establishment of new associations, training schools, and museums, all of which would enable the regeneration of Japanese art and antiquity after centuries of neglect. Dismayed at the lack of progress in such areas, Fenollosa returned to the United States in 1890, continuing to research and write in his capacity as an exhibition curator. His subsequent *Epochs of Chinese and Japanese Art: An Outline History of East Asiatic Design* drew on research conducted in Nara. This offered a detailed theorization of Greco-Buddhist art as the following excerpt illustrates:

> It was apparently in the western side of the Nara plain, close up under the sand hills, and a little north of the present town of Koriyama, that the first great experiments in Japanese Greco-Buddhist art were made. Here stands Yakushiji itself with the Toindo; and just south of it lies Shodaiji, an institution founded a little later, but probably on an early Buddhist site. Here, amid a mass of broken statues and interesting refuse, I found in 1880 a life-sized piece which seems to have been one of the original Greco-Buddhist models, or at least experiments. The Greekish modification of Indian drapery over the legs is under-cut in deep, catenary folds; the body, nude above the waist, shows strong markings of the primary muscular tracts; the long, tapering arm has been separately modelled and set into the shoulder with a plug; the neck is short, the head rather too large, but semi-Greek in profile, and a projecting plug shows where a top-knot was added to the Greco-Buddhist hair.[7]

But as Pai suggests, Fenollosa's theories of cultural diffusion did not stop with classical Greece. Persia, Rome, Babylonia were all seen as providing artistic ideas that traveled through India, China, and Korea en route to Japan, creating distinct stages of development. After Fenollosa left Japan, his former student Okakura Kakuzō remained committed to understanding Japan's past in relation to such long-distance connectivities. As a professor at the Tokyo Fine Arts School, he taught and studied world history through the lens of axial civilizations and used his position to promote the arts within Japan. But as Pai and Duara point out, with Okakura's career progressing against the backdrop of rising militarism and conflicts with China and Russia, his analysis of Japanese history directly spoke to his fears about the present.[8] Concerned about the country's descent into warfare, Okakura developed an account of civilization markedly different from that offered by Fukuzawa. Rather than seeing modernity and progress as bringing Japan closer to the West and thus away from a less civilized "backward" Asia, Okakura argued that Japan's culture was fundamentally part of the family of Asian civilizations, which, in their collective, were inherently more peaceful than Western civilization. But his efforts were not just tailored to a domestic audience. To present a more positive image of Japan internationally and rectify misconceptions held in the West, he wrote extensively in English. Books such as *The Ideals of the East with Special Reference to the Art of Japan*, published in 1903, were in part conceived to demonstrate that "Japanese rulers had from ancient times been responsible for the transmission of old customs, arts, rituals, and ceremonies."[9] In the book, Okakura directly challenged the Hellenic theory of cultural diffusion. Studies of the famed Ajanta Caves in India and sites in China constituted the evidence for an argument that the classical civilizations of Europe and West Asia were in fact part of a longer story of cultural diffusion that had its roots in early forms of Asiatic art. Instead of seeing Asian civilization as the recipient or derivative of the high cultures of the West, Okakura made the case that Buddhism and Confucianism form the bedrock of a continental culture that possesses unrivaled values and ideals, "a single mighty web" inherited by Japan:

It is in Japan alone that the historic wealth of Asiatic culture can be consecutively studied through its treasured specimens. The Imperial collection, the Shinto temples, and the opened dolmens, reveal the subtle curves of Hâng workmanship. The temples of Nara are rich in representations of Tâng culture, and of that Indian art, then in its splendour, which so much influenced the creations of this classic period—natural heirlooms of a nation which has preserved the music, pronunciation, ceremony, and costumes, not to speak of the religious rites and philosophy, of so remarkable an age, intact . . . Thus Japan is a museum of Asiatic civilisation; and yet more than a museum, because the singular genius of the race leads it to dwell on all phases of the ideals of the past, in that spirit of living Advaitism which welcomes the new without losing the old.[10]

Here, then, we see Okakura harmonizing tradition with the forces of modernity in an effort to retain continuities with both the Japanese past and a region yet to experience the societal and technological transformations Japan was undergoing. His classification of Japanese history into a "three-age system" reflected the international trend of archaeology of the time for constructing stylistic or technological typologies and linking them to phases of development. Diffusionist theories developed by Fenollosa were thus ordered into a triad of antiquity, middle age, and modern.

He came to see Japan as the "exhibition hall" of Asia as a region of civilizations, each with their respective cultural and religious roots but in their collective fundamentally different from the West. Japan was where these various traditions combined to produce the highest forms of cultural expression. Such ideas were integrated into the stance held by those on the left, who believed Japan's role as a "leader," indeed its responsibility, was to help the civilizations of Asia flourish. However, for those on the political right, victory in the Russo-Japanese War of 1904–1905 demonstrated that Japan could gain military and economic parity with the industrial powers of the West. The ideas of Okakura would prove critical to an ongoing commitment to pan-Asian histories in Japan after World War II and research initiatives that defined the contours of the Silk Road as a story of regional religious connections, most notably Buddhism. But to better understand how the "routes" of the Silk Road took on formal definitions within international policy in the 1950s, we also have to turn to another figure of significance in the development of late nineteenth-century Japanese identity, Shiratori Kurakichi.

Shiratori is widely regarded as the founder of the field of modern Asian history (tōyōshi) in Japan.[11] As Stefan Tanaka explains, for Shiratori, tōyōshi was the process of writing a deeper and more geographically expansive account of Japan's past. Crucially, his frustration with Europe's treatment of the East as culturally inferior and lacking its own history shaped both his choice of fieldwork location and his theorization of the region. This would have a bearing on how the Silk Road came to be thematically and geographically constructed after World War II. By the 1890s, he was dismayed at the lack of attention given to Korea by European scholars and sought the roots of Japan's past in the lands and people of Korea and Manchuria.[12] Some years later, he persuaded the South Manchuria Railway Company to fund a research department in its Tokyo branch dedicated to the history and geography of the two regions.[13] Perhaps most significantly, however, Shiratori's research interests shifted westward toward the steppe and northerly reaches of Central Asia. Through detailed accounts of the Mongols and nomadic groups, he began to construct a typology of Asian history based on a duality of north and south.[14] This, he claimed, transcended Eurocentric narratives of trade corridors between East and West, putting Asia and Europe on a par via an analysis of themes such as climate and conflict, which disconnected ideas of civilization from progress. Unshackled from European hierarchies, metaphors of conflict provided a lens through which Japan's imperial present could be interpreted.[15] He saw Asia as the home of civilization, with its climates and landscapes orienting the grand trends of history, as Tanaka explains:

> Shiratori divided the Eurasian continent, geographically and culturally, by the mountain ranges that ran from eastern Europe, along the Himalayas, to the Liaotung peninsula. The vast land to the north, the desert and steppes from Manchuria to the north shore of the Black Sea in southern Russia, was inhospitable, the cold climate and infertile ground inhibiting the natural development of high culture. The people of this region, whom he called *kiba minzoku* (horse-riding people), were basically hunters and gatherers; they were nomadic, simple, skilled horsemen and fierce fighters, and their leaders were autocratic. Because of this military prowess and a lack of resources, they often invaded and plundered others, especially civilizations to the south.[16]

Shiratori's ideas would prove formative in Japanese Oriental Studies right through to World War II. Significantly, this brought the regions of the Eurasian Steppe, its nomadic cultures, and the historical importance of the horse into the fold. Decades later, his work provided the foundations for a Silk Road "Steppe Route," whereby a team of Japanese scholars questioned Richthofen's reading of Eurasian history as a story of east-west flows, thereby stressing the need for understanding the connections between the fertile south and the nomadic north.

Japan's various attempts to construct a narrative for the nation and its people was a situation repeated across many countries during this late nineteenth-century period.[17] But the situation in Japan at this time—not least the ongoing debates about national security and the moral case for imperialist adventures—ensured that ideas about deep histories of transregional connectivity found a level of support not seen elsewhere in Asia, the flip side of which meant that they remained politically fraught areas. Of course, this took place within state efforts to build a new citizenry, whereby the threat of

European colonialism demanded a feudal system be replaced by a modern nation-state with a population connected to the emperor. As Koji Mizoguchi explains, this meant there were "safe" and "dangerous" periods of Japanese history to study, depending on whether they reinforced or undermined the genealogical continuity of the emperor. Even for those safe periods, the expectation of constructing appropriate narratives meant that only certain themes and forms of evidence were discussed.[18]

Japan had expanded its army presence in the region in the years following the First Sino-Japanese War of 1894–1895, and the defeat of a European power a decade later marked a turning point in Asia's political affairs and created a new platform for pan-Asianist alliances rooted in ideas of shared history. Duara notes that ideas about pan-Asianism were co-opted by both the left and right and as such "fed and resisted the nascent imperialism" of Japanese politics in this period.[19] There is also a body of scholarship that interprets the Greater East Asia Co-Prosperity Sphere of the 1940s in ideological terms and the quest for a regional order based on values different from those of Western imperialism. As Jeremy Yellen notes, this approach historically locates the Co-Prosperity Sphere as both "the ultimate political form of Pan-Asianism" and a "project to bring Japan to the center of global history."[20]

Searching for Buddhist Asia

In 1901, Ōtani Kozui, an important intellectual figure who would later become the chief abbot of one of Kyoto's most important temples, set off for London. As a scholar of Buddhism, Ōtani wanted to learn about the great finds made by European scholars in western China.[21] The installation of Shinto as the state religion after the Meiji Restoration marginalized Buddhism as a moral and cultural compass for a rapidly changing country. Ōtani's travels to Europe and other parts of Asia were thus driven by a desire to comprehend the compatibility of religion and modernity on the one hand and the possibilities of using Buddhism as a platform for a pan-Asian revival on the other. As Imre Galambos demonstrates across a series of fascinating publications, Ōtani traced this transnational shared heritage by organizing and sponsoring a series of expeditions to India, China, and other parts of Asia.[22] Of significance here are the three trips to Central Asia he oversaw between 1902 and 1914.

The Ōtani expeditions were designed to identify the "Buddhist culture and its cultural and artistic artifacts" that had been forgotten or buried in regions where Islam was prevalent.[23] After an initial trip spanning 1902–1903 to the ruins and caves of Kucha, Ōtani began work on a villa in Kobe designed to showcase and study the sacred texts and artifacts retrieved by the team (see Figure 4.1). A close relationship with the well-traveled architect Itō Chutā led to a building that drew on Mughal and Persian architecture, as well as Japanese elements, to give a sense of a shared Asian tradition.[24] During a follow-up expedition to Xinjiang and Mongolia in 1908, the team split into two groups. It was here that Ōtani's expedition entered the official British records and thus the story of Hopkirk's *Foreign Devils*.[25] The British consul in Kashgar suspected two members were spying for the Japanese government. On all sides of the Great Game, men gathering military intelligence had been masquerading as archaeologists. Having left their collected items at the British consulate to head south to India, one of the team members was refused entry back into China. Galambos has compared archive sources in Japan and

Figure 4.1 Villa Nirakusō, designed by Itō Chūta.
Credit Line: Department of Architecture, Graduate School of Engineering, University of Tokyo.

the UK to argue that there is little evidence to support the suspicions of the British.[26] On a third trip, spanning 1910–1914, team members gathered a wealth of items—including 250 manuscript scrolls from Dunhuang—transporting them back to Japan via Siberia on the Trans-Siberian Railway. Ōtani publicized the results of his three expeditions and communicated with scholars and associations across Europe. But he also endeavored to include Japanese Buddhist students and researchers in an effort to enhance their international reputations.[27] For Galambos, then, the importance of the team's search for ancient Buddhist relics, along with Ōtani's larger vision of a pan-Asian cultural past, was two-fold: "On the one hand, they tried to position themselves as part of the tradition of European exploration of Central Asia, which to some extent reflects Japan's contemporary aspirations to align itself with leading colonial powers. This European colonial element shines through in all narratives associated with the expeditions. On the other hand, they also claimed a connection with the medieval Buddhist pilgrimages through the Western Regions."[28]

Ōtani's contributions to pan-Asianist ideas were both significant and timely, given, as Sven Saaler and Christopher Szpilman note, that the concept was only beginning to appear in intellectual discourse in the early 1910s.[29] Pan-Asianist writers and other critics of European colonialism stressed regional solidarity, and by the 1920s such groups were holding conferences in China, India, and Japan. A visit by the celebrated poet Rabindranath Tagore in 1916 helped to cement ties with an Indian intellectual elite increasingly disillusioned with colonial rule. Nationalist and regionalist identities needed their historical roots, and in India decades of archaeology and the work of Alexander Cunningham on the seventh-century Chinese traveler Xuanzang demonstrated the long-standing ties between India and China. The spread of Buddhism also gave weight to an intellectual position that foregrounded harmonious, precolonial intra-Asian interactions. Tansen Sen thus concludes that ideas about contact zones among "Asian civilizations" served as the foundations for building ideas of cultural and political regionalisms.[30] Of course, all this would be facilitated by the new infrastructures of modernity. Railways and steamships carried Japanese visitors to the most sacred sites of Buddhism in India, most notably Bodh Gaya. Mark Ravinder Frost points to the role played by the region's network of museums, which displayed the items collected by travelers and scholars. In Calcutta, the India Museum was home to an extensive collection of artifacts from across the Central Asia region.[31] Crucially, then, the pan-Asianism that emerged in the early decades of the twentieth century constituted a geocultural imagination incorporating the regions, histories, cultural interactions, and religions that today come under the umbrella of the Silk Road. It advanced new narratives about civilization in Asia that were entirely disconnected from the canonical religions or major events of European history.[32] At a political level, such a reading of the past refuted Eurocentric visions of the world order, which had placed Western civilization at the center of universalist discourses of progress and enlightenment.[33]

Unlike some of his counterparts, Ōtani continued to engage with European scholarship that foregrounded the Europe-Asia nexus. Interestingly, the co-existence of these two geocultural imaginations—pan-Asianism and East-West exchange—also brought Japan into dialogue with the Ottoman Empire. For pan-Islamic intellectuals in search of a resolution to an expanding Tsarist Russia, Japan served as an inspirational model for Islamic modernity.[34] Ali Merthan Dündar demonstrates how this came to be expressed across the Turkic world via poetry and literature.[35] But with pan-Asianism underpinning the imperial ambitions of the Japanese ultranationalist right by the 1920s, anti-Russian sentiment in both Turkey and Japan fueled ambitions for a more united Asia. Esenbel argues that this situation encouraged a number of Turkish intellectuals to turn to geocultural histories as the connective tissue. Interestingly, ties between the two countries continue today via a number of Japanese-Turkish scholarly collaborations in Silk Road studies.[36]

If we turn to the early days of Japanese archaeology from this period, we also learn about forms of research and heritage management that become anchors for Silk Road imaginaries in East Asia in the 1990s. Hyung Il Pai explains how the search for evidence of the origins of Japanese civilization in Korea gathered momentum by the time the region was formally annexed in 1910. The restoration and beautification of ruins formed part of the colonial apparatus established for enticing Japanese settlers to the peninsula. After 1910, surveys conducted by Sekino Tadashi and colleagues from Tokyo Imperial University led to the reconstruction of numerous temples, all of which were by then formally documented as Japanese imperial possessions.[37] These were subsequently promoted by the Japan Tourist Bureau as picturesque destinations for those Japanese in search of their cultural and spiritual roots. The most spectacular restoration occurred at the sites of Kyŏngju located in the southwest, the cultural center and administrative capital of the Silla Kingdom (see Figure 4.2). Through conquests in the seventh century, Silla expanded its domain across the southern half of the Korean peninsula.

Japanese archaeologists argued that Unified Silla represented the height of Korean artistic achievement, one that was followed by stagnation and long-term decline. It was a narrative embodied in the ruins of Bulguksa and Sŏkkuram, and in a model reminiscent of the colonial practices of European powers in South and Southeast Asia, their restoration of crumbling staircases and hallways served as a metaphor for civilizational redemption and revitalization. Critically, Japanese experts and authorities thus presented themselves as the heirs to and guardians of a glorious past that, through its revival, would (re)unify both the Korean peninsula and East Asia as a single civilizational zone rooted in the peaceful practices of Buddhism. Such an appropriation of antiquity not just served to legitimize colonial rule in the peninsula but also provided the evidence for connecting Japan to the wider cultural orbit of China and India.

As a trained architect, Sekino Tadashi had played an instrumental role in establishing an ethos for preservation in Japan, and in viewing this as the responsibility of the state, he was highly influential in the creation of new acts, guidelines, and public awareness programs. In extending this philosophy to Korea, he saw the survival of temples and other structures as evidence of the peaceful coexistence of faiths and kingdoms stretching back centuries. Reaffirming the ideas of Okakura, Sekino also argued that the different forms of material culture passed down through the generations were evidence of the region's deep appreciation for the arts and, to quote Pai again, that preservation and restoration in the twentieth century demonstrated to the public and world "the steady progress of Japanese civilization."[38] By then, Hellenic theories of cultural diffusion had given way to accounts of trans-Asiatic connectivities compiled from scholars studying different regions. Ōtani's trips to China and Central Asia were instrumental in raising awareness in Japan about the dialogue of cultures and spread of Buddhism upward from India through Central Asia over a number of centuries. By this point, Buddhism had also become an important conduit for building international connections, as Judith Snodgrass demonstrates in her analysis of the World's Parliament of Religions, held as part of the 1893 Columbian Exposition.[39] Chapter 6 shows how this trend continues right through the twentieth century. I have also detailed the significance of the Unified Silla Kingdom here because this gains prescience for reviving diplomatic ties in East Asia at the end of the Cold War via a major international Silk Road collaboration led by UNESCO.

Figure 4.2 Site of Bulguksa, pre- and post-restoration.
Credit Line: Public Domain and photo by Author.

For the same reason, I also want to consider early attempts to craft maritime histories. In 1911, Friedrich Hirth and William Rockhill published their English translation of Zhao Rugua's (*Chau Ju-Kua*) thirteenth-century two-volume *Zhu Fan Zhi* (*Chu-fan Chih*), a title they translated as *Description of Barbarous Peoples*. Produced in the early thirteenth century, *Zhu Fan Zhi* shed new light on the extent of the trade ties between Song dynasty China and the Islamic world across the Indian Ocean. With Rockhill posted as the US government's minister to Russia, the translation was published by the Imperial Academy of Sciences in St Petersburg and stimulated great interest among scholars around the world.[40] But as Hisao Matsuda explains, by this time scholars in Japan had been studying the maritime histories of East Asia for more than a decade. They began around 1900 by examining ancient place names found in Chinese chronicles for Southeast Asia's coastal ports.[41] Pioneering work on southern maritime Asia was also undertaken on trade systems spanning a number of regions. In India, Paul Pelliot was one of a number of Sinologists who extended their analysis of long-distance overland cultural transmission in Asia to the maritime world. Kwa Chong-Guan suggests that French and Dutch archaeological agencies working across various sites in South and Southeast Asia steadily built up an understanding of the knowledge accumulated in India and China about the southern seas.[42] He explains how this inspired Indian historians, mostly Bengalis, to consider the sea more seriously, an intellectual movement that eventually coalesced into the Greater India Society in 1926 and studies of the historical linkages across the Bay of Bengal and down through Southeast Asia.[43] Again, we will see such ideas continue to evolve after the Second World War as these early Japanese studies and "Greater India" discourse become pivotal to the development of the Maritime Silk Road concept.

PART TWO

ADVENTURES INTO COSMOPOLITANISM

Adventure, exploration, and discovery have been defining themes of modernity. Many of the great figures of history, the heroes of nations, are those who set off in search of unknown lands, crossed uncharted seas, or walked and climbed untrodden paths. We admire the pioneer and those who are prepared to risk life and limb and endure hardship and uncertainty. Each century, each generation has created its new narrative of adventure and risk, new images of pushing the frontiers of humanity and of individual endurance. Sailing ships into remote island harbors comes from the same spirit, and speaks to the same hopes and ideals, as immortal words uttered while descending steps broadcast on television screens around the world. Such themes lie at the heart of the Silk Road story, and its entry into popular culture occurred at a moment when dreams of discovery and adventure had moved on from an exploration of Asia's more "remote" regions to the excitement of exploring the frontiers of a new age of car manufacturing. As we have seen, in the 1890s the story of Silk Road antiquity was wrapped up in ambitions to conquer space and terrain by rail. But as the term gains visibility beyond academia in the 1930s, new layers and themes are added, where the spirit of adventure, the freedom of independent travel, and the excitement of using untested technologies returns to the road.

Part Two addresses such themes, examining how the idea of a historical Silk Road has intersected with a twentieth-century spirit of adventure. "Traveling the Silk Road" has been instrumental in linking the past to the present and all that a journey of crossing continents entails. Politics and conflicts as well as ever shifting borders define the routes of modern Silk Road adventures. But the two chapters here also show how sojourners have undertaken their journeys within a symbolic economy of "retracing" pasts, supposedly following routes that previously linked the cultures and civilizations of Asia and Europe. To that end, we see the historical themes of cultures in contact identified in Part One consolidate in the present, whereby the Silk Road as metaphor for cosmopolitan worldliness is afforded to those privileged enough to travel its routes in the twentieth century. Traveling the Silk Road is without parallel in its promise of crossing unmarked cultural boundaries, an experience of encountering difference not just between self and other but between other and other, as regions, religions, and people are passed en route. Indeed, it might plausibly be suggested that part of the allure of its routes lies in their metaphorical qualities for life itself, where any sense of destination is of secondary importance to the journey.

Modern-day heritage and tourism, regarded by some as agents of neo-colonialism, have been instrumental in defining what constitutes the authentic, invariably valorizing those cultural expressions that speak of a singular root, whether it be ethnic, religious, or geographical. In this regard, the Silk Road has been somewhat of an outlier, with contemporary tourism discourses built on an ethnographic gaze that has "documented" facial features, languages, textiles, music, and cuisines as the tangible legacy of complex histories of movement and transmission. Traveling across lands is about encountering foods of fusion, hybrid architectures, and experiencing diverse cultural traditions. Together, the two chapters here also demonstrate how a history of Silk Road mobility emerges out of this ethnographic, come tourist, gaze. The nomad, Mongol horseman, and centuries of traders who crossed desert and ocean all become the anonymous archetypes of romance and the mystique of lost pasts. In depicting this story, Part Two begins in the 1920s, tracing the popularization of the Silk Road, as attempts to cross Asia and retrace the steps of the pioneers of Central Asian adventure reach new audiences via newspapers, magazines, personal travelogues, and silent film. One of the arguments advanced here surrounds the distinct visual culture that formed around the overland Silk Road, where the icons of mobility that connect past and present—the tent, camel, and horse—combine with an ethnographic gaze of exotic peoples and endangered traditions, the type of process Bruno Latour suggests enables complex phenomena to be comprehended by different audiences.[1] With Silk Road worldliness also coming from the sense of an expedition to unknown and foreboding lands, in the 1990s traveling through extreme climates and terrains took on additional impetus when the appeal of simpler, more friendly ties between East and West was at its height.

Silk Road adventure has recruited its celebrated pioneers. Whether they set off in 1930 or 2010, modern-day travelers have invariably found meaning in their voyage by following the routes taken by cosmopolitans of previous centuries, namely Marco Polo, Ibn Battuta, or Xuanzang. Born in Tangier in 1304, Ibn Battuta traveled nearly three times the distance of Polo. All but ignored in the West, across the MENA region he has become synonymous with a cosmopolitan Islam and integral to the story of regional trade and exchange. Interestingly, as the idea of a Maritime Silk Road continues to gain currency, his accomplishments are now reaching new audiences. From the ninth century we have the writings of Abū Zayd al-Sīrāfī, who compiled various reports of seafarers across the Indian Ocean, texts that form part of one of the most important depictions of long-distance travel left to us, *Accounts of China and India*.[2] Farther east in Asia, a number of traveling scholar-monks are likewise celebrated as the embodiment of Silk Road cultural transmission. At the beginning of the fifth century, Faxian left China for India, traversing Central Asia in search of Buddhist scripture. Two centuries later, Xuanzang completed a 17-year journey through India. Their efforts to diffuse ideas through teaching and the translation of texts played a formative role in the establishment of Buddhism in East Asia, a legacy that is commemorated today via statues and temples across India, China, Taiwan, and Southeast Asia. More broadly though, our iconic travelers play a crucial role in the story, that of friendship. Xuanzang and Ibn Battuta, like Polo, are celebrated for their ability to negotiate suspicions and build trust across cultures and as such embody the "spirit" of the Silk Road. Not surprisingly then, they have come to occupy a central role in Silk Road historiography. In 2017, Valerie Hansen, a renowned figure in this field, argued that accounts of their travels and encounters form part of an archive of texts and maps around which a new history of the Silk Road can be written.[3] Susan Whitfield takes an alternative approach to this history of mobility, highlighting various archetypal characters—the pilgrim, soldier, merchant, courtesan, and horseman—to tell the story of "life along the Silk Road."[4]

In the limited space available here, I take a very different approach from those of these authors, focusing on the popularization of Marco Polo's *The Travels* via modern translations and adaptations of his story for film, television, and stage. This means the discussion is primarily about Silk Road imaginaries in the West, and parallel studies could, and should, be undertaken for Ibn Battuta, Xuanzang, and others. Arguably, however, Marco Polo has become the most recognized traveler associated with the term, and his story has continued to garner considerable interest around the world.[5] In China, *The Travels* were studied and discussed among scholars and travelers at the beginning of the twentieth century.[6] We do not know exactly from *The Travels* what route the Polos followed, and yet in the pages that follow we see authors and journalists throughout the twentieth century repeatedly framing their own journeys as a retracing of his footsteps along the Silk Road. Such writers have thus contributed to a conflation between his 24-year-long voyage and the pre–Christian Era trade routes identified by Richthofen. The broad arc of his journey, from Italy to China and back again, replicates the points of connection signposted by Richthofen, Pelliot, and others. It is a geographical coincidence that has been pivotal in creating a seemingly coherent narrative of East-West connectivity that spans thousands of years. Indeed, somewhat strangely, modern Silk Road adventures and tourism have been built around texts written six centuries apart that describe events separated by a millennium and a half.

Part Three of this book discusses a major Silk Road international collaboration led by UNESCO at the end of the Cold War, which identified histories of maritime Islam, nomadic cultures of the Eurasian Steppe, and connections between Korea and Japan, among other themes. But even today these have yet to penetrate Silk Road tourism, which, as Chapter 6 here shows, continues to gravitate around the "exotic" ruins, cities, and museums of the former Soviet republics of Central Asia and northwest China. Rarely, if ever, are Rome, Aleppo, Palmyra, Baghdad, or Jerusalem—a key stop for Polo—marketed by the tourism industry as Silk Road locations. In countless documentaries and travelogues, Xi'an is described as its eastern terminus, but Rome continues to be the seat of a once-great empire and civilization. A project to develop the Western Silk Road is cited as one way this might change over the coming years, a theme returned to in the final chapter in relation to new forms of Silk Road consumption and adventure emerging on the back of Belt and Road.

5

The Car-tographies of Adventure

> Farther toward the north this highest upland on our globe slopes
> down to the vast desert of Chinese Turkestan, the western contin-
> uation of the great Gobi and a part of ancient Cathay, as China was
> called in the diaries of Marco Polo. This region was the goal of our
> expedition, and the fact that great portions of the country had never
> before been explored lent added interest to the undertaking.
>
> Hellmut de Terra, 1931[1]

Until now, the story of the Silk Road's emergence has centered around manuscripts, archaeological finds, and theories of cultural transmission. But in turning to the ways in which the concept started to capture public imagination in the run-up to World War II, we need to shift focus to the romance of adventure. We have already seen the importance of rail in the Great Game competition for antiquities. But as the fascinating volume edited by Nile Green shows, these communication infrastructures also drew other travelers into and across the region.[2] Much of the political writing of empire—the reports and diaries of explorers, spies, and bureaucrats—remained secret. But once stories of Central Asia's landscapes began to circulate, a number of poets, writers, and artists set off in search of its "mysterious," sparsely populated landscapes.[3] As Green notes, "by the late 1890s, the Trans-Caspian Railway was already becoming a tool of culture by offering easier access to the region to artists, intellectuals, and journalists from western Europe."[4] In essence, these travelers used a number of representational strategies to capture Central Asia as a "remote" and "vast" region for audiences back in Europe. The introduction of new communication technologies, namely long-distance telegraph lines, would also transform expedition journalism. In 1907, the much-celebrated Peking-Paris road race captivated audiences with the ambition of traveling from northeast Asia to Europe by car. Conceived as a

The Silk Road. Tim Winter, Oxford University Press. © Oxford University Press 2022.
DOI: 10.1093/oso/9780197605059.003.0005

media event, the race involved five cars, each setting off with a journalist on board, with stories telegraphed en route to editors in London and Paris. After traversing the Gobi Desert, the cars pushed across Siberia toward Moscow and on to the French capital. The expedition's makeshift infrastructure included camels carrying gasoline to temporary service stations. Not surprisingly, newspaper stories of such grand adventure inspired others to pack their bags, including a number of lone women travelers. The arrival of the first guidebooks further eased the logistics of independent travel to the region, and in 1912 Baedeker published its first guide for those wanting to venture from Russia across to East Asia. The English-language version—*Russia, with Teheran, Port Arthur and Peking; Handbook for Travellers*—followed two years later.[5] The guide included the now familiar sections on the history, culture, and types of landscape travelers were likely to encounter, as well as the logistical details of hotels, restaurants, and rail connections. There was no mention, however, of antiquities or manuscripts. Although the accounts of Stein, Hedin, and others had by then attracted considerable attention across metropolitan Europe, it would be some decades before their insights into the region's complex history were picked up by Baedeker and other guidebooks.[6]

To capture the sense of adventure and risk, travel writing on Central Asia during the early twentieth century often invoked the figure of Marco Polo. The son of a Venetian merchant, Marco set off for Asia with his father and uncle in 1271. Together they would travel more than 20,000 kilometers over a 24-year period. On return to Venice, Polo was taken captive by the Genoese during a sea battle and imprisoned. There the romance writer and fellow inmate, Rustichello of Pisa, wrote an account of his voyage. Scribed in a hybrid Franco Italian, multiple translations helped the manuscript to quickly gain attention across Europe. Readers were given an evocative picture of Mongol life and Kublai Khan's embattled relations with China on the basis of Polo's extended stays in his court. At some point the original manuscript was lost, but as Nigel Cliff notes in his own 2016 translation, around 150 different versions have survived. He thus suggests that *The Travels*—arguably the most famous travelogue of all time—"stands as the book that revealed the East to the West and formed Europe's idea of Asia."[7] John Larner has also traced its reception through the centuries. In the 1300s, *The Travels* was viewed as a tale of wonders, but it subsequently came to be recognized for the geographical insights it offered on Asia, inspiring, among others, Christopher Columbus. Larner argues that it then fell out of favor, often being discredited, only to be revived in the nineteenth century, achieving "cult status as a work of scholarly and romantic interest."[8] For Sinologists, *The Travels* was a particularly valuable reference source, with Paul Pelliot among those citing it to interpret histories of connection within and across Central Asia. In the case of Victorian Britain, Polo's reputation and popularity was further enhanced through Henry Yule's 1871 translation, a text that added new maps and garnered a prestigious Royal Geographic Society award. As mass tourism continued to grow in Europe, so too did interest in Polo, in part through the popularity of publications like the *National Geographic Magazine*, which launched in 1888. Placing strong emphasis on "world culture," the magazine featured numerous stories on Asia, and with photography included from the early 1900s onward, it frequently reproduced imperialist epistemologies.[9]

Of particular relevance here are a number of articles on China and other parts of Central Asia from the 1920s and 1930s. In 1927, William Morden's piece *By Coolie and Caravan across Central Asia* explained how Marco Polo "first brought word" of the Pamirs.[10] The following year, J.R. Hildebrand dedicated an entire article to *The World's Greatest Overland Explorer* at the same time that Broadway was staging *Marcos Millions*. Unlike the first-hand travelogues common to this period, Hildebrand's 63-page article was a condensed interpretation of *The Travels*, citing Yule's "famous summary" at various points along the way.[11] Interestingly, however, dozens of photographs of local landscapes and scenes of people weaving, cooking, or herding animals connected 1920s Georgia, Persia, and China to Polo's thirteenth-century text through the familiar trope of an unchanging Orient. It was an approach that produced some extraordinary examples of "othering" through stereotype. For the portrait of a man identified as a Kurd, the addition of a caption "A Pirate of the Persian Plains" was justified because he "comes of a race that holds a world-endurance record for fighting and longevity . . . Marco Polo called the Kurds 'an evil generation, whose delight is to plunder merchants.'"[12] Extensive reference to Polo in *National Geographic* articles on Persia and the regions of Central and East Asia thus underpinned a narrative of grand exploration and adventure. But it was also an Asia discovered and depicted through a distinctly ethnographic gaze. A consistent picture of immutable peoples and technologies was offered through scenes of agriculture or domestic craft and what by then was a well-crafted genre of "exotic" portraiture.[13] Within this framing, there were few, if any, references to the archaeological discoveries discussed in Chapter 3, and although numerous articles during this period cited the use of silk in the making of clothes and rugs, they rarely explored its history as a commodity of trade.[14]

In the 1920s, air travel began to open up previously remote areas of Central and West Asia. By then, however, tourism in large parts of the region had come under the purview of Soviet central planning. Intourist, the newly formed state travel agency of the Soviet Union, set about creating a new geocultural imaginary of Eurasia for Western tourists. Marketing campaigns for the agency's offices in Europe and the US promoted road trips to the mountains of Georgia to see the "Peoples of the Caucasus" or the landscapes of Soviet music.[15] Posters and brochures for the Trans-Siberian Railway promised a unique 12-day experience seeing the diverse landscapes and cultures of a Soviet Union stretching from Europe to the "Far East." And for those tourists wishing to venture farther south, train tours visited "the modern comforts of Baku" and onward to the oil-producing regions of Iran.[16] In other words, Soviet narratives of tourism shared the same ethnographic gaze as those of the *National Geographic Magazine* but did so in ways that advanced the idea of a union of integrated, yet culturally distinct republics. As we saw in the studies of Hirsch and Sarkisova cited in Chapter 3, within the Soviet Union museums and *Kulturfilms* were among the technologies used to create a public discourse around national populations and their ethnic categories. In western Europe, those who saw Sven Hedin's film on his Sino-Swedish Expedition, which began in 1927, also learned about everyday life of the Uyghurs of Xinjiang and Mongols of the Gobi Desert region. Hedin's expedition involved land surveys and the establishment of meteorological stations on behalf of Lufthansa, with the airline scoping possible refueling stations as part of a plan to connect Berlin with Peking. German filmmaker Paul Liberenz documented their journey, returning home to make the silent film *With Sven Hedin across the Deserts of Asia*.[17]

By the early 1930s, *National Geographic Magazine* authors began inscribing deeper histories to the different groups they encountered in Georgia, Mongolia, Northwest China, and elsewhere. Notable here is the German geologist Hellmut de Terra, who traveled to China in the late 1920s. In a 1931 article titled *On the World's Highest Plateaus*, Marco Polo featured once again, as did photographs of women operating looms and portraits of groups wearing formal dress.[18] Around the time of publication, de Terra had taken up an academic post at Yale University, working on the geological and archaeological material gathered from his trips. He was most likely familiar with Richthofen's geological studies of the area, and so made reference to a "silk-trading road" in his article. With the three members of the expedition separating to follow different routes along the way, the Swiss photographer

Walter Bosshard and German geographer Emil Trinkler skirted along the southern rim of the Taklamakan Desert in search of artifacts. de Terra explained the broader context of their finds:

> Ruins of Buddhistic shrines containing a number of painted statues, Chinese coins of the third century of the Christian Era, and several implements pointed to one of the old settlements already mentioned in the annals of the Tang period. At that time a silk-trading road existed which connected this faraway land with eastern China, and it was along this road that an exchange not only of merchandise but subsequently an interchange of Western and Eastern civilization, took place. Through Alexander's famous campaign to Bactria, Greek influence came into this country and some time later became strong enough to mold the cultural character of the then more civilized races.[19]

Walter Bosshard published his own account of the trip in the book *Hazards of Asia's Highlands and Deserts*. There he explained the plan of retracing the footsteps of Stein, Le Coq, and others in the hope of finding further artifacts and gold.[20] In describing the context of Stein's findings, he also cites "the Chinese pilgrims Fa-hien and Hsiang-Tsang" as valuable information sources testifying to the legacy of Khotan as an intersection "on the old Silk Road, along which developed Asiatic trade with the West."[21]

On Road Testing

The arrival of modern car industries in Europe and the United States was transforming the nature of adventure. By the 1930s, the golden age of long-distance expeditions by car had well and truly arrived. Manufacturers sought publicity through the newspaper column inches that would inevitably follow any grand adventure. Since the early 1920s, André Citroën had helped to fund an all-male expedition across Africa, and in 1931 he sponsored the Citroën-Haardt Trans-Asiatic Expedition. Two convoys of seven vehicles were to meet in northwest China, with one team, led by Georges-Marie Haardt, setting off from Beyrouth and the other, led by Victor Point, departing from Peking. Vehicles were fitted with caterpillar tracks in preparation for deep Himalayan snow and the sands of the Gobi. In addition to mechanics and drivers, the project included artists, photographers, and cameramen, as well as experts in geology and archaeology.[22] Writing in 1933, Stewart Blacker noted that the arrival of robust vehicles greatly eased the task of carrying the bulky equipment required for conducting these different forms of research, including the new audio and film recordings favored by ethnographers of the early twentieth century.[23] The expedition stretched to 10 months because progress was slowed by episodes of temporary imprisonment and administrative delays caused by the domestic politics of China. Plans to extend the trip to Southeast Asia and beyond were canceled after Haardt's failing health and subsequent death from pneumonia in Hong Kong (see Figure 5.1). The success of André Citroën's previous expeditions ensured international media interest in the project, even before the team departed in April 1931. To publicize the expedition to the English-speaking world, the *National Geographic Magazine* correspondent Maynard Owen Williams—who found fame reporting on the opening of Tutankhamen's tomb in 1923—was invited along. The *New York Times* further explained why the magazine and its parent organization, the National Geographic Society, got involved:

> [their] journey will traverse areas which have been little visited by Europeans since Marco Polo's time, skirt some of the world's highest mountains, lofty plateaus, cross vast deserts and come upon tribes and racial remnants of ancient peoples whose habits and habitats are virtually unknown.
>
> Two cars will be devoted to the taking of one of the most comprehensive geographic-vocal motion pictures ever made. This phase of the expedition, requiring special scientific and technical experimentation, is being conducted by Pathé-Natan, Paris. The scenic wonders of Innermost Asia and the customs and the costumes of the peoples there will be photographed, both by the black-and-white and the color camera; and native dialects, songs, chants and rituals will be preserved in sound records. The expedition will carry a radio sending station for the purpose at all times of keeping in touch with Paris. This sending station will be utilized by the National Geographic Society's representative in filing dispatches to the society's headquarters in Washington, which, in accord with the society's invariable custom, will be released simultaneously to all press associations and newspapers desiring news of the expedition's progress.[24]

Here, then, we see the convergence between anthropology and the spectacle of grand adventure facilitated by the new technologies of motorized

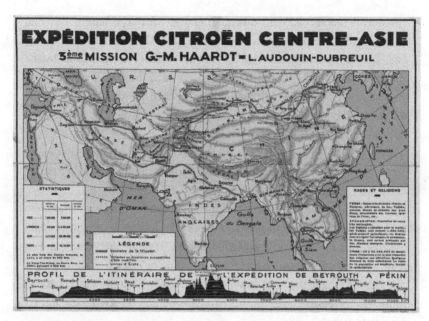

Figure 5.1 Map of Expédition Citroën Centre-Asie, 1931.
Credit Line: Public Domain.

vehicles and shortwave radio. The latter enabled daily updates to reach media outlets and amateur radio associations on the other side of the world, in the United States.[25] The onboard artist Alexandre Jacovleff was charged with capturing the cultural diversity of Asia through portraiture, for, as the *National Geographic Magazine* put it in one of two stories on the expedition, "nowhere else in the world can one find a greater conglomeration of races" (see Figure 5.2).[26] The route taken by the teams was in part shaped by the international politics of the moment. After departing Beyrouth, at that time administered by France under the mandate system, their plan was to enter China via western Turkestan. But with Moscow suspicious about a cargo of recording and camera equipment, access was denied, forcing the team to enter China via a more treacherous Himalayan route. Such logistical considerations were lost in media reports, which repeatedly linked their crossing of Asia to the routes followed by others before them:

> We pass east in automobiles along a part of the way which Marco Polo followed, and also along the medieval silk caravan routes from Cathay to the Mediterranean.
>
> Georges-Marie Haardt, June 1931[27]

The world's oldest road—the caravan trail over which the famous Venetian merchant Marco Polo travelled to China in 1272 AD—has been at last conquered by a modern automobile. It is believed that the work done by the Haardt Expedition in blazing a trail across China may be of considerable importance. If Marco Polo's trail can be opened for regular automobile travel, it will constitute an important artery between the rich resources of Central Asia and the cities of the Chinese coast.

Gnowangerup Star and Tambellup-Ongerup Gazette,
Western Australia, September 1932[28]

Part of [the expedition] follows the line of Alexander the Great's march to the Indus; part of it is the old silk route which for hundreds of years brought the treasures of China to the Mediterranean Sea. On the Pamirs and in Hunza the expedition will in part follow the trace of Younghusband 40 years ago. From Kashgar, through the old Gobi Desert to Peking, a nearly parallel route was traversed in 1893 in the reverse direction by Younghusband six years before that.

Times (London), March 1931[29]

In March 1934, *La Croisière Jaune*—the result of the thousands of hours of footage taken on the trip—reached French cinemas after lengthy editorial disagreements. Audiences were told the team was following "La vielle route des caravanes de la soie: celle de Marco Polo."[30] Its English version, *The Yellow Cruise*, was shown in the US just over two years later, with reviews again misleadingly stating "the route was virtually the same as that traversed by Marco Polo 600 years earlier."[31] In 1935, *An Eastern Odyssey*, the English version of Georges Le Fèvre's account of the expedition, was also published.[32] As other *National Geographic Magazine* writers returned to the region, the portraits and landscape scenes sketched by Jacovleff appeared in other articles, including one by Edward Murray on his time *With the Nomads of Central Asia*.[33] Here again readers learned about the customs and everyday cultural practices of the various "tribes" and "races" Murray encountered during his trip. Of note here is the distinct attention the article gave to histories of movement and cross-cultural interaction to frame an anthropological reading of the different groups living in the region.[34] Murray relayed details about interviews he conducted on language dialects, headdress, or the different forms of yurt design. Marriage practices described as holding "morals unchanged since Polo's time" were also cited to present the sense of a nomadic existence unchanged over centuries.[35]

Georges Le Fèvre was among a number of authors publishing books on their travels through Central Asia at this time. Of particular importance here are three travelogues by Ella Maillart, Peter Fleming, and Sven Hedin; authors who also had a significant impact in introducing the concept of the Silk Road to new audiences. Born in Switzerland, Maillart had reached the Olympics as an athlete, but a desire for adventure took her to the remote regions of the Soviet Union. In China she met Fleming, a British travel writer who had also ventured east using the Trans-Siberian and Turksib railways. From Beijing, at that time Peking, together they left for Kashmir in India. Maillart's described their seven-month journey in the 1937 book *Oasis Interdites: de Pékin au Cachemire*, and Fleming published *News from Tartary* in 1936.[36] In this he referred to Chinese Turkestan as the "forbidden province," describing it in the following terms:

Figure 5.2 Drawing of Barum Khan by Alexandre Jacovleff.
Credit Line: Public Domain.

For most travellers, and all merchants, the road from China into India lies, as it has lain for centuries, through Sinkiang along that ancient "Silk Road" which is the most romantic and culturally the most important trade route in the history of the world. The Silk Road takes—or used to take—you through Sinkiang to Kashgar and the Himalayan passes by one of two alternative routes; the first (a road now practicable for wheeled traffic) running along the line of oases which fringe the Takla Makan on the north, below the foothills of the Tien Shan or Celestial Mountains; the second (sandier and less well watered) skirting the Takla Makan on the south and backed by the Kuen Lun Mountains, behind which mass the 20,000 foot escarpments of the Tibetan plateau . . .

In the spring of 1935, however, to have attempted to enter Sinkiang by either of these routes would have been most inadvisable. The bloody civil war, or succession of civil wars, which had ravaged the province in 1933 and 1934 was indeed believed to be in abeyance. The capital, Urumchi, and with it the cause of the self-appointed provincial government, had been saved from the invading Tungan rebels in January 1934 by Soviet troops and aeroplanes operating—inadmissably and unavowedly—on Chinese soil.[37]

Fleming relayed in some detail the challenges and risks of getting in and out of China, a theme that would reverberate in the travel writing of the 1980s. That same year, 1936, Sven Hedin's *Sidenvägen* appeared in Swedish, with an English translation *The Silk Road* published two years later. By this point, Hedin's international fame was considerable, and the book further popularized the idea and terminology of the Silk Road (see Figure 5.3).[38] He acknowledged Richthofen as the author of the term and Albert Herrmann for his detailed study *Die alten Seidenstrassen zwischen China und Syrien* of 1910. To extend Herrmann's account of trade routes between China and Syria, Hedin also cited evidence of silk fragments discovered in the Mediterranean, thereby informing readers that "the whole Silk Road, from Sian via Anhsi, Kashgar, Samarkand and Seleucia to Tyre, is 4200 miles as the crow flies and, including bends, something like 6000 miles, or one-quarter of the length of the equator."[39] Crucially, however, the book was first and foremost a travelogue, further cementing his reputation as one of Europe's most intrepid explorers.

In 1938, Goldwyn released *The Adventures of Marco Polo*, a film Iannucci and Tulk argue dispensed with any sense of geographical specificity to present East and West through dichotomies of "civilized and primitive, active

Figure 5.3 Portrait of Sven Hedin on a camel.
Credit Line: CPE Media Pte Ltd. / Alamy Stock Photo.

and passive, noble and wicked, male and female, dominant and submissive" (see Figure 5.4).[40] In a departure from *The Travels*, Polo was presented as a conquering lover, seducing and saving "the passive eastern female."[41] But as Suzanne Akbari reminds us, the question raised by the films of this period is which Orient were they presenting: the erotic fantasies of Ottoman and Persian lands; the ascetic Buddhism of the Indian subcontinent; or the mysterious civilizations of Cathay?[42] In its modern depictions, the story of Marco Polo embraced them all in a seamless geography of romantic adventure. In this quintessential story of journeying east, the Orient started in the Holy Lands of the "Near East" and stretched across to the mountains of Tibet and plains of Mongolia and China beyond.

For those readers hoping to visit regions depicted in *The Travels* or those visited by Hedin and the Citroën-Haardt expedition, international events intervened. The descent into global conflict meant tourism to Central Asia— which had begun to gather momentum in the 1930s on the back of media spectacles and the opening of regional airports—came to an end. World War II had already broken out in East Asia with the Second Sino-Japanese

Figure 5.4 Promotional poster for the 1938 Goldwyn film *The Adventures of Marco Polo*.
Credit Line: Public Domain.

War, and Soviet Central Asia entered a particularly dark time with Stalinist purges, forced collectivization, and brutal labor camps affecting millions. At the very moment Hedin's book was popularizing the Silk Road, he was becoming involved in German politics, an association that would draw him into controversy and forever tarnish his legacy. But as war broke out in Europe, there was just time for one last team to venture east to showcase the products of motoring, this time those from America. In June 1939 Lawrence

and Margaret Thaw left Paris for Asia on a trip designed to prove the reliability and strength of specially designed Chevrolet trucks and a Buick car.
Once again publicity was sought through print and radio journalism and the
now-reliable documenter of adventure, the *National Geographic Magazine*.
Their 1940 article *Along the Old Silk Routes: A Motor Caravan with Air-
Conditioned Trailer Retraces Ancient Roads from Paris across Europe and Half
of Asia to Delhi* told their story.[43] Scenes of the vehicles departing the modern
urban centers of 1939 northern Europe sat in distinct contrast to an Orient
once again portrayed through traditional dress, agriculture, and customary
festivities, with further "color" coming from the urgency of "escaping" regions of France and Germany preparing for war. The Thaws explained the
premise of their trip in the following terms:

> The Great Silk Route! What visions of mile-long caravans of camels laden
> with spices and of the tramping march of invading hordes these words
> conjure up! Stretching east from Beyrouth or Antioch (Antakya) on
> the Mediterranean, it was known to Darius before Alexander and to the
> Assyrians before Darius. Imperial Rome used it as a direct means of com-
> munication with the East. By it Greek merchants, coming through Antioch,
> crossed the deserts of Mesopotamia (now Iraq). They paused at the mighty
> city of Baghdad before passing through the defile of the Zagros Mountains
> to reach the great trading center of Tehran and its near-by Caspian ports.
> After putting behind them the deserts of eastern Persia and the two-mile
> high passes of the Hindu Kush, they crossed the Khyber and other passes to
> the gold and spices of India.
>
> In the 7th century parts of this mighty caravan route of the dead past were
> traversed by the Chinese pilgrim Hsüan Tsang. Six centuries later Marco
> Polo followed similar parts of its tortuous course. Changes were made in
> the great land route from time to time as a result of new geographical dis-
> coveries or political complications, but the general direction remained the
> same.[44]

An interesting detail here is their identification of Beyrouth as the western
end of the Silk Road, an idea they possibly acquired from the Citroën-
Haardt expedition, which was also mapped and reported in the same magazine some years earlier, as previously noted. In a documentary made for the
Thaws by the petroleum company Esso, cinema audiences were given insight
into the technical challenges of changing oils and lubricants on the side of

sand-covered roads and the historical context of nomadic families encountered along the way: "since time immemorial the camel has carried the wealth
of Asia over the vast spaces of the East, from China all the way to Africa."[45]
After reaching Afghanistan, instead of heading farther into Central Asia and
onward to China, the expedition turned south to India. Noticeably absent
then were the lost cities and archaeological finds of the Tarim Basin seen in
Chapter 3 and described by Sven Hedin in his Silk Road travelogue published
less than two years earlier. But while the Thaws might have taken an alto-
gether different approach to "The Great Silk Route," their account drew on
ideas and images that had formed around the Silk Road narrative in the interwar period and that would appear again and again over the second half of
the twentieth century.

6

Closed Worlds, Open Minds

By the early 1950s, the ethnographic gaze toward the nomads of Central Asia had changed. With China and the eastern regions of the Soviet Union closed to foreign travelers and journalists, *National Geographic Magazine* turned to Mongolia. Chapter 9 explains the different ways that Genghis Khan emerged as a metaphor for violence during World War II, standing in for Japanese and Soviet expansion and aggression. But with Mongolia's nomads living along the remote frontier zones of Chinese and Soviet territory, the magazine portrayed them as escaping the clutches of communism, such that their mobile lifestyle symbolized freedom and liberty. In a 1954 article, *How the Kazakhs Fled to Freedom*, Milton Clark wrote: "my wiry, high-spirited hosts were the remnants of hordes of saddle-bred nomads who had fled the Communist regime which Red China had imposed on their native Province of Sinkiang. . . . On the march from Sinkiang the tribesmen faced incredible odds: continuing Chinese Communist attack, desperate food and water shortages, mysterious illness, and untracked mountain and desert wilderness. Yet they heroically fought through to freedom."[1]

Some years later, William Douglas returned to the region and painted the same picture. Portrayed as a "pawn between powerful neighbors," an embattled Mongolia exemplified the wisdom of containing the "virus" of communism and the threats it posed.[2] Reflecting upon the nomadic groups he met, Douglas noted "these people still appear to have open minds. Yet the Mongolians are far removed from Western culture, so distant from the influences of Judeo-Christian civilization, so unaware of the West's great books and humane letters, that if they long remain in an isolated pocket between the Soviet Union and China, they may evolve into ideological puppets. If that should happen, it would be a tragedy, not only for a warm and stout-hearted people but for the free world."[3]

Interestingly, *National Geographic*'s ethnographic discourse strongly chimed with the political commentaries of a Mongolian nomadic culture under threat appearing in the *New York Times* and other US newspapers around that time.[4] Although nomads continued to cross mountain and

The Silk Road. Tim Winter, Oxford University Press. © Oxford University Press 2022.
DOI: 10.1093/oso/9780197605059.003.0006

stream by horse, for everyone else the age of roaming was over. The new realities of Cold War Asia had well and truly put an end to trans-Asiatic car expeditions. Jan Myrdal and Gun Kessle's 1958 road trip to Afghanistan in a Citroën 2CV—perhaps a modest attempt to invoke the spirit of the 1930s— was a rare exception. But in a world where the East and the West were cleaved in two, and with Central Asia no longer open for tourism, the romance of a great Silk Road—imagined as history and retraced as adventure—had lost its currency. This did not mean it disappeared from view completely. Chapter 8 explores the different ways it remained relevant for scholars and journalists seeking to interpret the political events of the period. But in the realms of film, theater, television, and museums, interest in the Silk Road dwindled everywhere throughout the Cold War period, except in Japan. Indeed, rather than celebrating the different cultures of the Silk Road, as we see today, music, literature, and theater were often deployed for soft power as Moscow and Washington engaged in a competition of enlightened civilization in their attempt to secure influence and moral superiority.[5] During this period, only a few authors from the West were able to write first-hand accounts of time spent inside China. In the early 1960s, Luce Boulnois gained access to remote areas through her role as a translator and researcher at France's National Centre for Scientific Research (CNRS). Her subsequent *La Route de la Soie*, with an English version following three years later, was one of the few attempts to theorize the Silk Road from this period. In an account that once again featured Marco Polo, Boulnois focused primarily on the production and trade of silk itself.[6] This brought the discussion up to the early twentieth century, wherein the role of the southern French city of Lille and Japan in the global silk industry was discussed alongside the geopolitics of transboundary infrastructures.

In the late 1970s, Central Asia was thrust back into the international spotlight through the Soviet invasion of Afghanistan. As we see in Chapter 9, expert media commentary on these events also breathed new life into the Great Game metaphor. But this meant that some interesting shifts were required in how the geography of the Silk Road was depicted. In researching his book *An Adventure on the Old Silk Road*, the BBC journalist John Pilkington was forced to skirt along Central Asia's political frontiers. With much of the East-West route depicted by Richthofen off-limits, Pilkington claimed to be "retracing" the route taken by Polo through Turkey, Pakistan, and up along the Afghan border to Kashgar. In a similar vein, Jan Myrdal's 1980 travelogue, *The Silk Road: A Journey from the High Pamirs and Ili through Sinkiang and Kansu*, recounted the frustrations of obtaining travel permits for Afghanistan and a lifelong ambition of completing "a real journey: following Marco Polo's route eastward."[7] A strong sympathizer of Maoism, Myrdal focused on the role of Xinjiang in twentieth-century Sino-Russian relations and the various ways in which the region was being transformed through master plans targeting industrialization and modernization.

In effect, then, in the three decades after World War II, popular culture in the West rarely turned to the theme of East-West cultural connectivity for inspiration. Of course, the Silk Road remained an evocative idea, and those interested in world history were able to find summaries of the concept in encyclopedias or more lengthy explications in books like *East to Cathay: The Silk Road* by Robert Collins, published in 1968.[8] But with Western archaeologists not welcome across significant portions of the Eurasian continent, there were no grand discoveries to feed media and public interest. The Silk Road was a history relegated to the distant past, its cultures and economic flows lost to the new ideologies of nationalism, industrialization, and, for many, communism. In distinct contrast to the late twentieth century, few were imagining how the Silk Roads might be "revived" for the modern era. Instead, and as the examples cited here illustrate, where the term is used it was often folded back onto the international affairs of the period, with authors lamenting the wars and violence in areas where traders and pilgrims "once" freely wandered. In the West, both China and the Soviet Union were constructed as enigmas whose cultures and governments were best treated with suspicion. Not surprisingly, as the idea of the Great Game reentered circulation, Rudyard Kipling's *Kim* found a whole new audience.

By way of contrast, however, Nile Green provides us with a somewhat different narrative from that time in his examination of the 1975 visit to China by the renowned Iranian author and critic Mohammed-Ali Eslami Nodoushan. Inspired to learn more about forms of Sino-Persian exchange, Nodoushan visited a number of cities, commencing his journey in Beijing. His travelogues illustrate that the Silk Road, *rah-e abrisham*, which, as Green puts it, was well established by then as a "borrowed Persian concept." As with Pilkington, the limitations of rail determined his routes, with Nodoushan using Russian lines of the early twentieth century to cross borders and China's limited network to move between its cities. Although he was shown various sites of industrial development and infrastructure, his key priority was to see the archaeological remains of entangled pasts. As Green explains:

Nodoushan's own imagination was captured by the historical sites which he was allowed to inspect. This was all the more true of those sites he was able to conceptually associate with the "Silk Road" (rah-e abrisham), a term which he used repeatedly when describing them. If this was the main historical concept he used to connect what he saw in China with the history of Iran, alongside it Nodoushan deployed a series of antique labels to evoke, for himself and his readers, a further sense of shared history. For example, he referred to Beijing as Khanbaligh, the Turkic and Persian name for its Yuan era predecessor from the time when both China and Iran were ruled by the Mongols. Similarly, for the inland provinces he used the pre-modern Persian name of Machin. However, it was on visiting the famous Longmen Grottoes in Henan province and the city of Xi'an, along with their associated museums, that Nodoushan made fullest use of the "Silk Road" concept to connect what he saw in China to the ancient Iranian history that was so central a concern of his other books.[9]

The events of the period would also descend upon the depiction of Marco Polo across film, stage, and even children's cartoons. In 1953, *Xanadu: The Marco Polo Musical* toured military and civilian theaters in Germany, Austria, and Italy. After graduating from Harvard, William Perry and William Wheeling were drawn into the US army, and upon posting to Germany they wrote the score for a musical produced by Seventh Army Special Services. Songs from the play were also rebroadcast on the American Forces Network radio service over a number of years. Among the early films of this period was the 1962 Italian production *L'avventura di un italiano in Cina*. A co-production involving five countries, the film was distributed internationally under the titles *La Fabuleuse aventure de Marco Polo* and *Marco the Magnificent*.[10] Iannucci and Tulk reflected upon the casting of actors, concluding that the film was "even more stereotypical in its presentation of alterity than its predecessors (a German Horst Buchholz as an Italian, a Mexican-American Anthony Quinn as the Mongol Khan; and an Egyptian of Lebanese/Syrian descent, Omar Sharif, as 'The Desert Wind')."[11] The idea of a demonic East even reached children's entertainment via *Marco Polo Junior Versus the Red Dragon*. This Australian-made fantasy animation told the story of a distant descendant of Polo and his task of slaying a red dragon in time to rescue the princess. Interestingly, a few years later the Hong Kong kung fu industry took Polo's story in the direction of flagrant blood spilling. A collaboration between the renowned Chinese director Chang Cheh and Hong Kong's largest film company Shaw Brothers, *Marco Polo* told the story of assassination attempts on Kublai Khan and the Italian visitor's role in protecting the court. Elaborate sword and kung fu fights reproduced the stereotype of a noble West and violent East. Evidently, such motifs resonated with Western audiences as commercial success came with the film marketed in various countries under the title *The Four Assassins*.[12]

An entirely different depiction of Polo's travels came in 1982 via an acclaimed American-Italian co-production for television. For Iannucci and Tulk, the four-part miniseries is among the most successful at "recreating the words and world" of Polo.[13] Marco is less the sexual conqueror of previous films and presented more as an earnest learner attempting to mediate cross-cultural misunderstandings and suspicions. Much of the first quarter of the series focuses on the tensions between Polo's father and uncle and a Venetian Senate who see little point in supporting a trip to a land of "blood thirsty savages."[14] For the Senate, civilization ends at the frontiers of Christendom, and the Mongols are among the many barbarian powers that pose an existential threat to the West. Here, then, we see one of the most careful treatments of Polo as the archetypal cosmopolitan, comfortable in intercultural settings and well equipped to mollify the suspicions of both Venice's most powerful Catholics and the court of Kublai Khan. The one exception to this narrative of crossing cultures is his romantic liaison in Mongolia. Iannucci and Tulk ask whether the choice of a Caucasian woman reflected the circumstances of production: "why not a Chinese actress as a love-interest, as abhorrent a thought as that was, apparently, to the Chinese co-sponsors of the film?"[15] Much of the series pivoted around the relationship between the Great Khan and Polo, one built upon their shared interest in other worlds, a tolerance for different religions, and a strong sense of fairness. Here again, then, we see the ideals of free thought and the journey that only an open mind can take being trumpeted as the lesson of history and the real legacy of *The Travels*.

In the tensions of the Cold War, such ideals were easily lost to fear and suspicion. Shortly before Richard Nixon's much-celebrated 1972 visit to China, the Italian filmmaker Michelangelo Antonioni imagined himself as a modern-day Marco Polo in accepting an invitation from Mao Zedong to make a documentary on everyday life in the country.[16] A five-week trip led to the three-and-a-half-hour film *Chung Kuo*, shown on Italian television a year later. Furious at the depiction of an impoverished, backward, and docile China, the Beijing government denounced the film as Western propaganda. Tens of millions of Chinese were drawn into meetings in schools, factories, and communes to publicly denounce the film, despite not having seen it.[17] The Italian government and local Chinese diplomats also attempted to prevent *Chung Kuo* being shown at the 1973 Venice Biennale Exposition, even declaring the famed *Teatro La Fenice* theater unsafe.[18] Organizers determined to honor free expression rapidly found an alternative venue. As Umberto Eco explained in an article on the incident: "Antonioni—the anti-Fascist artist who went to China inspired by affection and respect and who found himself accused of being a Fascist, a reactionary in the pay of Soviet revisionism and American imperialism, hated by 800 million persons."[19] In his narration, Antonioni described his own endeavors in terms of Marco Polo's adventures in China, a reference Eco used in expressing sympathy with the filmmaker's near-impossible task of delivering an ethnographic gaze of alterity without causing offense in an environment of tense geopolitics.

By contrast, Mao's willingness to host foreigners in 1972 did sow the seeds for a more successful Silk Road diplomacy project with Japan. Close on the heels of Nixon was Japanese Prime Minister Tanaka Kakuei. To publicize this moment in the normalization of relations between the two countries, Tanaka's delegation included a film crew from Japan's state broadcaster, NHK. During the trip, the idea of a Silk Road documentary was floated. After several years of negotiation, a partnership between NHK and China Central Television (CCTV) was established, and with filming commencing in 1979 Japanese film crews were granted unprecedented access to China's northwest provinces at a time when the wider region was entering the turmoil of the Soviet-Afghan War and Iran-Iraq conflict. The series focused primarily on a corridor from Xi'an across to regions bordering Pakistan and the Soviet Union and was broadcast in 12 parts in 1980. Kawamoto Tetsuya, chief producer of the series, captured its significance for the Japanese public: "If a Japanese wants to look into his past, he travels to Nara, if he wants to go one step further, he's got to go to the Silk Road."[20] The addition of an English soundtrack enabled the documentary to be sold and broadcast in an additional 35 countries, and many still regard the series as *the* definitive Silk Road documentary. At the same time, NHK was also producing a second television series set in Northwest China that was shown in more than 52 episodes in Japan between 1978 and 1980. Dubbed and renamed *Monkey* for international export, *Saiyūki* retold one of the most famous works of Chinese literature, *Journey to the West*, attributed to the sixteenth-century author Wu Cheng'en. The novel depicts the travels of a seventh-century Buddhist monk and scholar. Fantasy action scenes and a memorable soundtrack meant that

Monkey enjoyed a cult following in multiple countries. This was followed some years later by *The Silk Road*, which became the country's most commercially successful film of 1988. The famed Mogao Caves featured in a story of love and violence as local mercenaries attacked and regional powers fought for supremacy. In the face of imminent attacks on Dunhuang, the film's hero Zhao hid hundreds of manuscripts in the nearby caves for safekeeping. This, along with *The Grand Exhibition of Silk Road Civilizations* held in Nara that same year, of which we will hear more shortly, accelerated Japanese tourism to northwest China.[21]

Doors Begin to Open

In China, the social and economic reforms of the 1980s opened up new opportunities for travel and media projects that raised awareness about the country's cultural ties to Central Asia. For example, Che Muqi, an editor at People's China Press, fulfilled a lifelong dream of returning to regions in the northwest he first visited in the 1950s. For decades, Che had read about Xi'an as a gateway of cultures and about the invention of silk and its spread to the West. He greatly admired Zhang Qian, who had led hundreds of men over many years, conducting diplomatic relations on behalf of the Han court. Che thus wanted to travel to the ancient cities, pass through mountains, experience the deserts, and better understand the role Zhang played "in opening up the Silk Road."[22] As a Chinese citizen able to freely travel across remote areas, in his 1989 book *The Silk Road, Past and Present* he told the story of his travels around the Taklamakan via the northern and southern routes. Although the book does not specify his dates of travel, it does describe an encounter with the NHK documentary team, thus placing his time there around the late 1970s, early 1980s. Interestingly, Che explains how Japanese reporters and tourists "wearing the tags of Silk Road groups" made finding a hotel room in Urumqi difficult and that preparations for a camel trek into the desert included a visit to the city's Xinjiang Museum, from which he recalled reading exhibits produced by Chinese archaeologists and various artifacts carrying Silk Road labels.[23] Che's book coincided with the hugely popular 25-part television adaptation of Wu Cheng'en's *Journey to the West*. The renowned author and cultural critic Yu Quiyu also began traveling across the country to capture layers of Chinese culture and history by foregrounding links to the outside world. Republished in 1992 under the title *A Bittersweet*

Journey through Culture, the text included a chapter on Xinjiang in which Yu described Kashgar as a city enriched by connections made possible by the Silk Road:

> This was a place where all travelers, explorers, Buddhists, and merchants had to stop. No matter going out or in, they all suffered this harsh testing ground, but they faced greater tests before, maybe the Pamir, maybe the Takla Makan Desert. Therefore, they purged their souls, picked themselves up, and prepared to risk their lives on the road again. For many people, this was the last station for their lives; for others, this was the new starting point, filled with generousness, fortifying them for their subsequent departure. Whether as terminal or starting point, here was a place for heroes' pouring wine and sacrificing. Every inch of air in Kashgar bore the dumb guttural sounds of such men. The world yearned for the connection from here time and time again.[24]

In 1984 Lonely Planet published their first guide to China. As more and more provinces gave access to foreign travelers, one of the ways to reach Xinjiang was via Pakistan.[25] For those travelers seeking rest after the arduous and lengthy trip, John King, author of the 1989 edition of *Karakoram Highway: The High Road to China*, cautiously recommended the former Great Game consulates of Britain and Russia as among the hotel options in Kashgar. Given both of these closed in 1949, he described the former as "a melancholy place, neglected and seedy" and the latter as "stoic and crumbling."[26] Remote mountains, bureaucratic hurdles, and bus journeys along crumbling roads were the ideal ingredients for authors of adventure and escapade. And with Chinese and Soviet Central Asia among the last regions of the world to "open up" to late twentieth-century tourism, "adventures along the Silk Road" inevitably became the narrative of choice for writers, photographers, and journalists alike. David Hatcher Childress, a writer known for his belief in fanciful histories, traveled to Xinjiang in search of its "lost cities," citing Sven Hedin as his guide to the "varied cultures" of the region.[27] He, along with those more widely read authors of this period such as Colin Thubron and William Dalrymple, invariably included evocative descriptions of the anxieties and hurdles of obtaining visas and crossing heavily guarded borders.[28] Tales of an evocative world of Silk Road borderless connectivity were framed, somewhat ironically, by the risks and excitement of negotiating heavily policed frontiers.[29]

The opening up of Central Asia also enabled the luxury travel market to cash in on the allure of the Silk Road and the possibilities of experiencing a region before others. Much like Southeast Asia at this time, tour operators selling high-end, small-group holidays promoted the region, as opposed to individual countries, for the long-haul markets of Europe and North America. In a parallel to the "romance of Indochina," tourists could "follow" or even "sample" the Silk Road by visiting "the highlights" of each country before moving on. From 1993 onward, those tourists seeking the romance of steam could take the Bolshoi Express from St Petersburg, arriving in Tashkent in Uzbekistan two weeks later. Mahogany interiors and a 1920s-style bar enabled passengers to travel to "the main centres of the legendary Silk Road," regions "never before reached in such comfort."[30] But with the newly independent Central Asian republics suffering from grossly inadequate tourism infrastructures, tour operators set about building itineraries in and around regional hubs, using specially commissioned vehicles, accommodation, and aircraft.[31] The commencement of direct commercial flights from Europe meant Tashkent became a gateway for tours to Bukhara and Samarkand, promoted as "one of the great medieval trading centres, a place where the caravan highways—of the Silk Road from China, the trails to India and to Marco Polo's Europe—all met and crossed."[32] Not surprisingly, Japan led the way in the development of more mainstream tourism into the region. By 1994, the Japan Tourist Bureau was selling around 2500 Silk Road tours per year, around 90 percent of which focused on China. Trips farther west to former Soviet republics involved dealing with convoluted and expensive visa policies, a legacy of Cold War suspicion and alignment.[33] Indeed, to promote tourism to the region, visa policy reform was one of the first tasks taken up by the World Tourism Organization as it launched its own programs for Central Asia in 1993.[34]

In a period of major social and economic transition, international tourism thus represented an important catalyst for a series of wider developments. Cynthia Werner, for example, has noted the sector's importance in creating all-important cash flows as Kyrgyzstan and Kazakhstan transitioned away from socialist central planning models toward capitalism.[35] And as Erica Marat explains, tourism also played a key role in the way governments strategized their national brands for post–Soviet era growth. She suggests that the challenge was reaching three types of international audience—businesses, politicians, and tourists. Focusing primarily on the first two and the development of public relations strategies, Marat argues that both Kazakhstan and Uzbekistan promoted themselves "as crossroads of civilisations and cultures."[36] Under Nazarbaev's leadership, the government of Kazakhstan began promoting the country as a new economic and political power for the region. To that end, their Ministry of Foreign Affairs ran international advertising campaigns proclaiming that the country was uniquely "located right at the crossroads of civilizations and for this reason it blends away, in a most harmonious way, all the contrasts between the East and the West."[37]

Fascinatingly, such ideas extended to the justification for moving the country's capital from Almaty to Astana in 1997. Marat cites a 2005 publication in which Nazarbaev explained "that Astana can rightly be called the centre of Eurasia, since it is located between Europe and Asia and thus has soaked up the cultural heritage of both West and East for centuries."[38] She goes on to explain how Uzbekistan took this idea further via a branding strategy that foregrounded tradition and culture in an attempt to create an image that countered the country's political reputation. This new era of openness was economically buttressed by an influx of aid across a number of sectors, including heritage and tourism.[39] An early collaboration between UNESCO and UNDP in Uzbekistan, *Rebuilding the Silk Road*, focused on the conservation of monuments and historical urban cores, as well as the revival of handicrafts for cultural tourism.[40] In 1994, the *Samarkand Declaration on Silk Road Tourism* also paved the way for international cooperation in areas such as hospitality services, information technology, and tourism marketing.[41] A Silk Road logo was adopted, and marketing campaigns were developed to promote Central Asia in international travelmarts, at trade fairs, and in the emergent world of online marketing.[42] A decade later, UNDP funded the *Silk Road Initiative*, an interregional scheme designed to promote trade and investment through tourism in an effort to achieve gender equity and poverty reduction targets laid out in the Millennium Development Goals (MDGs).

In important ways then, Western tourism to post–Cold War Central Asia reestablished the themes of the 1920s and 1930s. It was once again a region where adventures were to be had and where "exotic" cultures, past and present, were to be encountered. From the early 1990s onward, however, part of the mystique of the Silk Road, particularly for Western tourists, came from the region's inaccessibility over a number of decades, a region enshrouded in a politics of East-West suspicion and a world unknown lying beyond metaphorical curtains and walls. But as the Silk Road came to be marketed and authored as the "once in a lifetime trip," some interesting questions arose as to where such histories were to be found. Put simply, traveling the Silk Road meant visiting Central Asia. As Cynthia Werner notes, a quite specific visual culture set in for how the region was, and continues to be, marketed and depicted.[43] The obligatory camel—photographed, sketched, and filmed with its unique shadow cast onto sweeping sand dunes—symbolizes off-road adventure and a life of wandering. The cobalt tiles of mosques set against desert skies signify the heritage of antiquity preserved through time, and iconic portraits tell a story of lives seemingly untouched by the trappings of modernity. As authors of the *National Geographic Magazine* once again traveled the region, depictions of a brutal, marauding Genghis Khan prevailed during the 1990s, eventually giving way to stories of trips that "retraced" the steps of Marco Polo.[44] What we see here then is a region undergoing momentous transitions framed by a Silk Road geocultural imaginary built up over a number of decades. Growing interest in the Silk Road during the 1990s meant such processes intersected with, and were reinforced by, a publishing boom in Silk Road popular history, a genre that frequently tapped into the nostalgia for European exploration and the great age of archaeology, such that the discoveries and adventures of Sven Hedin and Aurel Stein added further romance to the story.[45] Interestingly, this template now extends to other regions. In 2016, for example, the United Nations World Tourism Organization (UNWTO) launched The Western Silk Road Tourism Development initiative. In laying out a roadmap for a project designed to facilitate thematic connections across the Mediterranean and Caspian and Black Sea regions, the UNWTO acknowledged that the concept of a Western Silk Road remains poorly defined and that investments were required for branding and marketing.[46]

Conclusion

Together, these two chapters have explored how an ethnographic, come tourist, gaze has contributed to the grand narrative of the Silk Road. A genre of overland adventure and escapade during the interwar period further reinforced the sense of European progress and technological superiority, and the "right" of its citizens to whimsically roam and conquer the extremes of nature and political frontiers of others. In the various references offered here, we also get the sense of how insights gained from the expeditions of the early 1900s formed part of the reading for the travelers of the 1930s, a number of whom were trained scholars. Strong public interest in travelogues, published via magazines, newspapers, and books, or the new vistas being created by film enabled their accounts to reach ever-larger audiences. But in contrast to nineteenth-century rail, the car symbolized independence, the type of free movement enjoyed by those of the thirteenth century. A "caravan" of vehicles traveling by "road" also offered an evocative parallel to those camel caravans of the ancient Silk Road. The addition of geological and—perhaps most significantly—ethnographic expertise crystallized the sense of traversing Asia, where crossing continents and the great cultural divides of East and West were revealed in ever-changing faces, clothing, and language sounds. In both text and image, the ethnographic Silk Road is thus one of "colorful" cultures "lost" in time. In a continuation of the themes explored in Part One, we see the ties between science and the geopolitics of empire that Bennett, Chang, Lyons et al., and others have documented for the late nineteenth century appear again.[47] This time it is adventure, rather than discovery, that provides the veil, whereby the gathering of knowledge is cloaked in the romance of Marco Polo and the heroism of teams crossing continents.

The themes discussed here also help to explain why ideas about trade networks of the early Christian era documented by scholars in the *fin de siècle* come to be connected with Marco Polo's travels of the thirteenth century, as the idea of a silk route or road surfaces in the public imagination. Marco Polo had created the imaginary of terrains unknown, of pioneering travel, and of discovering the peoples of Asia. We have seen, that in citing his travels, expeditions hoped to cement themselves in history, and over the decades journalists have tried to create romance for their armchair travelers. His steps were there to be "retraced" both on map and in person. Here, then, the cartography of sweeping arcs—traced on paper and animated in the new media of film and radio in the 1930s—connected continents to create a vista of male adventure. Documenting such processes helps to explain how the Silk Road imaginary comes to be "extended" through time and space. Geographically, Polo helps to refocus the story beyond its nineteenth-century Central Asian origins toward West Asia and up into southern Europe. But the examples of Beyrouth under French administration during the 1930s and the Soviet-Afghan War of the 1980s illustrate that in these vague, amorphous geocultural imaginaries of the historical connections between Europe and the "Far East," context, politics, and even coincidence shape the narrative in tangible ways.

The Travels indicates that Polo traversed regions conquered by Alexander the Great and described by Ptolemy. Perhaps more significantly though, his journey coincidently began from the same mercantile Italy described by Richthofen in his account of the silk trade between China and Rome during the Han dynasty. As such then, as the idea of a Silk Road becomes more widely known, Richthofen's pre–Common Era trade routes are overlaid with an account of East-West travel written one and a half thousand years later. But as expeditions of the early twentieth century "retrace" his route, their inability to enter Soviet territory meant that they were forced to route through Afghanistan and enter China via British India. It's only when such an example is located within the larger histories of expedition and adventure seen here do we begin to see how the Silk Road, as a highly evocative and compelling geocultural history, reassembles culture and geography, dissolving events and centuries into a sweeping arc of time.

PART THREE
A ROUTE TO PEACE?

In the 1950s, the Silk Road emerges as a vehicle for peace, harmony, and intercultural dialogue, values that are best advanced by cooperation between governments and between people divided by ideologies and borders. Dialogue between Eurasia's cultures and civilizations—enacted through the peaceful exchange of ideas and technologies, religions, and goods—has been a narrative of history fit for the challenges and violence of the twentieth century. The popularity of the Silk Road has grown on the back of its unique value in the diplomacy of peace and friendship, both in the aftermath of war and in those moments when the threat of conflict looms large. Taking up such themes, the two chapters that follow reveal its history as a resource for nongovernmental and intergovernmental institutions promoting peace and reconciliation across a variety of bilateral and multilateral contexts.

Throughout the twentieth century, the past has yielded to the forces of nationalism and statecraft that have tied populations to territories and, in many cases, notions of ethnocultural purity. As I noted earlier, the Silk Road has been deployed since World War II to counter this hegemony of "rooted" pasts and the forms of enmity they give rise to. Its emergence as a mechanism for international policy and collaboration bears testimony to the political commitment held by many over the past hundred years to construct and reconstruct a world in, and of, dialogue. For reasons explained in Chapter 7, it required the efforts of UNESCO and interest from Japan to keep the light on transcultural and transboundary histories at a time when the world was divided by the Cold War. Transformational in East-West affairs, the 1990s was a period when the diplomatic and collaborative qualities of the Silk Road could fully come together for the first time.

In a 1993 issue of *Foreign Affairs*, Samuel Huntington claimed that civilizations were about to clash.[1] Enshrined as a vehicle for crossing borders and building trust, the Silk Roads promised another future. As Chapter 7 explains, the circumstances surrounding Silk Road multilateralism were significantly different from those of the post–World War II era: Western media outlets readily celebrated UNESCO's activities; Japan had successfully reintegrated itself into the so-called international community; reforms in China were paving the way for an economic and cultural revival; and countries across the world were deeply invested in the long-term stability of Central Asia, for reasons discussed in Part Four. As the language of "thawed" relations in a post–Cold War world became increasingly tired, fresh metaphors capable of making sense of the new realities were required. A story of internationalism, peace, and the cultural enrichment that comes from civilizations in harmonious dialogue had found its political moment.[2]

As debates about culture and civilization have continued to gain traction in the UN since then, the visibility, indeed political expediency, of histories of transmission and exchange have duly followed. As Chapter 8 shows, Xi Jinping's choice of UNESCO's headquarters for his speech on the merits of civilization was far from arbitrary. The Chinese government's ambitions to develop the cultural components of Belt and Road, namely people-to-people ties, share distinct discursive similarities with the organization's previous hopes for the Silk Roads, but elevate them to become new forms of geocultural power. By invoking the concept of civilizations in dialogue and the importance of building mutual respect and peaceful relations, Xi has taken ideas that rolled around the corridors of UNESCO in the 1950s and 1980s and "revived" them for the twenty-first century.

Within this story we see the Maritime Silk Road form as an idea. First mooted by Japanese scholars in the 1950s, this parallel to the overland route is given considerable visibility through museum exhibitions in Japan in the 1980s and then by UNESCO via its Roads of Dialogue initiative. This process forms part of the fascinating story of how the politics of peace and diplomacy at particular moments has had a tangible impact on the ways in which the Silk Road has come to be mapped, both geographically and thematically. Various examples are cited to illustrate this. Post–Second World War, Japan's desire to rebuild international goodwill helps to stretch the Silk Road as far east as Nara. The isolation of China during the 1950s and 1960s means that little or no attention was given to Suzhou, Xi'an, or Quanzhou, cities whose histories are readily tied to the Silk Road story today. By the late 1980s, Silk Road fever hits Japan, with the city of Nara holding a major exhibition on the topic, shipping in 30 tons of sand from Central Asia. Visitors to The Sea Route exhibition learned about trade from artifacts loaned by the Syrian Ministry of Culture, a scenario that would be essentially impossible three decades later. As we will also see, the celebration of the Unified Silla Kingdom in 1991 carries distinct symbolic value for a Korean peninsula separated by heavily guarded fences at a moment when the geopolitical cards of the region were being reshuffled.

By focusing on international cultural policy and cultural sector collaborations, Part Three adds another layer of explanation to the evolving cartography and story of the Silk Roads, revealing why places and histories move in and out of focus as the geographic and institutional parameters of conflict and peace-making alter. But in adopting this lens we also see the political capital gained by celebrating exchange along the Silk Road as a source of civilizational enrichment. The cases of Japan and China indicate how a vision of Eurasian history as connectivity has given form to cultural nationalisms, as identities are grounded in civilizational pasts whose geographies span far and wide. A discourse of peace and cooperation has thus been a story of accumulated power on the international stage. We see this most vividly today in Belt and Road, an issue that is given greater attention in Part Four.

7

A Divided World

It is said that Joseph Stalin was unfazed by the news from President Truman that the US had developed a new weapon of unprecedented power. Both men, along with Winston Churchill, were gathered in Potsdam negotiating the postwar security landscape of Europe. A week later, the bombings of Hiroshima and Nagasaki marked the beginning of a new age for humanity. But as Stalin discussed the carving up of Germany, his Soviet spy networks—which would later become infamous in the annals of Cold War history—ensured that he was aware of the progress made by the Manhattan Project team. At that moment, August 1945, the unprecedented destruction of World War II was giving way to a phase of international cooperation, peace, and reconstruction. The wartime alliance, formulated in the Declaration by United Nations of 1942, had paved the way for a new architecture of postwar multilateralism, buttressed by the Big Four—United States, Soviet Union, China, and Britain. As the US entered the war, Franklin D. Roosevelt envisaged that these four powers would be the guardians of peace within their respective spheres of influence. His plan largely survived the lengthy negotiations and resistance from smaller countries, and a Security Council made up of 15 members, with the "Four Policemen" as permanent members, formed part of the UN Charter of June 1945. As Robert Hilderbrand notes, the idea of great-power solidarity across regions appealed to Churchill and Roosevelt and most likely Stalin. Dividing up Europe addressed the obvious ideological schisms between Britain and the Soviet Union, and for Roosevelt greater autonomy over a single region gave comfort to isolationists back at home lobbying against his plan.[1] He also optimistically hoped that an embattled China could curtail Soviet ambitions in Asia. But as we now know, these wartime plans for postwar social and economic development through a global web of international cooperation failed to materialize. Competing ambitions in the alliance on show at Potsdam were the source of growing suspicions after 1945, and as the political face of eastern Europe continued to change under Soviet influence, relations with the United States rapidly broke down. The subsequent rise of communist parties in southern Europe

The Silk Road. Tim Winter, Oxford University Press. © Oxford University Press 2022.
DOI: 10.1093/oso/9780197605059.003.0007

and elsewhere, many of which received Stalin's support, provoked fears that western Europe might follow. By 1947, the contours of a new ideological divide were becoming clearer, and with Stalin forbidding leaders from the Eastern Bloc to accept the aid of the United States' Marshall Plan a year later, the struggle to create domains of influence and loyalty—which would dominate world affairs for the next four decades—had begun. Historians now acknowledge that the atomic power unleashed on Japan and further developed via thousands of tests after the war both threatened and preserved the peace. But the world was divided as never before, as the United States led a Western Bloc alliance committed to containing the expansion of a communist East.

Part Four explores the shifts in geopolitical thinking during this period. Of note here though are the ways in which this new Cold War, together with an ongoing civil war in China and superpower proxy war in Korea, created a series of ideological, cultural, and physical barriers across the Eurasian continent, all of which precluded the types of mobilities and connections described earlier. Decolonization accompanied the geopolitical imperative to construct power blocs and buffer zones, with borders busily drawn up to demarcate newly sovereign nations. The entry of charismatic non-white statesmen to the postwar order also led to solidarities around rebutting the sense of Western racial superiority, which lurked within the international system.[2] Put simply, the world had entered a time when there was little appetite within many national and international political systems for recognizing the entanglements of Eurasian cultures and histories. With Asia and the Middle East among the first regions to be drawn into proxy wars, the cultural past was subjugated to a complex array of political presents. The task of nation-building demanded narratives that shored up ethnic, cultural, and geographical boundaries. Icons and traditions needed to be symbolically enshrined and, where necessary, invented. In large parts of the Middle East, archaeology was reoriented toward Islamic—and in the case of Israel, Jewish—nationalism. In the Soviet Union, researchers continued to use Marxist formulations of history to subsume nomadic groups within a periodization of agrarian economics that culminated in a productive national present.[3] Elsewhere, Hinduism or Buddhism served as the bedrock for claims of homeland.[4] In other words, as political leaders across the region invested in the practices of statecraft, there was little impetus for nurturing an identity politics rooted in histories of transboundary connectivity or cultural exchange. This was particularly the case in northwest China, where Mao moved to isolate Xinjiang from the rest of the country and treat it as a buffer zone against the Soviet Union. As Dru Gladney, Michael Clarke, and others have documented, such a strategy involved removing "external influences through the neutralization of the region's historical, ethnic, cultural, religious and economic linkages to Central Asia."[5]

In the formulation of the United Nations, it was recognized that the challenge of establishing long-term peace extended far beyond high-level political agreements. It was hoped that education, science, and culture could be the weapons of peace, and UNESCO was given the responsibility for mobilizing them as venues of international cooperation and dialogue. But as William Preston Jr et al. demonstrate in their book *Hope & Folly*, UNESCO's ideals and long-term goals were quickly sucked into the hostilities of the Cold War. UNESCO's commitment to universality and internationalism was the foundation for a series of initiatives oriented around the "free flow" of ideas. Newly emergent mass communication technologies, namely radio and television, were optimistically perceived as vital to the "crusade for truth and tolerance."[6] But in the propaganda war of the 1950s, both Moscow and Washington sought to influence, and on occasions curtail, UNESCO's activities. Preston Jr traces US attempts to embed a language of "free markets" in the work of those in Paris hoping to promote the "free flow" of information. But with UNESCO staff resisting US pressure in their commitment to "reducing the obstacles to the movement of ideas," suspicions grew.[7] Both sides considered the ideals advanced by UNESCO to be of immense political consequence, as each sought to increase their spheres of influence around the world. Nowhere was this more charged than in the Third World of Asia. As numerous studies have shown, Turkey, India, Iran, Malaysia, and Vietnam were among the ideological battlegrounds of the period, wherein both superpowers influenced affairs by all means possible.

For the intellectuals and political leaders of Asia's newly independent countries, decolonization raised fundamental questions about the economic, political, and cultural nature of sovereignty. Faced with the challenge of establishing new national securities between two great power blocs, many chose to steer a middle course. It was a geopolitical disposition that eventually led to the non-aligned movement of 1961. The Bandung Conference, held six years earlier in Indonesia, proved to be a significant landmark along the way, gathering together "the largest ever grouping of new entrants into the international system," harnessing the now famous "Bandung spirit" (see Figure 7.1).[8] United Nations representatives attending the conference were told that more needed to be done to protect the developing countries

Figure 7.1 Bandung Conference, a meeting of Asian and African states, 1955.
Credit Line: World History Archive / Alamy Stock Photo.

of Africa and Asia from the economically and culturally destructive forces of the Cold War. The following year, 1956, many of the Asian participants at Bandung met again in Delhi to formally request UNESCO to provide ideas and initiatives that could help to forge another paradigm of East-West relations, one that better represented their interests, and created an equity and mutual respect reflective of the realities of decolonization.[9] In response, UNESCO launched the East-West Major Project on the Mutual Appreciation of Eastern and Western Cultural Values in 1957. This hugely ambitious initiative was conceived to stimulate cultural relations and the interchange of "cultural values" across regions, most notably between Europe and Asia. Lasting almost a decade, the multi-country project covered the spectrum of the humanities, with religion, art, folklore, music, craft, literature, and archaeology among the themes for events and publications. Not surprisingly, international collaboration remained an ever-present prerequisite for activities and funding, but equally, and crucially here, the core concept for framing these different spheres of culture was transmission and exchange. In this regard, the initiative directly spoke to the precariousness of the moment, for as Laura Wong puts it, the East-West Major Project represented "an unprecedented intergovernmental effort to engage states in dialogue around cultural identities in the midst of redefinition and rising ambiguity about the meaning of East and West."[10]

Shortly after the project's launch, the Japanese National Commission for UNESCO organized an International Symposium on the History of Eastern and Western Cultural Contacts. Events took place in Tokyo and Kyoto over a two-month period toward the end of 1957. In preparation, around 20 Japanese specialists produced a background document, *Research in Japan in History of Eastern and Western Cultural Contacts: Its Development and Present Situation*.[11] As the title suggested, the report summarized the history of Japanese scholarship on Asia over the course of the twentieth century, incorporating the work of many previous scholars. Extensive reference was made to the Silk Road. However, the editors critiqued its conceptualization as a land bridge between China and the Mediterranean, arguing that this was too narrow for understanding the depth and complexities of a historically connected continent. To address this, three primary forms of connectivity were identified: the Steppe Route; the Oasis Route; and the Sea Route. This differentiation has proved critical to the development of the Silk Road concept ever since, particularly within international cultural policy, as we will learn. An introductory essay by the respected scholar of Central Asia, Matsuda Hisao, summarized the team's rationale and the body of Japanese research they drew upon. Here, he recognized the contribution of European scholarship, noting the expeditions to Central Asia of the *fin de siècle* and their role in shaping our understanding of the historical ties along the Oasis Route. The essay made clear, however, that an expanded analysis of three separate routes could only come from the insights gleaned from Japanese studies conducted before World War II. The report was thus structured around this work.

Matsuda accounted for the emergence of scholarship during the Meiji era, summarizing the different themes and places that gave form to Japanese Oriental Studies: factors that differentiated it from its European counterpart. Exploration of the Steppe Route, he suggested, "best reveals the creativity of the Japanese orientalists"; contributions to knowledge that had been inadequately recognized by the West.[12] The work of Shiratori Kurakichi—including his extensive studies in Mongolia of the north-south connections down to China and India seen in Chapter 4—was offered as one such example. The vast majority of prewar Japanese orientalists uncritically viewed Mongolian nomads as the "uncivilized" inferior to the Chinese.[13] Although Shiratori reinforced this distinction through his theory of a barbarous north and civilized fertile south, his focus on the importance of Mongol power to the broad arc of history meant that "Japan was released from the habit of centering on China and readjusted to the viewpoint of the opposition between north and south."[14] Identification of a Steppe Route also drew on his histories of Uyghur migration and nomadic peoples, as well as the work of other scholars on tribes and archaeological material recovered from the region.[15]

In mapping out the Oasis Route, the report featured a series of essays summarizing the corpus of knowledge accumulated by Japanese researchers. The incorporation of this into a single, integrated geography led to a route defined in the following terms:

> The Oasis Route passes through Dry Inner Asia, and runs from East to West of the southern part parallel to the Steppe Route of the northern part which connects Ukraine, Kazakhstan, Zungaria and Mongolia. It starts from Iraq or Armenia, through the oasis of Iran to the oasis group of Western Turkistan (Transoxana), and from there, on the one hand, connects with the Steppe Route which runs east from the north of the Aral Sea, and, on the other hand, joining the route that passes over the Hindu-kush Range from India, passes Panni, becomes two caravan roads going through the north and south of the Taklamakhan Desert, and passes the Tarim Basin. Then on the eastern side of the T'ien-shan Mountains branches into the route to Mongolia and several mountain passes that connect to Zungaria. On the other hand, at the south of Lob-nor, it branches a road to Zaidani-Koko-nor Region, while the main road goes through Tun-huang by the oasis bridge of Kan-su and reaches North China.[16]

It was noted that comprehending the scale of exchange and connection across these different regions posed significant challenges, not least the need to master multiple languages. Here, though, Japanese Oriental Studies had some distinct advantages over its European counterpart, with many researchers able to "excel in the reading and analysis of the Chinese records."[17] Renowned scholars of the 1920s and 1930s were acknowledged for their insights on religious and cultural transmission across Central Asia and China.[18] To account for the diversity and complexity of the route, a combination of thematically and geographically constructed essays cited previous studies on the Chinese military, alongside a synthesis of Japanese knowledge about "The Uighur Period," said to span the late eighth century through to the thirteenth.[19] It was recognized that there had been incomplete and contradictory studies conducted, with the latter problem often caused by the translation of texts that inaccurately depicted events. It was clear that prewar scholars struggled with the veracity of Iranian versus Chinese accounts and the shortcomings of Ptolemy's *Geography*.[20] For the Sea Route, those working and studying at the Imperial Universities of Tokyo and Kyoto had played a key role. Most significant, however, was Taihoku Imperial University, which ran a course on the "History of the South Sea Area" in the years leading up to World War II. Fujita Toyohachi and Kuwabara Jitsuzō were cited in the report as pioneers in the field, with the latter publishing a landmark study on long-distance Chinese sea trade. By the 1930s, Japan had built up a substantive body of work on maritime Southeast Asia and the trade routes established by both Japan and China in the centuries predating the arrival of European vessels. Matsuda's introduction also noted the contributions made by the Research Bureau of the South Manchuria Railway Company, as noted in Chapter 4. Their histories of Manchuria and Korea were thus folded into a wider analysis of east-west, north-south connectivity.

The various essays included in the report thus demonstrated the scope of work conducted under the umbrella of oriental studies in Japan in the first half of the twentieth century. Dozens of academics and students, some of whom were discussed in Chapter 4, created a paradigm of scholarship toward Asian history that remained largely intact in the postwar period. They shared an interest in the themes of transmission and connectivity with their European colleagues but interpreted them in different ways and by exploring other regions came to some quite different readings of the past. As we have seen, Japanese scholars looked beyond the narrative of east-west to include north-south routes and attempted to read the cultural development of Asia as a series of historically connected peoples and civilizations. Although UNESCO ostensibly set out to document knowledge about histories of contact between Europe and Asia, this report retained the emphasis on intra-Asian connectivities that we saw in the Japanese accounts of long-distance connectivity of the early 1900s. Indeed, the 1957 study repeatedly emphasized that the West is not merely Europe but includes Central Asia, India, Persia, and Asia Minor, to use the terminology of its editors.[21] Such a conception of geography, I would suggest, reflects the complex political environments within which Japanese scholars operated, in both the early 1900s and post–Second World War period. Moreover, in looking back to Ōtani's fears concerning rising nationalism in the early twentieth century, I would argue that in producing material for UNESCO, the 1957 team hoped that their knowledge could provide a counter to the ultraconservatism and iso-lationism present in Japan in the postwar years. But given that the country remained under US control until 1952, even some of those on the left har-bored resentments toward the West. As Ann Sherif notes, artists and intellectuals occupied a complex space in postwar Japan, with many reluctant to "blindly conform to Western- or Eastern- bloc values, politics, and aes-thetics" and instead finding a "third way."[22] Establishing the precise political dispositions of each contributor to the report is beyond the scope of this dis-cussion. Nonetheless, what we do see here is a team of scholars committed to histories of internationalism who regard Japan as intimately tied to Asia and thus see part of their task as creating three continental routes along which the roots of Japanese civilization can be traced. UNESCO's primary aim with the East-West Major Project was to facilitate dialogue between Europe and Asia. As a key component of the project, this 1957 study contributed to that aim but did so in ways that reflected a complex geopolitical moment, and the in-tellectual dispositions it created.

Moreover, an initiative to stimulate understanding of the cultural and commercial links that had knitted the Eurasian continent together over cen-turies took place at a time when the superpower of the region was the Soviet "East." Not surprisingly, the US government perceived such projects as giving considerable advantage to Moscow. As Preston Jr indicates, by the late 1950s UNESCO was treated with deep suspicion in Washington, with the Heritage Foundation among those feeding the media with stories to discredit it. The State Department also resented UNESCO's unwillingness to join their anti-communist struggle, with disagreements over interpretations of the "free-flow" of information in the propaganda war. By then, members of Congress were regularly denouncing UNESCO, frustrated in their inability to subvert internationalism with national security interests. Since 1950, the CIA had been secretly funding programs for historians, cultural critics, and other intellectuals around the world via the Congress for Cultural Freedom. With offices in more than 30 countries, the controversial program was one of the weapons in the war of ideas and images, and the struggle to propagate them as universalist ideologies.[23] Preston Jr thus suggests that "a miasma of con-gressional distrust enveloped the word 'culture', and initiatives in its name were often met with indifference or hostility," particularly for those projects involving non-aligned countries, which—with the State Department failing to understand "the complex realities of the Third World"—were invari-ably perceived to be pro-Soviet.[24] In a political climate where aligning with

UNESCO was seen to be holding an anti-US position, there was little incentive for media outlets to publicize, let alone celebrate, attempts to reunify the east-west frontiers of Eurasia. By implication then, few if any stories on UNESCO's Silk Road initiatives appeared in the Western media, a situation that was in marked contrast to the coverage they would receive three decades later.

Despite this, the project's impact would prove to be lasting. First, it served as a bridge between the pan-Asianism of the early 1900s and Silk Road policies introduced at the end of the twentieth century. Meetings in Tokyo and Kyoto and the publication of an overview of Japanese scholarship on the "History of Eastern and Western Cultural Contacts" were also instrumental in defining the concept of the Silk Road as a platform for international cultural policy and cooperation. As we will see shortly, the three routes serve as the template for additional Silk Road projects in Japan over the coming decades and for UNESCO at the end of the Cold War. Moreover, the project introduced the idea of a sea route to the world of international policy, creating a platform for a Maritime Silk Road discourse to emerge from the 1980s onward. Finally, and perhaps most significantly, it also marked an important landmark in the Silk Road's trajectory as a vehicle for peace, and for friendships and solidarities that defy borders.

In Japan, engagement with UNESCO represented a uniquely valuable opportunity in the task of rebuilding relations across Asia and Europe. In 1951, the Japanese government signed a peace treaty with 48 nations in San Francisco. The concept of the Silk Road enabled Japanese scholars and bureaucrats to project the image of a Japanese civilization defined by centuries of peaceful relations. Politically, the country was under pressure from Washington to lead an East Asian axis of containment. As Makoto Iokibe explains, Japan had taken the path away from cooperative diplomacy in the 1930s, steering instead toward military expansionism. The postwar Yoshida Doctrine reversed this with pacifist policies emphasizing "expansion through cooperation."[25] The biggest challenge lay in rebuilding cultural and political ties with China, a country enduring the upheavals of Mao's vision of a communist state.[26] Alignment with the US also precluded any possibility of nurturing formal diplomatic and trade ties with the PRC. Indeed, China did not attend San Francisco, and the Soviet Union refused to sign. In such an environment then, informal forms of cooperation via nongovernmental actors took on particular significance, and here again Buddhism offered opportunities for building bridges through a language of peace and mutual respect.

Silk Road Diplomacy

It was within this space of informal diplomacy that Daisaku Ikeda, a Buddhist educator and peacemaker, operated over a number of decades. During a career of extraordinary energy, Ikeda led or assisted with the founding of numerous associations, schools, and research institutes dedicated to the promotion of peace through Buddhism, as well as publishing several hundred articles on the topic. From 1960 to 1979 he held the position of president of the Soka Gakkai lay Buddhist organization, a position from which he also founded Soka Gakkai International, a community-based Buddhist association dedicated to promoting peace. In the late 1960s, anti-communist and anti-Chinese feelings remained strong in Japan, and Ikeda ignored death threats in his call for the country to restore relations. In the years that followed, his commitment to international dialogue extended to the broader geopolitics of the Cold War. After the fall of the Soviet Union, Ikeda would publish a series of "in dialogue" texts, including one with Mikhail Gorbachev on the benefits of understanding the experiences of Buddhism and communism in the twentieth century for the construction of a global humanism for the twenty-first. But his efforts at bridging the Eurasian political divides of the post–Second World War period began in the mid-1960s via projects that used music as a platform for "developing mutual understanding and respect among people of different races and nationalities."[27] The Min-On Concert Association, an initiative he founded in 1963, developed programs specifically targeted at building relations between the people of Japan and different communities living across the Soviet Union. This continued to gather momentum through the 1970s, first with a major concert in Moscow, followed by the funding of research teams to conduct studies of musical traditions across Central Asia and the Middle East. Framed as a celebration of East-West cultural exchange and a project to "transcend national, ethnic and language barriers," the collaboration was given the title "Musical Voyages along the Silk Road." Speaking at the opening of the 1975 Moscow concert, Ikeda explained the logic of using the Silk Road as a point of reference for promoting peace:

> Individuals with a global view of the human condition agree that the best way to unite the hearts and minds of all people is through cultural networking on the broadest possible basis. In my travels I have heard people everywhere speak of their desire for East-West cultural interchange. At

no time in history has there been as great a need for a spiritual Silk Road extending all over the globe, transcending national and ideological barriers, and binding together peoples at the most basic level. Cultural interactions that are a spontaneous manifestation of the popular will can turn suspicion into trust, convert hostility into understanding, and lead the world away from strife toward lasting peace.[28]

Eleven further concerts followed, involving in excess of 400 performers from more than 20 "countries along the historic Silk Road," an ambitious antecedent to Yo Yo Ma's Silk Road Ensemble, launched in 1998.[29] The project capitalized on the "Silk Road fever," which Kazutoshi Nagasawa argues emerged in Japan around that time.[30] Scholars from Kyoto University, the University of Tokyo, and Nagasawa's own Waseda University also led the charge in a new wave of research in South and West Asia, with the Silk Road commonly added to the titles by publishers to increase sales.

During the 1980s, the Mogao Caves near Dunhuang were also becoming a venue for Sino-Japanese cooperation in conservation and heritage diplomacy. The Japanese painter Hirayama Ikuo visited the site in 1979 for the first time, and over the subsequent years his financial contributions and success in securing additional funds from the Japanese government would lead to a new center for conservation, research, and exhibitions. Former Japanese Prime Minister Takeshita Noboru was among those invited to the 1994 opening ceremony, an event that included the unveiling of the monument commemorating Hirayama's efforts pictured in Figure 7.2. Its inscription reads:

> In recognition of the renowned Japanese artist Hirayama Ikuo, chairperson of the Japanese Chinese Friendship Association and honorary research fellow of the Dunhuang Academy, for his dedication to Dunhuang Studies and continuing support of Dunhuang Academy scholars. In October 1989 Professor Hirayama donated two hundred million yen to the Dunhuang Academy Foundation. With this monument we express our gratitude to Ikuo Hirayama for his friendship and support.
>
> Dunhuang Academy, August 1994.

Back in Japan, and to return to the 1960s, fascination with the Silk Road was given a further boost by the 1964 Tokyo Olympics. Since 1936, the carrying of the flame across borders in the weeks preceding each Games had

Figure 7.2 Monument to Hirayama Ikuo, Mogao Caves, Dunhuang.
Credit Line: Photo by Author.

been a symbolic ritual of "peaceful inter-cultural communication and exchange."[31] With the Olympics held in Asia for the first time in 1964, organizers
in Tokyo infused this symbolism with additional motifs. The runner chosen
to light the cauldron, Sakai Yoshinori, was born on the day of the Hiroshima
bombing, and global television coverage of this 19-year-old athlete striding
round the stadium to great cheers suitably emblematized a country successful in its peaceful reconstruction. Added to this was the symbolism of the
flame's route. The convention of its departure from Athens meant it would
travel West to East, across Asia. A route that saw the flame pass through

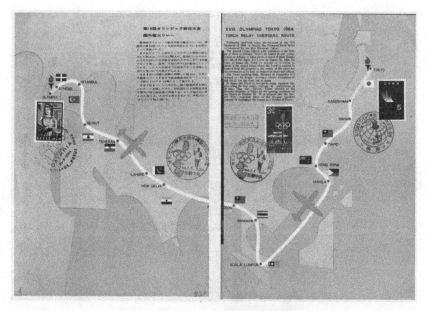

Figure 7.3 Southern Silk Route stamps souvenir issued for 1964 Tokyo Olympics.
Credit Line: Ministry of Posts and Telecommunications (Japan).

cities in Turkey, Iran, Pakistan, India, and Malaysia, among others, was officially badged as "an international relay along the southern Silk Road."[32] Interestingly, the logistical complexities of crossing land-based borders meant that the vast majority of its journey took place in the air, with Japan Air Lines brought on board as its custodian (see Figure 7.3). In anticipation of such publicity, the airline launched its own Silk Road route in October 1962, connecting Tokyo to Europe via Bangkok, Karachi, and Kuwait. Prospective passengers were promised the opportunity to "travel Asia's legendary caravan route at almost the speed of sound" (see Figure 7.4).[33]

The previous chapter noted the hugely successful NHK/CCTV co-production *The Silk Road* and the beginnings of Japanese tourism to northwest China in the 1970s. With the popularity of the Silk Road remaining high, NHK entered into another collaboration, this time with the city of Nara to host *The Grand Exhibition of Silk Road Civilizations*. The cementing of the city as a focal point of internationalism and transregional Buddhism during the Meiji era had by then evolved into the idea that Nara represented the "eastern terminus" of the Silk Road. Estimated to have cost in excess of US $80 million, the 1988 exhibition featured 30 tons of sand from the Taklamakan and attempts to recreate the desert's harsh climate with heaters

Figure 7.4 "Fly JAL's new 'silk road' to Japan." Promotional advert for Japan Air Lines, 1962.
Credit Line: Public Domain.

and dehumidifiers.[34] To push Nara's significance in the story of the Silk Road beyond Buddhism, the organizers revisited the three-route model developed in 1957.[35] Here, though, the two land routes were combined into *The Oasis and Steppe Routes*, with two additional exhibitions dedicated to *The Route of Buddhist Art* and *The Sea Route*. International collaborations were established for each, with a number of countries lending artifacts for display. Government ministries from France, Iraq, Italy, and the Soviet Union sent items for *The Oasis and Steppe Routes*. The Musée Guimet, for example, supplied artifacts from Afghanistan collected by Paul Pelliot and others. Museums from other cities in Japan also supplied items obtained from Central Asia and Iran. To produce the exhibition for *The Route of Buddhist Art*, items were procured via agreements with India, China, South Korea, and Pakistan. Maritime archaeology collaborations between Tokyo's Ancient Orient Museum and the Syrian Ministry of Culture meant that the story of *The Sea Route* across the Indian Ocean was told through items recovered from the seabed off the coast of Syria and national museums in Aleppo and Damascus.[36]

To explain the concept of the three routes and how they better reflected "the plural form of the word used by Richthofen" rather than the singular Silk Road more common to English, the former director of the Ancient Orient Museum and professor of archaeology, Egami Namio, provided a detailed essay *The Silk Road and Japan*. Once again, Japanese Oriental Studies underpinned his analysis. But Egami also indicated how the international collaborations for the exhibition had added new pieces to the jigsaw. He cited, for example, recent Soviet archaeological discoveries around fortified settlements in the region then known as West Turkestan. In his identification of trade routes down through Iran and across China or the importance of long-distance travelers such as Buddhist monks, to cite just a few examples, Egami's broad aim was to tell the story of the "goods and people that flowed between the East and the West and the magnificent, exotic culture brought to China and Japan by way of the Silk Road."[37] In this respect, despite using the framework of these three distinct, multidirectional routes he reverted back to a European Silk Road of East-West connectivity. Some years later, Nagasawa observed that this shift toward framing Japan as an East deeply entangled with the West had been a trend of the "Silk Road fever" of that time, as authors and journalists aimed to capture the popular imagination of a Japan that was successfully restoring its reputation with Europe and the United States.[38] Perceptive to the exhibition's attempts to stitch the country into a narrative celebrating harmonious relations between East and West, the *Los Angeles Times* noted: "Strictly speaking, Western scholars have traditionally defined the Silk Road as the overland trade route between Istanbul, Antioch and Tyre, and the ancient Chinese capitals of Xian and Luoyang. But Japanese academe has stretched it out a little, from Rome to Nara."[39] Egami's essay appeared in a series of highly detailed catalogs produced for the exhibition. These catalogs also featured introductory texts by the international partners brought on board to provide artifacts for the three separate themes. Each explained their basis for participation:

Today as science and technology continue to progress rapidly, a need is strongly felt among us to reexamine our past and to try to understand the principles of cultural development with reference to the origins of civilization. As we look into the histories of peoples around the world, we realise that communications beyond national boundaries, for instance, exchange of ideas and discoveries, cultural exchange and trade, have always been major factors contributing to social development. Needless to say, one outstanding symbol of such meaningful, rich exchange among various peoples and cultures of the world is the Silk Road, a great link between East and West . . . I would like to express my sincere gratitude and respect for your interest in our exhibits and my strongest hope that this exhibition will be of some help towards mutual understanding between the peoples of Japan and the Soviet Union.

Gurii Ivanovich Marchuk
President, Academy of Social Sciences, USSR[40]

The Iraqi Antiquities displayed in this Exposition represent the most precious pieces. These antiquities cover all historical periods of the civilization of Iraq, since the existence of human race up to now. The antiquities which are exhibited is a good evidence for the good relations between Iraq and Japan, the two well known countries in history. These archaeological items also express Iraqi goodwill for peace and progress for humanity. I hope that the winged-bull . . . explains this message which Iraq has addressed to you. This statue combines the power of the bull and the intelligence of man, and he has the ability to fly from place to place expanding peace and love.

Dr. Muayad Sa'id Damerji
Director General, Department of Antiquities and Heritage, Iraq[41]

It is of great significance that Japan is hosting the Silk Road Exposition in Nara concurrently with the Seoul Olympics, to take place in September by virtue of cooperation between East and West. The Silk Road, historically linking East and West in cultural exchange, served an essential pathway of cultural empathy . . . I am sure that this Exhibition will further the mutual understanding between East and West.

Chung Han Mo
Minister of Culture and Information, Republic of Korea[42]

Figure 7.5 Commemorative stamp and envelope for Nara exhibition, 1988.
Credit Line: Ministry of Posts and Telecommunications (Japan).

The Nara exhibition proved to be a successful exercise in public diplomacy, raising awareness about Japan's deep cultural and religious connections to Asia. To mark the event, Japan's Ministry of Posts and Telecommunications issued a set of commemorative stamps and envelopes (see Figure 7.5). There were clear benefits of extending this to the international stage. In the postwar era, the country had created a distinct international footprint in the areas of development aid and peace diplomacy. Back in the 1960s, the government had taken a leading role in the establishment of the Asian Development Bank, and countries in Southeast and Central Asia received funding and technical assistance from JICA (Japan International Cooperation Agency) for infrastructure and development projects.[43] In the 1980s, Japan invested heavily in Cambodia's postwar reconstruction, and by then Hiroshima had become a pivotal node in the international networks lobbying for nuclear disarmament and a cessation of Cold War hostilities.[44] In effect then, the Silk Road represented a uniquely valuable platform for moving into new sectors of cooperation and further projecting the image of a country facilitating international peace and dialogue between East and West. Such developments are the focus of Chapter 8.

8

Civilizations in Dialogue

> Conflicts and disagreements are unavoidable between various na-
> tions due to their differences in historical development, social
> background, cultural tradition and lifestyle. These conflicts and
> differences can be resolved through dialogue and exchanges on an
> equal footing and in the spirit of mutual respect. It is wrong to place
> the civilization of one's own nation before other civilizations and
> ignore or even despise other civilizations, make much ado about
> the differences between civilizations, or attempt to stir up conflicts
> between various civilizations, for they are detrimental to prog-
> ress of world civilization and to the lofty cause of world peace and
> development.
>
> Jiang Zemin, Saudi Arabia, 1999[1]

In 1988, UNESCO launched The Integral Study of the Silk Roads: Roads
of Dialogue. Encouragement had been coming from the Japanese government for some time, and media reports indicated a possible arrangement
involving Japan providing 90 percent of the funding on the back of commercial sponsors hoping to cash in on Silk Road fever in the country.[2] In its initial
set-up, though, additional funds were sourced from Oman, South Korea, and
France for a multilateral program of workshops, meetings, and public events
intended to last five years.[3] In retrospect, the project proved extraordinarily
timely, despite the fact that those involved in its planning could not have anticipated how East-West affairs were about to change so profoundly. Against
a backdrop of a collapsing Soviet Union, the decision was taken to extend
Roads of Dialogue for an additional five years, with it eventually wrapping
up in 1997. Vadime Elisseeff, whose own life course and academic training
led him to be one of the architects of the 1957 UNESCO project, was appointed as chairman of the UNESCO International Consultative Committee
for the duration of the project. Born in St Petersburg and of French descent,

The Silk Road. Tim Winter, Oxford University Press. © Oxford University Press 2022.
DOI: 10.1093/oso/9780197605059.003.0008

Elisseeff grew up in Paris. His father was employed at the Japanese embassy, having been one of the first foreign students to study at Tokyo Imperial University and then moving to the University of St Petersburg to complete a PhD on the Japanese poet Bashō. For Vadime, a Paris education included diplomas in Chinese and Japanese and led to a passion for East Asian art, in part through his attending the classes of the sinologist Paul Pelliot. In a career spanning university teaching, museum directorship, and advisory roles to governments, he moved back and forth between Paris and East Asia, primarily Tokyo.[4] In Paris he also undertook roles for UNESCO and ICOM promoting cultural relations between the two regions. Coming to the 1988 Silk Roads project at the age of 70, Elisseeff was thus ideally placed to understand its broader significance. In an interview conducted in 1990, he indicated the broad philosophical approach he was attempting to foster: "history—that is, the philosophical explanation of the world—tends to be compartmentalized, but history is not linear. It is more of a branching process. For example, many aspects of the Silk Roads have already been studied, often very thoroughly. However, the connections between these aspects seem to have been somewhat neglected, . . . hitherto, international cooperation has often been viewed as a process of channelling international contributions into a national study, rather than as an international study in its own right. Unesco is in a unique position to rise above nationalist fervour."[5]

Administratively, Roads of Dialogue evolved quickly and within 12 months received the support of national coordinating committees in Canada, China, France, Iran, Iraq, Mongolia, Oman, Pakistan, Poland, Republic of Korea, Syria, Thailand, Turkey, USA, and USSR.[6] Cooperation between these countries was, once again, oriented around three principal routes: Desert, Steppe, and Maritime. To examine these routes, Elisseeff and his team laid out an ambitious program of academic and public events, drawing on the expertise of nearly 500 scholars.[7] Upon invitation, contributors were explicitly encouraged to expand upon existing ideas about Silk Road history, an approach that led to conferences and exhibitions dedicated to a diverse array of topics, including nomadic culture, harbor cities, food, and Arab seafaring, as well as to less familiar routes of connectivity, such as the inter- and intraregional connections of East Africa and Southeast Asia.[8] The expeditions component—designed to follow the three routes—is particularly revealing of the diplomatic and conceptual factors that shaped the project's implementation. The first of these, undertaken in 1990, involved a team of more than 40 experts and journalists following the

Desert Route from Xi'an to Kashgar over a two-week period. A year later, the Steppe Route in Central Asia was traversed, with the Nomads' Route in Mongolia and the Buddhist Route planned for 1992 and 1995, respectively. To ensure international media coverage, television crews from China (CCTV), South Korea (MBC), and Japan (TV Asahi), as well as radio and print journalists from multiple countries, were invited as expedition guests.[9]

A fifth expedition involving more than 100 scientists and 45 media representatives followed the Maritime Route from Venice to Osaka in 1990–1991. For the 154-day trip, they were loaned a military troop carrier, the *Fulk al-Salamah* (Ship of Peace) and a television crew by His Majesty Sultan Qaboos of Oman. Sixteen countries hosted the expedition. For its launch, Federico Mayor, then UNESCO's director general, joined the ship, announcing:

> The purpose of the Integral Study of the Silk Roads is to heighten contemporary awareness of the need for dialogue by highlighting the historic opportunity for mutually enriching understanding and communication between the different civilizations linked by these roads . . . the starting point of [this] expedition is Venice—city of Marco Polo, the "West's window on the East."[10]

Given the number of journalists on board, a series of stories and publications about the expedition were produced. They included two books by Chinese photojournalist Sun Yifu, one in Chinese, the other in English, titled *A Voyage into Chinese Civilisation, from Venice to Osaka; UNESCO Retraces the Maritime Silk Route*. Here I offer a number of quotes from the book to illustrate how a project celebrating routes, flows, and connections still comes to be narrated through the frame of civilizational centers and cultural diffusion, in this case amplifying China's historical significance. Interestingly, this occurs in ways that return us to the previous discussion of Marco Polo, who once again becomes the definitive reference point giving specificity to East-West encounters. In Sun's account of Venice as "the largest trading port in Europe during the 12th century," he notes that "the most outstanding representative of cultural exchanges between Europe and China during that period was Marco Polo . . . [*The Travels*] revealed China's wealth, vastness, property and civilization, creating a stir in Europe."[11]

After leaving Venice, the ship traveled through the Suez Canal flying the flag of the United Nations, making 20 stops before eventually reaching Japan. More than 120 debates and lectures were held on board, and 17 international seminars and two colloquia took place in port locations. In his multiple reports from on board, the French political scientist, François-Bernard Huyghe explained how expedition scholars delivered lectures on the routes and connections being "retraced," including a number of talks on the fifteenth-century voyages of Zheng He from China to Oman. In East Asia, the *Fulk al-Salamah* sailed between China, South Korea, and Japan, with media stories highlighting how they had been culturally entangled through the Silk Road. Here then, the story of the Unified Silla Kingdom came back into focus, this time framed as "the age of friendship" both within the region and with the worlds of Persia and Arabia. As Chapter 5 noted, such friendship narratives are metaphorically conveyed through stories of long-distance travelers, and on this occasion it was the reports of the ninth-century Persian geographer Ibn Kurdadbih.[12] The expedition visited sites in the Kyŏngju area, including those restored by Japanese archaeologists in the early 1910s, notably the Bulguksa Temple, discussed in Chapter 4 (see Figure 4.2). In his account of the expedition's visit to the area, Sun Yifu also explained how "Buddhism was introduced to the Silla Dynasty by China" and that the "foreign historians on the expedition team found relics in Kyŏngju astonishingly similar in style to relics of the same period in China, showing China and Korea share the same cultural roots."[13]

To coincide with the expedition, the National Museum of Korea opened its first-ever *Art of the Silk Road* exhibition in Seoul. But here the focus was on Central Asia, with the museum showcasing its "Ōtani Collection," which, as Young-pil Kwon notes, is comprised of around 60 wall paintings and 1700 artifacts removed from temples and tombs.[14] In a repeat of the cultural politics of colonial Japan, the Korean peninsula was once again connected to the story of Nara, the final stop in East Asia for the *Fulk al-Salamah*. To signpost diplomatic ties with China, the ship also stopped at the Japanese port of Hakata, where "in the eighth century the imperial court sent monks and students to Chang'an, present day Xi'an."[15] The expedition team then traveled onward to Osaka to learn about diplomatic and religious connections with China. Finally, they traveled by bus to Nara. Their attention focused on one building in particular, Shōsōin, which served as the repository for the city's famed Tōdaiji Temple. This, it was suggested, best exemplified Japan's connection to the Silk Road:

> The immense log building was thus a storehouse of art which reached Japan
> from China along the Silk Roads. For thirteen centuries the Shoso-in has

preserved these treasures in a state comparable to that which modern technology could be expected to achieve. It is a mysterious and, for scientists who would like to understand its secrets, a somewhat frustrating place. Scholars who have studied the collections have identified many works produced by T'ang craftsmen with materials brought to China from across the sea: ivory and rhinoceros horn from India, tropical timber, pearls and tortoiseshell, wood from Indochina, metal artefacts from Persia and Sogdiana. The objects in the emperor Shomu's collection had a considerable impact on Japanese society, introducing a new taste for foreign arts and thus contributing to the opening of Japan to the outside world. The treasures of Shoso-in possess a symbolism which is perhaps even more powerful than their outstanding aesthetic qualities. They remind us that the silk roads were not only a conduit for trade in everyday commodities, and that the travellers who for centuries braved great risks as they wended their way in caravans, across steppe and desert or plied the oceans in their fragile craft were also serving an inexhaustible appetite for beauty.[16]

With much celebration of Buddhism as the shared heritage of peace and dialogue in East Asia, Nara was once again declared to be "the eastern terminus of the silk roads."[17] There, on 9 March 1991 a final symposium was held, which celebrated the project's key findings and diplomatic successes. Once again, Sun Yifu offered an account of Nara that leant heavily toward the cultural and religious influences from China. Accordingly, he explained that the "Chinese scholars on the expedition toured the ruins of Heijokyo. The buildings were modelled after those in China's Tang Dynasty Chang'an" and supplemented the text with photographs of displays of ceramics from Jingdezhen and artifacts that "resemble some in China in Xu Fu's time."[18]

It is hard to imagine such a heritage diplomacy initiative for East Asia succeeding today given the increased tensions over disputed islands, the South China Sea, and the production of World War II propaganda for nationalistic purposes. China's Belt and Road Initiative has also created a Maritime Silk Road imaginary that excludes Japan, an issue I return to later. But back in 1991, the final leg of the expedition back to Oman provided an intriguing moment in the diplomatic ambitions of the project. With the First Gulf War at its height, the Sultan's loan of the *Fulk al-Salamah* enabled Oman to project a timely message of its commitment to peace. Huyghe also captured the upheavals of the time and his sense of disorientation as the ship came into port in Muscat: "The distant noise of war reached us but was somehow muffled. And this helped to remind us of the strangeness of our adventure, causing us to look at the world with new eyes. One specialist pointed out that the presiding geniuses of our journey, Marco Polo and Ibn Battuta, had been able to roam freely through the then known world without being arrested or murdered. What was their secret? What signs of peace did they use, what code of salutation? Our voyage could be an occasion for meditating upon the rituals that defuse aggression in different cultures."[19]

Additional expeditions were planned for the years that followed, with a number being successfully completed, as mapped in Figure 8.1. Roads of Dialogue also spawned numerous international archaeology projects, study centers, and its own fellowship program named after Hirayama Ikuo, the Japanese painter and goodwill ambassador to UNESCO whom we saw in the last chapter.[20] Applicants submitted research proposals on Silk Road gardens, bazaars, calligraphy, and silverwares, to cite just a few examples.[21] As Appendix A indicates, across Asia and Europe museums joined in. Berlin hosted *The Heirs of the Silk Roads: Uzbekistan*; the Hungarian National Museum in Budapest put on *Eastern Roots of the Ancient Hungarian Culture*; and Quanzhou organized *Islamic Culture along the China Coast*. Paris became the unrivaled Silk Road exhibition capital, with residents visiting *In Search of Sinbad: The Maritime Silk Road* among many others. These events, along with the project's expeditions and publications, had a dramatic impact on the international visibility of the Silk Roads.[22] In March 1993, the *New York Times* proclaimed that "a fascinating new chapter in the epic of the legendary Silk Road was being written."[23] The article proceeded to explain some of the ways in which imagery from NASA space shuttle flights—which, by then, was being made available to teams of international researchers—afforded new interpretative possibilities for previously remote regions:

> Geologists plan new radar surveys from space to map ruins of long-abandoned caravan stations half buried in desert sands. Teams of anthropologists have been searching for stone tools and fossils that could reveal traces of the first humans to migrate to eastern Asia, showing that they probably followed the route that became the Silk Road. The Silk Roads Project, begun in 1990 [*sic*] by Unesco, is bringing together a variety of scholars from 90 countries for field trips along parts of the route and seminars to exchange research findings. "The Silk Road has become fashionable," said Dr. Denis Sinor, a historian of Central Asia at Indiana University in Bloomington and

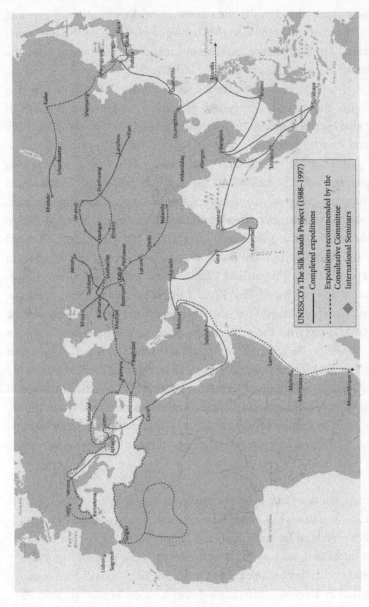

Figure 8.1 UNESCO Silk Roads of Dialogue Project, 1988–1997, modified from UNESCO, *Integral Study of the Silk Roads: Roads of Dialogue* (Paris: UNESCO, 1997).

Credit Line: Courtesy of Toyah Horman.

coordinator of a Unesco study of the languages used in communicating along the trade route.[24]

For UNESCO, the project directly addressed the organization's core aims: that of promoting intercultural dialogue and peace among nations. As the project came to a close, Doudou Diène noted that the "fundamental aim is to create the right conditions to raise people's awareness of the necessity of restoring the cultural dialogue of the Silk Roads as a way to promote a culture of peace and tolerance—so necessary in the world of today."[25] In a similar vein, Federico Mayor placed the project's significance within the instabilities and changes of the period: "Through this project, UNESCO has sought to shed light on the common heritage, both material and spiritual, that links the peoples of Eurasia. To generate an awareness of the different civilizations' shared roots and to foster the concept of a plural world heritage that embraces the masterpieces of nature and culture in all countries is, in the final analysis, to encourage attitudes of openness and tolerance, so necessary in an essentially interdependent world."[26] The project was also significant in raising visibility about the idea of a Maritime Silk Road. In the early iterations of the three routes, the lack of knowledge about maritime histories, combined with the primacy of Richthofen's account, meant that the bulk of attention was given to land-based flows and mobilities. The themes and locations covered by UNESCO and its partners gave greater equity to land and sea, a process that had a major impact on raising awareness about a maritime Eurasia.

A Politics of Heritage, from Roots to Routes

UNESCO's two initiatives were separated by 30 years and by a world that had profoundly changed. By the 1990s, the Silk Road had become fully established as a platform for heritage diplomacy, a metaphor for peace and dialogue across borders, and the "bridge" between East and West. Since the end of World War II, the concept of heritage had flourished within various international policy circles, with awareness driven largely by UNESCO's own World Heritage program, which began listing in 1972. It was a system that reinforced a paradigm formed in Europe over a number of centuries and that had stabilized into a modern conservation movement at the end of the nineteenth century. In the aftermath of two world wars, the task of building a list of the heritage of humanity was, not surprisingly, oriented toward safeguarding the spectacular and irreplaceable. By implication, the majority of sites added to UNESCO's increasingly prestigious register followed a particular pattern, whereby utmost importance was given to preserving the authenticity of the incomparable and unique.[27] This privileged buildings and archaeological sites that bore the legacy of great civilizations past. Despite criticisms of Eurocentrism, World Heritage quickly emerged as a system that many countries outside Europe saw as bestowing prestige and legitimacy on their historical "achievements." For those undergoing decolonization, international recognition of their cultural and civilizational "roots" invariably fed into domestic politics and the articulation of common ties around religion, ethnicity, and the idea of a collective past.

In its success then, World Heritage teetered between fostering national pride and, simultaneously, fueling antagonism toward others. In other words, the UN had developed an "olympics for culture" on the premise of safeguarding for future generations but which invariably took on a culturally centripetal imperative, a signification of material pasts around which identities would revolve and be drawn in. By the early 1990s, there was a growing recognition that a correction was needed in this balance between nationalism and internationalism. In 1994, a group of UNESCO experts met in Madrid to discuss the idea of adding the concept of "cultural routes" to the World Heritage framework. The Silk Roads was identified as one of the quintessential examples of transnational pasts that could help promote intercultural dialogue. Unlike the project of 1957, Roads of Dialogue placed considerable emphasis on the conservation and protection of material culture and historical sites. Expedition trips highlighted the fragility of archaeological landscapes in Pakistan, Mongolia, and elsewhere, stories enthusiastically reported by an international media sector that never tires of the romance of loss and the lost, salvation and redemption.

The political impediments of 1990s Central Asia meant that it would be some years before ministers and experts sat around the table to formally plan World Heritage nominations for the Silk Roads. But the Madrid meeting and the momentum it created had a significant and lasting impact on raising awareness about transboundary "cultural routes" and their importance to both world history and the dark sides of modern nationalism. In addition, the different components of Roads of Dialogue, together with the public interest it generated, acted as a catalyst across the international conservation sector. Post-launch, the Los Angeles–based Getty Conservation

Institute initiated a project for conserving the cave murals at Mogao, the site of Aurel Stein's discoveries near Dunhuang. Five years later, the International Dunhuang Project started as a collaboration between institutions in London, Beijing, Berlin, Kyoto, St Petersburg, and Dunhuang itself. Through the co-ordination efforts of the British Library—and the curatorial team of the Stein Collection—the project established a long-term program to conserve and digitally reproduce the manuscripts and artworks exported at the beginning of the twentieth century.[28] In China, a Maritime Silk Roads Study Center in Fuzhou planned through UNESCO's support tapped into growing interest in a maritime past, a history previously shunned by the state because of its associations with the humiliation of encounters with European naval power. Newly opened research centers for maritime archaeology searched for shipwrecks along China's southern coast, and by 1996 sufficient material was recovered for a public exhibition, the details of which I will return to shortly. By bringing in the World Tourism Organization, UNESCO also looked to develop sustainable tourism industries in countries that were "opening up" after decades of relative isolation.

As we saw earlier, 1990s globalization was a watershed, whereby those invested in restoring East-West relations and respect across cultures turned, or in some cases returned, to the Silk Road. Clearly, UNESCO played a major role in this. Elisseeff's approach to dialogue and peace had evolved from that pursued in the East-West Major Project. The latter gave explicit recognition to civilization as a concept, but the prevailing ideas and politics of the time meant that India, Iran, and other participants primarily represented themselves as the originators and centers of culture.[29] Decades later, multi-lateralism found an easier platform once buttressed by a more explicit recognition of the idea of civilizations in dialogue. By then Central Asia was also capturing the public's imagination as the "crossroads of civilization," as we have seen. Roads of Dialogue thus took such ideas and themes to a vast mul-tilateral platform, whereby the language of "cultural routes" linking the East and the West offered the reassurance of better times, a renewal of histories, at a moment of global precarity.

The arrival of Mohammed Khatami into office in Iran in May 1997 trig-gered significant shifts in the country's economic and foreign policies. In response to Huntington, he proposed the concept of "Dialogue among Civilizations." In his fascinating account of Khatami's policy, Edward Wastnidge explains how it became an important pillar for building bilateral, regional, and multilateral relations.[30] By 2001, it was installed as UN policy as the organization launched its own "Year of Dialogue among Civilizations." Two years earlier, the Japanese diplomat Kōichiro Matsuura had been elected as director general of UNESCO, having served as chairperson of the World Heritage Committee for the previous decade. With the arts and traditional cultural practices seen as key resources for promoting exchange, tolerance, and mutual learning, Matsuura committed UNESCO's full support to the initiative, with multiple projects created across its education, science, and culture divisions.[31] A year of events around the world, together with the intense debates following 9/11, meant that civilization had become one of the key vectors of international affairs and the structures of multilateral governance designed to address them.

Exhibiting the Silk Road

Interestingly, at the same time that UNESCO set about opening up the geographies and timelines of the Silk Road, museums and galleries located in Asia, Europe, and North America closed it back down to the geographies of Central Asia. This occurred primarily because their efforts to tap into the growing interest in the concept revolved around their own collections, those forms of material culture that traveled outward from Central Asia in the decades leading up to World War I. One of the legacies of the events documented in Chapters 3 and 4 is the translocation of tens of thousands of objects and manuscripts to state-funded galleries, museums, universities, and libraries located in several countries. In St Petersburg, for example, the Institute of Oriental Manuscripts holds around 19,000 items, the majority of which are Buddhist manuscripts. Across the city, the State Hermitage Museum holds Buddhist murals, textiles, and other artworks.[32] In Germany, in excess of 30,000 items, which together make up the Turfan Collection, are divided across a number of locations.[33] Manuscript fragments are kept in the Berlin Brandenburg Academy of Sciences and the Berlin State Library. Those objects deemed to be "artworks" are housed in a museum that changed its identity from Ethnological, to Indian Art, to Asian Art over a number of decades. Items gathered by the Japanese monk Ōtani Kōzui are distributed across a number of locations, including museums and libraries in Kyoto, Fukuoka, Nara, and Tokyo, the National Library of China, and the National Museum of Korea, which holds around 2000 pieces.[34] British Great Game hauls primarily reside in the British

Library, the British Museum, the Victoria and Albert Museum, and the National Museum of India, Delhi.[35] Items acquired by the Swedish explorer Sven Hedin have been dispersed across Sweden, Russia, United States, and China. Langdon Warner's trips of the 1920s means that the Harvard Arts Museums hold a variety of wall painting fragments, sculptures, and wooden objects.[36] And finally, in France, the Bibliothèque Nationale and Musée Guimet hold in excess of 30,000 books, manuscripts, paintings, and statues.[37]

Over the course of the twentieth century, a number of these collections moved between institutions and even countries, partly for storage purposes but in some cases to facilitate their exhibiting. One notable example was the shipping of objects collected by Sven Hedin to Chicago for the 1933–34 "A Century of Progress" World's Fair. Hedin persuaded the wealthy Chicago industrialist Vincent Bendix to fund the construction of a replica of the Wanfaguiyi Hall of Jehol from the Qing summer retreat of Chengde to represent China at the fair. To decorate the inside of the hall, Hedin supplied a mix of furniture, textiles, a temple bell, a prayer wheel, and statuary, which, as Roskam explains, was "all artfully arranged around a representation of the bodhisattva Guanyin" (see Figure 8.2).[38]

But it would take the changes of the 1990s before the above institutions began curating and interpreting their Central Asia collections through the imaginary of the Silk Road (see Appendix A). Interestingly, however, in contrast to the Nara exhibition discussed in the previous chapter, which offered three principal routes spanning oceans and regions, public audiences in Europe and North America learnt about the great explorer-scholars of the *fin de siècle* and the evidence they found of cross-cultural contacts within Central Asia. In 1995, the *Sérinde, Terre de Bouddha: Dix siècles d'art sur la route de la soie* opened in Paris, an exhibition that brought together objects from a number of partner institutions. Among the exhibition's centerpieces were manuscripts acquired from Dunhuang by Paul Pelliot. The following year, the city of Edinburgh was the venue for *Gateway to the Silk Road— Relics from the Han to the Tang Dynasties*. In October 2001, the Asia Society Museum of New York opened its doors to the public for an exhibition titled *Monks and Merchants: Silk Road Treasures from Northwest China*. By the early 2000s then, the number of Silk Road–themed exhibitions began to proliferate, in part driven by various collection–based collaborations oriented around creating new modes of conservation, digital archiving, and research. One further attribute, the photograph, added a distinct aura to the Silk Road

Figure 8.2 Replica hall for 1933–34 World's Fair in Chicago, containing objects supplied by Sven Hedin.

Credit Line: Donald G. Larson Collection on International Expositions and Fairs, Special Collections Research Center, Henry Madden Library, California State University, Fresno.

imaginary depicted in the museum. Many of the expeditions returned home with significant collections of negatives. The British Library, for example, holds more than 10,000 prints, negatives, and lantern slides taken by Aurel Stein over a 40-year period. Similarly, in Paris, the Mission Pelliot Archive stores more than 1500 images. Depicting scenes of desert adventure—of men astride camels and horses, and among camp sites and archaeological ruins— these grainy black and white images inserted the all-important ingredient for drawing in public audiences: romance. Integrated into museum displays, and presented for both their archival and evocative qualities, photographic images reproduced the classic tropes of an Orientalist visual culture, whereby the idea of "lost civilizations" rediscovered by heroic male adventurers delivered a real-world Indiana Jones narrative to the public.

Interestingly, it would be in China that the Maritime Silk Road gained currency as a museological concept, notably through the exhibition *The Maritime Silk Route: 2000 Years of Trade on the South China Sea*, organized by Guangzhou Museum and Hong Kong's Urban Council in 1996.[39] This drew on items recovered by the country's newly opened maritime archaeology research centers. What we see occur then in this post–Cold War era is a Silk Road imaginary stabilizing around certain objects that came to be arranged and presented in ways that created an aura of romance and mysticism around a story of mobility, transmission, and carriage. But in the material representations of the Silk Road outside China, the opportunity to showcase existing collections meant that land-based histories and those forms of connectivity within Central Asia remained the point of focus. In this regard, we see an interesting time-lag in the development of the Silk Road narrative across different cultural sectors. In the 1990s, UNESCO worked to broaden its geographies, themes, and timelines, while some years later Silk Road museology continued to close it down to one particular region and spectacle of material culture. It is a combination, I would suggest, that has contributed to some of the confusions and ambiguities that characterize popular Silk Road imaginaries today, as noted in Chapter 1.

Jumping forward to 2019, however, reveals a different picture. To coincide with the International Conference on Dialogue of Asian Civilizations, held in Beijing, the National Museum of China organized the public exhibition *Sharing a Common Future: Exhibition of Treasures from National Museums along the Silk Road*. As with Nara in 1988, a number of countries loaned artifacts, and given that the exhibition explicitly referred to the Silk Road's "revival" for the twenty-first century, it was little surprise to see each country was a Belt and Road partner. But this meant that the Silk Road was depicted via items from Latvia, Poland, Slovenia, Romania, and Cambodia, as well as the more familiar Japan, Kazakhstan, and Mongolia.[40] Interestingly here, it also led to a distinct expansion in the material culture that was brought under the umbrella of a Silk Road geocultural imaginary, namely wardrobes, clocks, European forms of dress, Omani pottery, and dinnerware from Eastern Europe, to cite a few examples (see Figure 8.3).

Figure 8.3 2019 exhibition *Sharing a Common Future: Exhibition of Treasures from National Museums along the Silk Road*, Poland exhibit.
Credit Line: Photo by Author.

The Road Becomes a Belt

Of course, this exhibition and intergovernmental conference is one of the many initiatives that have been organized as part of the cooperation architecture advanced within the Belt and Road framework. As we will see in greater detail in Chapter 10, Beijing has adopted the Silk Roads as a metaphor for an immensely ambitious plan for connecting up Eurasia. Primarily interpreted as a project of networked infrastructures—physical,

Figure 8.4 Xi Jinping speech at UNESCO headquarters, 27 March, 2014.
Credit Line: Abaca Press / Alamy Stock Photo.

institutional, digital—Belt and Road includes multiple ingredients that were rarely, if ever, discussed in post-launch media stories and think-tank reports that grappled with understanding its long-term geo-economic and geopolitical implications. Less than six months after giving his initial Belt and Road speeches in Kazakhstan and Indonesia, Xi Jinping traveled to UNESCO's headquarters in Paris to confirm China's commitment to fostering intercultural and intercivilizational dialogue in challenging times (see Figure 8.4). The rejuvenation of China, Xi proclaimed, was not merely economic but the revival of a civilization that can help to guide the world toward sustained peace and harmony. The mechanism for delivering this would be a Silk Roads "revived" for the twenty-first century. Such lofty aspirations for a new cultural multilateralism were directly aligned with the founding principles of UNESCO, as the following excerpts of his speech indicate:

Since its inception in 1945, UNESCO has faithfully lived up to its mandate and worked untiringly to enhance trust and understanding among the world's peoples and promote exchanges and mutual learning among the various civilizations. China attaches great importance to its cooperation with UNESCO and stands ready to get more involved in its activities. . . . Civilizations have become richer and more colorful with exchanges and mutual learning. Such exchanges and mutual learning form an important drive for human progress and global peace and development. . . . The ocean is vast for it refuses no rivers. All civilizations are crystallizations of mankind's hard work and wisdom. Every civilization is unique. Copying other civilizations mechanically or blindly is like cutting one's toes just to fit his shoes, which is not only impossible but also highly detrimental. All achievements of civilizations deserve our respect and must be treasured. . . . History tells us that only through exchanges and mutual learning can a civilization be filled with vitality. If all civilizations can uphold inclusiveness, the so-called "clash of civilizations" will be out of the question and the harmony of civilizations will become reality.

Xi Jinping, UNESCO headquarters, 27 March 2014[41]

Shortly afterward, international cooperation programs celebrating Silk Road culture(s) began to appear. In Astana, the Silk Road International Cultural Forum held its inaugural event, with a second forum taking place in Moscow a year later in 2015. The Silk Road International Arts Festival expanded its ambitions rapidly, with annual events in Xi'an featuring calligraphy, painting, and photography exhibitions, as well as performances by artists from more than 80 countries. Annual Silk Road film festivals were also launched in the wake of Belt and Road, and in 2015 the China Silk Road Foundation initiated a collaboration with the UK-based 1001 Inventions for exchanges and events on the history of science. In Beijing, the Silk Road International League of Theaters (SRILT) brought together more than 60 theater companies from 20 countries, the majority of whom are Belt and Road partners. Speaking at the league's inaugural symposium in October 2016, Ding Wei, vice minister and committee member of the Ministry of Culture, PRC, indicated that this formed part of a broader strategy of cooperation programs: "We have created cultural events such as cultural years, art festivals, film festivals and tourism promotions. All the endeavor has contributed to the mutual understanding among China and countries involved in the Silk Road."[42]

Domestically, a multitude of Silk Road projects now contribute to the project of national and cultural rejuvenation.[43] As Maria Adele Carrai and others have noted, under Xi Jinping, the Communist Party increasingly looks to China's cultural past to build patriotism and national pride: the "China Dream of Great Rejuvenation." In considering such developments, Millward observes that this involves orchestrating history, culture, and heritage in ways that connect the modern polity that is China to the more amorphous entity that is Sinic civilization.[44] The aim of such an endeavor is to give form to the idea of a civilizational state, one that has distinct qualities and values, which stem from 5000 years of continuous history. To that end, the hugely popular television series *National Treasure* talked of "the cultural blood-line" of the nation in 2019.[45] The Silk Road narrative is woven into this by suggesting that China was engaged with the outside world through trade, diplomacy, and cultural exchange over many centuries. It thus follows that the country contributed to, and learned from, the outside world through commodity trade, the transmission of scientific knowledge and religious values, and peaceful inter-polity relations. But it also means that certain aspects of the Silk Road, namely the removal of artifacts from sites in and around the Taklamakan Desert have come to be associated with the century of humiliation. In Beijing's National Museum of China, for example, an exhibition titled *The Road of Rejuvenation* includes a number of photographs of archaeological sites from the early 1900s. Notably, a grainy picture of Paul Pelliot reading manuscripts by candlelight—an image frequently reproduced by Western authors and museums as an iconic moment in the "golden age" of Silk Road research—is given a caption that translates as "The French explorer Paul Pelliot was stealing treasures from the Dunhuang Caves" (see Figure 8.5). Reviving the Silk Roads for the twenty-first century then is, in part, about restoring, and giving new life to, the cultural achievements of China's past.

Indeed, in the era of Belt and Road, Dunhuang's famed Mogao Caves have become an important venue for cultural-sector diplomacy. An international music forum held there was followed by an annual Silk Road International Cultural Expo. Designed to promote heritage tourism and international cooperation, the expo pulled together performers from 70 countries, with several thousand delegates attending its conferences. That same year, 2016, the city of Gavin in Iran hosted the Silk Road Mayors Forum meeting, with participation by UNESCO. A month later, cultural exchanges of the ancient Silk Road were the basis of discussions about developing joint tourism strategies during a meeting of the Iran-China Friendship Society in Tehran.[46] In 2016–17, the movies *Kung Fu Yoga* and *Xuanzang* were produced as India-China collaborations. Branded as Belt and Road people-to-people projects in China, both films focused on the civilizational and Buddhist histories that conjoined the two across the Himalayas. And in 2014 the Silk Roads were finally added to the World Heritage List. An intergovernmental committee

法国探险家伯希和正在敦煌石室中盗宝。

Figure 8.5 Image of Paul Pelliot in Dunhuang, National Museum of China, *The Road to Rejuvenation* exhibition. Caption on Photograph: "The French explorer Paul Pelliot was stealing treasures from the Dunhuang Caves."
Credit Line: Photo by Author.

to advance collaborative nominations had been operational since 2009. The first to be listed, The Silk Roads: The Routes Network of Chang'an-Tian-shan Corridor, is comprised of 33 sites, 22 of which lie in China, 8 in Kazakhstan, and the remaining 3 in Kyrgyzstan (see Figure 8.6).[47] The extensive resources and negotiations required for World Heritage nominations mean that additional Silk Road listings involving multiple countries will be an inevitably

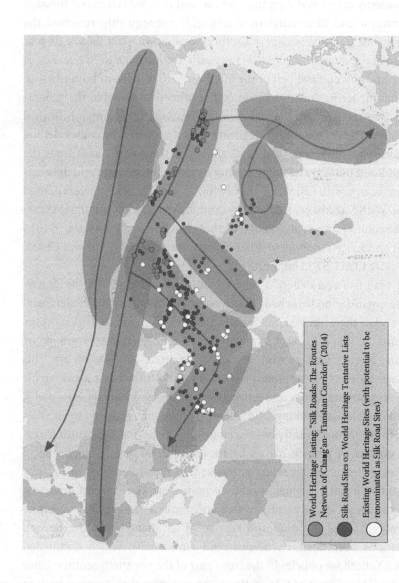

Figure 8.6 Map of sites for Silk Road World Heritage listing and Belt and Road economic corridors.

Credit Line: Courtesy of Toyah Horman.

World Heritage Listing: "Silk Roads: The Routes Network of Chang'an–Tianshan Corridor" (2014)

Silk Road Sites on World Heritage Tentative Lists

Existing World Heritage Sites (with potential to be renominated as Silk Road Sites) slow process. But for countries like Kazakhstan, such projects form part of a broader strategy of international cooperation around Silk Road culture. In 2015, President Nazarbayev spoke at UNESCO's headquarters to launch his new Academy of Peace, stating that "we can best counter extremism through inter-cultural and inter-religious dialogue."[48] Subsequently renamed the Centre for the Rapprochement of Cultures to align with UNESCO's 10-year program of the same title, activities were said to contribute to "the revival of the spiritual and cultural belt of the Silk Way."[49] Crucially, in both physical and symbolic terms, investments in culture directly map on to the geographies of Belt and Road. In the case of World Heritage, for example, historical Silk Road corridors identified for listing directly overlay the routes Beijing has identified for Belt and Road development. In the case of Kazakhstan, the Belt and Road Initiative has significantly increased investment and development assistance, with Chinese loans funding thousands of kilometers of road and rail. With Nazarbayev's Astana government strategically aiming to transform the country into a gateway of trade between East and West Asia, in 2015 alone it announced more than 40 infrastructure collaborations with China, worth more than US $33 billion.[50]

Less than five years after Xi Jinping's 2014 visit to UNESCO headquarters, the organization launched "phase two" of its Silk Road multilateralism. At the end of the Cold War, Silk Roads: Road of Dialogue expanded on the trade and cultural flows that dominated early Silk Road historiography by including themes such as Arab seafaring, ceramics, and Persian art. This continues today via a program oriented around 18 thematic areas: architecture; traditional sports and games; agriculture and botany; astronomy, navigation, calendar-making, and astrology; food and gastronomy; textiles and clothing; medicine and pharmacology; paper-making and printing; ceramics, porcelains, pottery, tile, and glass; coinage and metals; language and literature; religion and spirituality; music; traditional painting; calligraphy and manuscripts; carpet-making and decorative arts; artistic performances; and philosophy. Not surprisingly, such an approach foregrounds transmission, mobility, and diffusion and represents an attempt to move beyond designations over territory, origins, and authenticity, which dominated UNESCO's heritage policies in the latter part of the twentieth century. Since 2017, the UN Alliance of Civilizations—an initiative that stretches back to 2005—has also organized and supported various Silk Road ventures.[51]

Many further examples could be cited to demonstrate how Belt and Road has ushered in a new era of cultural-sector cooperation in Asia, with a multitude of museum and gallery exhibitions, theater performances, fashion shows, and film and music festivals all celebrating the countries, cultures, and "spirit" of the Silk Roads. I have argued elsewhere that this celebration of transboundary, transcultural "shared" pasts has rapidly become a forum of heritage diplomacy through which China exercises new forms of geocultural power. Channeling the Silk Roads as a dialogue between civilizations figures into the vision of a resurgent China, a country seeking to reclaim its place at the heart of international affairs. Belt and Road has further raised concerns about China's growing influence in the Asia region. Andrew Scobell notes that "while China is relatively peaceful, it has begun acting more belligerently and more threatening."[52] A foreign policy built around reviving a history of peaceful trade and cultural exchange thus represents a strategic attempt to placate anxieties and present Chinese investment and networked infrastructure projects as benign and of benefit to all. In my previous book, *Geocultural Power*, I elaborated at length on the potential that China's co-opting of the Silk Roads holds for generating new narratives of Asian and world history. Belt and Road constitutes a political economy within which the study, publication, and exhibition of intra-Asian and Afro-Asian connectivities will occur. But I have also argued that with China driving so much of the research and funding in this space, the risk of Sinocentric depictions of the past is significant. The remaining chapters here build on this discussion by offering a more detailed account of the Silk Road's evolution as a platform of foreign policy. Together, they examine aspects of Belt and Road that provide a lens for viewing the Silk Road in geopolitical and world-ordering terms.

PART FOUR

GEOPOLITICS

In 2018, renowned international relations author Robert Kaplan proclaimed that Eurasia was entering an era of weakened state power and fading empires.[1] Borders were receding, and the Westphalian model of states in competition was becoming less relevant. In the coming decades, Kaplan argued, the political map of the region will look more like "medieval times," such that we are witnessing the "return of Marco Polo's world." More specifically, he cited Laurence Bergreen's description of Polo's travels across a "complex, tumultuous, and menacing, but nonetheless porous" Eurasia as the precise lens through which we should interpret the region's geopolitical future.[2] The essay was first written for the Pentagon's Office of Net Assessment before being republished in book form two years later. For Kaplan, Marco Polo represents Asia seen through Western eyes and thus a figure to which his readership can relate. But this also allows further historical parallels to be drawn, including the intersecting power structures of Persia, described as "history's first superpower in antiquity," and Pax Mongolica and the conquests of Kublai Khan:

> It was trade routes, not the projection of military power, that emblematized the "Pax Mongolica." Mongol grand strategy was built on commerce much more than on war. If you want to understand China's grand strategy today, look no further than Kublai Khan's empire. Yet, for Kublai Khan it didn't altogether work. Persia and Russia were beyond Chinese control, and the Indian subcontinent, separated from China by the wall of the Himalayas, with seas on both sides, remained its own geopolitical island. All the while, though, the Great Khan strengthened his base in what always has been Chinese civilization's arable cradle, in central and eastern China, away from its Muslim-minority areas of the western desert. In all of this, the geopolitical characteristics of Marco Polo's world roughly approximate our own.[3]

Here, then, Marco Polo also stands in for the world of the Silk Road, which, he suggests, "provides as good an outline as any for defining the geopolitics of Eurasia in the coming era."[4] In this regard, Kaplan is referring to China's Belt and Road Initiative. Picking up Beijing's rhetoric of "reviving" the Silk Roads for the twenty-first century, he compels his readers to pay attention to the historical parallels now playing out. Deployed in this way, Marco Polo is used as a metonym for a region of the world and a particular moment in its history. The question remains, though, of whether he is using the Silk Road as metaphor or as a point of empirical comparison. In stating "the current Chinese regime's proposed land-and-maritime Silk Road duplicates exactly the one Marco Polo traveled, there is no coincidence," it appears as though history is more than just a resource for building analogies.[5] Put simply, the thesis is that the twenty-first century shares distinct characteristics with the thirteenth. But Belt and Road does not duplicate exactly the route taken by Marco Polo. Rather, the overland and maritime Silk Roads are invoked by the Chinese government to signal themes such as long-distance connectivity, exchange, win-win cooperation, and dialogue. And more broadly, the absurd contention that borders are receding to the extent that Asia mirrors "medieval times" is misleading to say the least. Evocative as it may be, an analysis tabled to the US government stacks one metaphor for understanding the past, Marco Polo, upon another, the Silk Road, with the latter now well established as both a stylized, aesthetic reading of Eurasia's history and, as the two chapters that make up Part Four reveal, a concept used for branding foreign policies and their analysis today.

The idea of Marco Polo's world provides an example of how the Silk Road has become both analogy and metaphor in foreign policy strategies and for analysts seeking to interpret the geopolitical implications they might hold. Martin Medhurst et al. have argued that the terminology and metaphors used by analysts during the Cold War did not merely reflect its realities but played a formative role in constructing them. He suggests that the period was constituted by "the discourses that call it into being, sustain, structure, and ultimately define it."[6] Indeed, I would agree that acts, actions, and their consequences are revealed and concealed by the contours of the language deployed to interpret them. We have seen how the idea of the Silk Road has been entangled in geopolitics and imperial rivalry from its very beginnings. Chapter 3 demonstrated that ideas of "ancient" trade and long-distance cultural transmission emerged from the imperial project to remake land as territory through geography-defying rail projects. Chapter 9 turns to two other conceptual metaphors—the Great Game and Heartland—which prevailed in the political analysis of nineteenth-century Central Asia and have been subsequently recycled to interpret the major events of the twentieth. Since the 1990s, the Silk Road has entered this space as a concept for foreign policy and its analysis. As the chapter illustrates, all three are historically constituted conceptual metaphors, each holding quite different readings of the past. As such then, they construct different Eurasian realities and draw on different events and iconic men to do so. Genghis Khan is a metaphor of power emanating from the north, whereas Marco Polo has become a metonym of transcontinental trade routes and cross-cultural encounters. And, of course, one represents the dark, foreboding East, the other a noble West.

It is evident that Belt and Road further advances the popularization of Silk Road metaphors in the discourse of foreign policies, harboring most explicitly in the case of China's international ambitions and new forms of power within a language of friendship, dialogue, and cooperation. This raises important questions as the Silk Road also embeds itself in the nomenclature of analysis. The Cold War and Great Game signaled competition, moves and countermoves, tactics and resources. The Heartland points to territory, a cultural and political core, and is analogous with homeland, a concept that has underpinned modern discourses of nationalism. But as Chapter 10 argues, when used to anchor government policies, as well as nationalistic scholarship and journalism, the Silk Road and its associated metaphors conceal its geopolitical qualities and intentionally render infrastructure, multinational banking, and development aid as benign and of benefit to all. Looking forward, it is highly likely that those analysts pursuing more critical pathways will continue to grapple with the metaphorical concepts now in ascendancy, both constructing and deconstructing the new realities Belt and Road and its rivals bring forth. Kaplan's world of Marco Polo, as unhelpful as it is, will doubtless be one of several attempts to evocatively capture the shifts and transformations now occurring.

9
Metaphors of Power

The origins of the term Great Game are somewhat murky. Seymour Becker argues that John William Kaye, a British army officer, was the first to use it in his 1851 book *History of the War in Afghanistan*.[1] Becker notes that it took a number of decades for the expression to enter circulation and has come to be associated with Rudyard Kipling's 1901 novel, *Kim*. Widely read in Britain, Kipling's writings lent intellectual weight to the colonial project in Asia. Chapter 2 described the anxieties in London over Russia's ambitions to secure control over the "the strategic cockpit of the continent."[2] George Curzon, later Lord Curzon, published his highly influential *Russia in Central Asia* in 1889, a manuscript based on extensive travel in the region. This formed part of a debate about the changing nature of warfare and Britain's military strategy.[3] In 1902, Halford Mackinder contributed a book on British naval power. His legacy as one of the foremost geopolitical theorists of the period would, however, come from a single lecture delivered to the Royal Geographic Society in 1904.[4] In *The Geographical Pivot of History*, Mackinder argued that a historic shift was occurring, away from the sea toward land-based forms of power, with Russia presented as the primary threat facing Britain. The lecture and subsequent paper gained notoriety for the theory of the "pivot," a vast area reaching down from the Arctic and incorporating the Iranian plateau, Tibet, Afghanistan, Mongolia, Xinjiang, and Russian territory. This expansive region was surrounded by an "Inner or Marginal Crescent," and beyond that lay the "Lands of Outer or Insular Crescent." Mackinder's analysis was significant in releasing the idea of Eurasia from the confines of geology and initiating debate about the region as a political construct.

In subsequent years, he adjusted his original thesis, renaming the pivot as the "Heartland" and refining the argument into an aphorism that would capture the imagination of analysts for decades to come: "Who rules East Europe commands the Heartland; who rules the Heartland commands the World-Island; who rules the World-Island commands the world."[5] During the interwar period, the German geopolitical theorist Karl Haushofer

The Silk Road. Tim Winter, Oxford University Press. © Oxford University Press 2022.
DOI: 10.1093/oso/9780197605059.003.0009

took up his ideas, a trajectory that led to much speculation about how the Heartland thesis influenced the strategies of the German state in World War II. Geopolitical science had come of age, and in 1942 the American public was warned of the dangers it posed in an article published in *Life* magazine: *Geopolitics: The Lurid Career of a Scientific System Which a Briton Invented, the Germans Used, and the Americans Need to Study*.[6] Nicholas Spykman, a professor of Yale University, accepted the broad premise of Mackinder's arguments but countered the Heartland thesis by asserting that the continental periphery of Eurasia was the region most critical to world affairs. Spykman thus renamed Mackinder's Inner Crescent as the all-important "Rimland."[7] Preceding Mackinder's 1904 pivot theory by little more than a decade, the American naval historian Alfred Mahan had published *The Influence of Sea Power on History 1660–1783*.[8] Mindful of such ideas, Spykman anticipated the importance of the Indian Ocean in international affairs and thus the potential for naval power to "contain" the expansion of the Soviet Union. Indeed, as Fettweis notes, Spykman posited that it was the ways in which power could be "projected into and out of the Heartland" that mattered most and in updating Mackinder declared, "Who controls the Rimland rules Eurasia; Who rules Eurasia controls the destinies of the world."[9] It was a perspective that underpinned US containment policy during the Cold War.[10] Those who followed Spykman argued that the best way for the West to contain Soviet power was to strengthen the Rimland.

Such a reading of international affairs, Meinig argued in 1956, was helpful but risked subsuming complex events within evocative concepts. His opinion was that theories of the Heartland reworked by scholars and journalists inevitably came to be "loosened from their original context."[11] Mackinder's disciplinary home of geography—together with the prestigious context of his lecture—meant that the theory was often read as a spatial interpretation of international events and transitions: the "geo" in geopolitical theory. For the strategists of World War II, space after all was power, a dictum Haushofer urged upon his superiors.[12] In certain cases, the theories of Mackinder and Spykman were reduced to mere equivalences: the Heartland with land power and the Rimland with sea power.[13] Those more careful readers recognized that Mackinder's 1904 paper was essentially a treaty on the lessons of history: how conquests, invasions, and different power structures had been impacted by rivers and mountains, deserts and harbors. Reading the past in such terms, he argued, was vital for understanding the full implications of Russia's ambitions for a transcontinental rail network:

The Russian railways have a clear run of 6000 miles from Wirballen in the west to Vladivostok in the east. The Russian army in Manchuria is as significant evidence of mobile land-power as the British army in South Africa was of sea-power. True, that the Trans-Siberian railway is still a single and precarious line of communication, but the century will not be old before all Asia is covered with railways. . . . Is not the pivot region of the world's pol- itics that vast area of Euro-Asia which is inaccessible to ships, but in antiq- uity lay open to the horse-riding nomads, and is today about to be covered with a network of railways? . . . Russia replaces the Mongol Empire. Her pressure on Finland, on Scandinavia, on Poland, on Turkey, on Persia, on India, and on China, replaces the centrifugal raids of the steppemen. In the world at large she occupies the central strategical position held by Germany in Europe. She can strike on all sides and be struck from sides, save the north. The full development of her modern railway mobility is merely a matter of time.[14]

Mackinder had established a new template of analysis, one that concep- tualized political and military affairs in a reading of history constructed in spatial, climatic, and topographical terms. In this regard, the Heartland was as much a cultural-historical metaphor as it was a spatial one. As geopolit- ical theory evolved, these themes continued to resonate, influencing the for- mation of Eurasia as a concept for policy-makers and scholars alike across a number of countries. In 1968, Alastair Lamb published a book on the topic of Asia's frontiers and borders.[15] Arguing that insufficient attention had been paid to such themes, he set about revising Mackinder's thesis via a more elab- orate schema of regions. These, Lamb argued, had particular characteristics, such that mountains, rivers, and other landscape features had shaped the de- velopment of civilizations and the story of empires. Deserts and mountains were seen as barriers to expansion, with the metaphor of the wheel used to describe the Tibetan plateau as the "hub" around which everything turns:

Around the periphery of the southern half of this wheel with its moun- tainous hub lie three main regions of settled civilisation separated from each other by transitional zones. To the east is China, stretching in a cres- cent from the edge of the steppe system in Manchuria and Mongolia to the hills and fertile valleys of the South-east Asian mainland. In the centre is the Indian subcontinent, the home of Hindu culture, flanked by mainland South-east Asia on the east and by the Afghan highland on the west. In the west is Iran, another centre of a distinctive civilisation based on settled agriculture and urban life. To the north, Iran, by way of the oasis cities of Turkestan, is linked to the steppe system. To the east, Iran overflows into the valley of the Indus river and its tributaries. There have been plenty of periods in history—when all three of these major civilisation centres around the southern side of the mountain hub have been affected by the same broad historical forces. In general, however, the presence of the mountain hub has severely limited regional interactions. If we regard the mountain hub and its rim, the steppe road on the north and the peripheral civilisations on its south, as a single major geopolitical system, then for much of its history that system has operated as if it were an assemblage of unconnected subsystems.[16]

The frequent citation of Kublai Khan and Genghis Khan and their ability to "shatter established powers" helped Lamb to illustrate the themes of history he perceived helpful for understanding contemporary affairs.[17] Indeed, the citation of both men was yet another example of a popular image held in the West of the Mongols as savage fighters who conquered vast territories and inflicted extreme violence upon their victims. Within this, their cultural achievements invariably disappeared from view. In China, the Mongols have also long been constructed as the destroyers of civilization, descending from the north. But in the context of the Cold War, the West equated Mongol power with the threat of a Soviet nuclear arsenal, whereby the notion of civilization was elevated from a particular group or culture to the scale of humanity. Interestingly, Lamb's book made no mention of Marco Polo. Instead, his historical narrative, buttressed by carefully chosen individuals, provided the analytic for interpreting Asia's problematic frontiers and borders created in the wake of decolonization and the hostilities enveloping the region in the 1950s. Lamb cited disputes over Kashmir and the Sino-Indian boundary as among the areas where problems inherited from the Great Game took on new significance at a time when China, Russia, and the United States dedicated significant resources to maintaining buffer zones and lines of control (see Figure 9.1).

Not surprisingly, the period Lamb was writing in spawned a new lexicon of analysis, as journalists, authors, and policy-makers grappled with a world of seemingly intractable ideological and political divides. Robert Ivie uses Lakoff and Johnson's ideas about the systemic nature of metaphor usage to argue that a series of clusters emerged in US thinking and political discourse from the late 1940s onward. To cite just two examples, the notion of

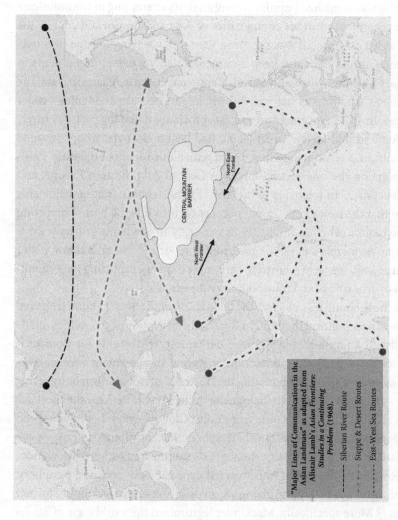

"Major Lines of Communication in the
Asian Landmass" as adapted from
Alistair Lamb's *Asian Frontiers:
Studies in a Continuing
Problem* (1968).

----- Siberian River Route

····· Steppe & Desert Routes

········ East-West Sea Routes

CENTRAL MOUNTAIN
BARRIER

North East
Frontier

North West
Frontier

Figure 9.1 Major lines of communication in the Asian landmass, modified from Alistair
Lamb, *Asia Frontiers: Studies in a Continuing Problem* (New York: Frederick A. Praeger, 1968).
Credit Line: Courtesy of Toyah Horman.

a "Game" included the terms "cards," "competition," "pawn," "play," "team," and "race."[18] Another cluster identified by Ivie, "Dark-light" captured the widespread use of "shadow," "nightmare," "smoke," "dawn," "abyss," "awakening," and so forth.[19] In addition to Spykman's Rimland concept, other spatial metaphors—"shatterzones," "containment," and Mackinder's "World Island"—also remained popular among analysts attempting to communicate the international relations complexities of Asia and Europe. Of course, the most well-known of all was the "Iron Curtain." Cleaving Europe into two, the Iron Curtain has since been commemorated via public monuments in Hungary and the Czech and Slovak Republics. Its East Asian derivate, the "Bamboo Curtain," was less well known, in part because of ongoing border changes. In 1979, reporters and analysts proclaimed that the past was reverberating and that a New Great Game had begun as Soviet troops invaded Afghanistan, a terminology that would return once again in the early 1990s in reports on the intersecting forces in Central Asia, Eastern Europe, and the Caucasus.[20] In reference to the first of these regions, Matthew Edwards argues that the New Great Game "became such an integral part of reporting on the region, whether implicitly or explicitly in academic journals, news bulletins, economic analysis or government reports."[21] Nearly a century after Kipling's *Kim*, the term seemed to carry new impetus, capturing the geopolitics of hydrocarbons and transboundary pipelines.

For those countries involved, the dissolution of the Soviet Union triggered a wave of new political thought. In Russia, the discipline of geopolitics finally established a foothold, having been denounced by the elite for decades.[22] As discussions gathered momentum, there was disagreement over whether Russia was best served by pursuing the "fortress" of isolationism or by acting more as an open "bridge" in dialogue with the West.[23] Perhaps the most detailed account of this has come from Edith Clowes, whose book focuses on the geographical and geopolitical metaphors that contributed to post-Soviet Russian identity.[24] Like others, she suggests that the translation of Mackinder into Russian in the early 1990s fostered debates about core and periphery, with the idea of a Heartland giving weight to ambitions of reclaiming former glories.[25] More specifically, Mackinder legitimized the world view of Russia as the cultural heart of Eurasia and arguments for expansion eastward.[26] Critical to this was the resurgence in Eurasianism at that time, described by Dmitry Shlapentokh as a "quasi-intellectual and political movement" with its roots in the late nineteenth century and post–Bolshevik Revolution period.[27] Intellectuals of Tsarist Russia used geohistorical theories to buttress "the

Russian state as a unified Eurasian great power."[28] In the 1920s, Eurasianism developed as a largely emigré movement, emphasizing the uniqueness of a Russian culture that combined Slavic and non-Slavic traditions. Crucially here, and as Shlapentokh notes, "Eurasianists also stressed the Asiatic ingredient of Russian culture and ethnicity."[29] Eurasia was seen as a single civilizational zone, one that could be identified by its cohesiveness and by its distinct differences with Western culture. Bassin argues that in its "classical" 1920s form, the West was primarily associated with Europe. But as such ideas resurfaced in the 1990s, Aleksandr Dugin and his followers argued that the center of gravity of Western civilization pivoted around Atlantic capitalism and thus, by implication, the United States. To justify this shift, neo-Eurasianism also left behind ideas of Eurasia as a single civilization in favor of a unified "political and ideological principle."[30] Clowes explains how Dugin "developed a Russocentric dream of a future Eurasian imperialist state system, centering in Moscow and the Russian north and Siberian east."[31] Dugin's ultraconservative ideas reached the meeting rooms of the Kremlin, and, not surprisingly, titles such as "The Mysteries of Eurasia" and "Absolute Motherland" also gave analysts in Washington cause for concern, not least because of the fascist ideology underpinning his dreams of a resurgent Russia.

In the game of reviving old ideas, analysts in the United States were not to be outdone. To cite just one example, Zbigniew Brzezinski, former national security adviser to the Carter administration, returned to the game metaphor, this time using chess to emphasize a situation of moves and countermoves and the multiple pieces—read countries—that needed to be moved into position. In the immediate aftermath of collapsed Soviet power, Brzezinski's analysis proved highly influential in understanding "The Grand Chessboard" that was forming.[32] Not surprisingly, debates in the US at this time also returned to the idea of a Eurasian Heartland, altering Mackinder's emphasis on Russia in favor of a focus on Central Asia and the South Caucasus. Brzezinski famously dubbed these regions as the "Eurasian Balkans," invoking a comparison with the countries of the former Yugoslavia to indicate a possible descent into regional conflict and turmoil.

To briefly summarize then, and to return to Mackinder and Kipling, what we see here are two distinct conceptual metaphor clusters—Heartland and game—which entered circulation in the opening years of the twentieth century and have been reworked and recycled ever since. Indeed, their popularity has not diminished among scholars of geopolitics today, as authors continue to announce the arrival of a New Great Game. Evidence of Russian expansionism gave this theory credence in the 1990s and early 2000s.[33] The growing influence of regional players since then, notably China, India, Iran, and Turkey, updates the concept, as does Belt and Road, which has also breathed new life into debates over Mackinder's model.[34]

The Return of Eurasia

The "seismic events" and "political shock-waves"—to cite the earthquake cluster that also gained currency in the early 1990s—seemed, however, to demand a new lexicon of political analysis and foreign policy. Alexander Maxwell traces such developments in relation to Poland, Croatia, and Czechoslovakia and their emergence as the "bulwarks," "bridges," and "frontiers" of European political discourse.[35] The case of Turkey is of particular relevance here. Lerna Yanik describes the transitions Turkish politicians made from being a "buffer" in the Cold War to acting as the "bridge" and "crossroad" between East and West. Switching to the latter, Yanik suggests, engineered discursive flexibility into foreign policy, enabling Ankara to pivot back and forth between Europe and the Middle East. At a more abstract level, it also allowed Turkish politicians to present the country "belonging equally to two different civilisations, Western and Eastern at the same time."[36] This was particularly useful as Turkey sought entry into the European Union. But in simultaneously looking eastward, the concept of Eurasia also opened up space for a revival of pan-Turkism, whereby strategic relationships were established with newly independent Turkic republics farther east.[37] It was at this moment of transition, a new East-West, that the notion of the Silk Road began to emerge.

For the former Soviet republics of Central Asia, the political transitions of the 1990s were accompanied by new international trade opportunities, not least on the back of a changing energy economy. Marlene Laruelle suggests that as these newly named countries attempted to gain market share and international recognition, they strategically branded themselves as being "at the crossroads" of a vast continent of established and emerging markets.[38] Kent Calder has described this period as the beginning of a "New Continentalism," as the Eurasian energy infrastructure sector developed in accordance with the new geopolitical landscape and increased demand from those undergoing rapid development, namely China.[39] With Beijing becoming a net importer of oil from 1993 onward, Turkmenistan, Iran, and Kazakhstan supplied oil and gas, a situation that required stable relations with intermediary countries and the upgrading of pipelines, seaports, and refinery facilities. This period also marked the beginning of a push to integrate the region via rail and road and the establishment of a number of bilateral and multilateral initiatives. In 1992, the UN Economic and Social Commission for Asia and the Pacific (UNESCAP) launched one such program, marking the beginning of a decade-long attempt to create intergovernmental agreements. As part of this process, the organization responsible for developing transborder cooperations in Central Asia, TRACECA (Transport Corridor Europe-Caucasus Asia), hosted various events including one in 1998 on regional development titled TRACECA—Restoration of the Historic Silk Route. By the mid-1990s, Central Asia was emerging from decades of relative isolation, with such initiatives "beginning to give a concrete shape to the idealized vision of an interconnected and economically successful Eurasian continent."[40] Newly independent countries endowed with an abundance of oil and gas were thus finding new friends in both Europe and East Asia. As Dennis Mootz notes, postage stamps are cheap to print and change and thus "can respond more quickly to the political changes and initiatives of a government."[41] Not surprisingly then, a number of Central Asian republics turned to the Silk Road as a motif to signal their new priorities and place in international affairs at a moment of momentous change (see Figure 9.2).

Figure 9.2 Silk Road–themed stamps issued by Uzbekiston Pochtasi, 1997.
Credit Line: Uzbekiston Pochtasi.

For Japan and South Korea, the new diplomatic challenges raised by the collapse of the Soviet Union led to a recalibration of their international aid strategies. In the mid-1990s, Japan embarked upon its "Silkroad Diplomacy" initiative, a foreign policy strategy that would evolve to stretch right across the continent. In justifying the government's engagement with Central Asia, Prime Minister Hashimoto Ryutaro stated that "Japan has deep-rooted nostalgia for this region stemming from the glory of the days of the Silk Road."[42] Progress slowed following Hashimoto's election defeat in 1998. Four years later, however, "The Silk Road Energy Mission" was launched.[43] This was followed by the Arc of Freedom and Prosperity Initiative in 2006.[44] Today, Japan remains committed to official development assistance (ODA) in Central Asia spanning multiple sectors, including JICA-funded Silk Road heritage programs in Iran. In 2014, the South Korean government launched its own "Iron Silk Road Project," an ambitious transcontinental rail initiative aimed at connecting northern Europe to East Asia. Interestingly, the geographical orientation of Seoul's Silk Road strategy differed somewhat from the one conceived in Tokyo. The Korean government added Mongolia and targeted strengthening economic ties with Uzbekistan and Kazakhstan, two countries with a sizable Korean diaspora that dates back to Soviet times.[45]

For much of the Cold War, Beijing governed the northwest province of Xinjiang as a buffer zone, preventing Soviet communism from spreading farther east. The 1990s, and China's increasing need for oil and gas from Central Asia, demanded a new strategy. The Chinese political elite were also increasingly aware that provinces in the northwest had fallen behind, primarily because the economic reforms of the Deng Xiaoping era targeted cities and regions in the southeast. In 1994, Li Peng, then Chinese premier, announced a proposal for a "New Silk Road" that would connect Xinjiang and its neighboring regions with the new republics of Central Asia and onward to the Middle East.[46] Years later, this strategy evolved into the Great Western Development Initiative, which supported the economic and infrastructure development of six provinces, five autonomous regions, and the municipality of Chongqing. In Xinjiang, disparities in living standards were targeted through urban, agriculture, and communication projects.[47]

In the United States and Europe, the debate about the new geopolitical importance of Central Asia extended beyond energy and diplomacy to questions of culture and religion. A number of scholars pointed to the risks posed by political Islam. The most discussed and critiqued thesis was that offered by Samuel Huntington. In 1997, a year after the publication of his book, the United States Congress introduced the Silk Road Strategy Act.[48] In broad terms, its aim was to strengthen democracy and foster economic development through enterprise and infrastructure projects in the South Caucasus and Central Asia. The bill was never passed, but in the aftermath of 9/11 and the US invasion of Iraq, the importance of nonmilitary interventions in these regions was emphasized by a number of Washington-based think tanks. One such report, by S. Frederick Starr, argued that Eurasian geopolitics was at a critical juncture and that the US government should invest in the development of a "new Silk Roads" comprised of "direct roads, railroads, and technologies for transporting gas, oil, and hydroelectric power."[49] Conflict in Iraq, together with the growing influence of the Taliban and al Qaeda and escalating demand for oil and gas from China and India, put the global energy sector under considerable strain. The heartland of Asia, it seemed, was once again the critical "pivot" of world affairs. In 2011, Hillary Clinton used Starr's report as a template for a New Silk Road Initiative. As Laruelle explains, the plan was to pull the countries of Central Asia and South Caucasus away from Russia, strengthen ties with Turkey, and simultaneously weaken the position of Iran. Speaking in southern India in July that year, Clinton told her audience:

> Historically, the nations of South and Central Asia were connected to each other and the rest of the continent by a sprawling trading network called the Silk Road. Indian merchants used to trade spices, gems, and textiles, along with ideas and culture, everywhere from the Great Wall of China to the banks of the Bosporus. Let's work together to create a new Silk Road. Not a single thoroughfare like its namesake, but an international web and network of economic and transit connections. That means building more rail lines, highways, energy infrastructure, like the proposed pipeline to run from Turkmenistan, through Afghanistan, through Pakistan into India. It means upgrading the facilities at border crossings, such as India and Pakistan are now doing at Waga. And it certainly means removing the bureaucratic barriers and other impediments to the free flow of goods and people. It means casting aside the outdated trade policies that we all still are living with and adopting new rules for the twenty-first century.[50]

Here, then, we see Clinton invoking yet another Silk Road geography, one that runs as much north-south as it does east-west, a spatial imaginary that also glided over the cultural and religious tensions of South Asia in its attempt to build a new regionalism. Laruelle subsequently argued that the Silk Road had become "the main metaphor that US officials use to frame their strategy for Central Asia and Afghanistan." The initiative eventually suffered from a lack of commitment back in Washington as key military and political positions changed hands. Nonetheless, the idea of the Silk Road had come into circulation among US think tanks, embassies, and federal agencies. Strangely reminiscent of the 1880s, debate ensued as to whether it should be deployed in the singular or plural. This time, however, the validity of the "s" was a geopolitical calculation, the degree to which the US plan should "colonize" similar Russian and Chinese projects in the region or whether it should become one of a number of "New Silk Roads."[51] And so while the ambitions of Clinton's team fell by the wayside, the idea of a new Silk Road for the modern era, envisaged around pipelines, transcontinental road and rail, energy production, and cross-border trade, had well and truly arrived.

By the late 2000s, it was becoming increasingly common for journalists, analysts, and bureaucrats to describe transboundary physical infrastructure projects in such metaphorical terms. To cite a few examples, in 2009 Andrew Kuchins wrote *The Northern Distribution Network and the Modern Silk Road: Planning for Afghanistan's Future.*[52] Likewise, Christina Yen constructed a triangular analysis of Iran–China–North Korea relations to consider trends in cross-sector collaborations, arguing that China was investing heavily to integrate itself into a "new energy silk road connecting the Persian Gulf, Caspian Sea, and Central Asia."[53] That same year, *Newsweek* described Beijing's plans for a high-speed rail network in the following terms: "If the ancient Silk Road was one of the first grand avenues of globalization, fueling trade from the Celestial Kingdom to medieval Europe, the new railroad will be the latest."[54] A year later, the Asian Development Bank proclaimed its accomplishments in energy, trade, and transport, publishing *The New Silk Road: Ten Years of the Central Asia Regional Economic Cooperation Program.*[55] And finally, Patrick Byrne argued that China and Turkey were "building a new Silk Road together," expanding trade and cultural ties and signing decade-long agreements for rail linkages connecting the two.[56]

In assessing this growing use of the Silk Road concept within foreign policy initiatives, Laruelle argues that it needs to be considered as a geopolitical imaginary. Her particular focus is on the United States, arguing that its Silk Road projects find their equivalence in Russia's Eurasianism. Together, these constitute "specific constellation(s) of worldview perceptions and political culture," which need to be taken seriously by theorists of critical geo-politics.[57] In this vein, Dadabaev analyzes the different approaches a number of governments adopt in their Silk Road strategies. He suggests that for Japan the Silk Road "implied the engagement of energy resources of gas and oil in Russia and other Soviet constituencies as well as human resource develop-ment." Whereas for China, "it means the construction of transportation hubs and infrastructure for its goods to penetrate related markets."[58] Dadabaev's account offers the occasional reflection on how these policies are framed by history, but he essentially understands the Silk Road as a geopolitical concept that emerged in the post–Cold War era.[59] To that end, he "argues against pos-itivist (realist and liberalist) interpretations of the engagement strategies of China, South Korea and Japan by suggesting that the Silk Road and its 'others' are socially constructed foreign policy agendas that arose from attempts by these states to react to changing foreign and internal environments."[60] In this fast-changing world of Silk Road geopolitics though, late 2013 would prove to be a critical period.

10

Geostrategic Revivals

The grand lecture hall of Astana's Nazarbayev University was the unlikely venue for the September launch of what has been described as "the most significant and far-reaching initiative that China has ever put forward."[1] Xi Jinping chose Kazakhstan to announce Beijing's plans to rebuild the Silk Road for the twenty-first century. Subsequent speeches clarified the concept and added an additional maritime route. A plan to link up Eurasia was thus formulated around two key routes: the 21st Century Maritime Silk Route Economic Belt and the Silk Road Economic Road. In the months that followed, analysts around the world struggled to comprehend its structure and aims. Speeches declaring new forms of regional cooperation, trade deals, and massive infrastructure investments have been broadly interpreted as a strategy for maintaining China's long-term economic growth and energy security, as well as the regional stability required for achieving such goals. As Chapter 1 noted, China's Belt and Road Initiative (BRI) is oriented around the ambition of a more integrated Eurasia across multiple sectors: transport, banking, education, energy, digital communications, heritage, and medicine, to name a few. Pipeline, port, and rail corridors running through northwest China and Yunnan are among the key pillars of Beijing's quest for securing its long-term gas and oil supplies from the Middle East and Central Asia. Conceived around five transboundary economic corridors and an overarching Eurasian Land Bridge, Belt and Road also significantly advances China's connections to East Africa and Europe. Fundamentally then, Belt and Road is an endeavor in connectivity.

By framing this strategy as the "revival" of the Silk Roads, Belt and Road places an evocative narrative of history front and center in a discourse of international trade and diplomacy designed to restructure the global economic order of the twenty-first century. More specifically, it recreates and remakes Eurasia's past in particular ways, whereby a politically expedient idea of history as entanglement, peaceful dialogue, and connection is crafted, around which bilateral infrastructure and multilateral trade take shape. Invoking

The Silk Road. Tim Winter, Oxford University Press. © Oxford University Press 2022.
DOI: 10.1093/oso/9780197605059.003.0010

the Silk Roads as a "shared heritage" of routes, trusted partnerships and co-operation puts in play a more subtle cultural agenda, one that is frequently overlooked in the analysis of Belt and Road. Here I want to return to Ivie's notion of metaphorical clusters to emphasize how this matrix of programs has led to certain ideas taking hold in the foreign policy discourses of governments, as well as in the scholarship that has emerged to interpret such developments. In a continuation of the 1990s, Belt and Road takes the idea of connection via infrastructure as the means to prosperity but advances it in significant ways. Since 2013, the Chinese Communist Party has used the idea of an ancient Silk Road to insert some key strategic concepts into the discourse of international cooperation. These are designed to help commu-nicate the core components of Belt and Road and—perhaps more impor-tant—to build the types of alliance demanded by the project and placate fears and anxieties about ascendant Chinese power.

Put simply, Belt and Road draws on the now well-established metaphors for the Silk Roads and appropriates them for geostrategic ends. Unlike the foreign policies emanating from Washington, whereby the Silk Road is os-tensibly signaling cross-border infrastructures, China is able to insert itself at the geographic and symbolic center of a narrative built around "trust," "harmony," "openness," and "dialogue." Win-win cooperation, Beijing proclaims, comes alive through "the silk road spirit": a shared history of "friendship." Closer inspection of the discourse deployed by Beijing and by its ambassadors located in different regions also reveals that Belt and Road draws on both the concept of the Silk Road as East meets West and the pan-Asianism inherited from Japan, with its emphasis on intra-Asian connectiv-ities. The speech given by Yang Jiechi, widely regarded as one of China's key foreign policy architects, to the Boao Forum for Asia in 2014 is indicative of such dynamics:

The Silk Road has given the people of Asia confidence to pursue inclusive cooperation. The Silk Road had enabled the East and the West to thor-oughly interact with each other in peace and equality in all possible areas. The network for trade running over the Eurasian continent way back in the early days brought benefits to all sides. . . . Some religions or sections of religion, after being introduced into China via the land and maritime silk roads, integrated with home-grown religions in China and coexisted with them in harmony. For the numerous Chinese and foreign envoys, merchants and the wise questing for scriptures and knowledge, it was the Silk Road, and the people who kindly assisted them along the way, that had made their journeys possible....

The Chinese philosophy values peace as being the most precious. The Chinese history shows a record of China in friendly relations with neighbors. And China's diplomacy honors the tradition of matching words . with deeds.... The Belt and Road initiatives China put forward fully reflect the commitment to mutual trust and mutual benefit. Chinese leaders have made it clear that in implementing the initiatives, China will uphold the spirit of "amity, sincerity, mutual benefit and inclusiveness", which guide China's diplomacy regarding its neighbors, and China will not interfere in other countries' internal affairs, or seek dominance over regional affairs or sphere of influence. The Belt and Road initiatives are for open cooperation, with economic and cultural cooperation being the focus. They are not aimed at creating exclusive blocks or compromising existing multilateral mechanisms. The lands and seas of Asia are broad, and the mind of the Asian people is only broader. We should stay committed to open regionalism and make sure that all cooperation initiatives and institutions play their due role and complement each other.[2]

For David Arase, Belt and Road represents a significant advance in China figuring out how to restructure the world around it, a process that involves weakening the advantages in world trade and finance held by the United States, and moving the dial in the balance of power across the Eurasia continent by displacing the influence of Russia in the Caucasus and Central Asia.[3] At the domestic level, Beijing's goals for BRI largely represent a continuation of previous efforts to develop and urbanize the country's less-developed inland regions of the northwest. The transformation of cities in Xinjiang and Tibet into commerce and urban transport hubs includes various forms of social and cultural violence on minority groups, including Muslim Uyghur communities. In its ambitions to simultaneously contain and connect these areas with neighboring Central Asian republics, Beijing declared it was committed to "reviving" the overland trade routes of previous centuries. This has led to a particular metaphorical language used among BRI partners, whereby historical "routes" and "links" stand in for twenty-first-century ambitions of pipelines and rail and road projects:

History shows that inter-regional and intra-regional trade has been one of the driving forces in ushering in prosperity and progress of mankind. . . . The ancient Silk Road, one of the most famous of such routes, was a great channel through which scores of countries exchanged goods, cultural traditions, and creative ideas. The advent of modern technologies and development of alternate routes gradually pushed this historical route into relative disuse. But the evolving geo-political realities and growing primacy of economic priorities has catapulted this relic of the past into a modern-day imperative.

One of the earliest steps taken by the Prime Minister, after taking office in June 2013, was to conclude the MoU on establishing the China-Pakistan Economic Corridor (CPEC) that would connect Pakistan with China's Western regions, through a network of roads, railways and fiber-optic linkages . . . . The CPEC has direct relevance to Dr. Wizarat's theme of revival of historical trade routes, especially the Silk Road, which, as she points out, commenced with the construction of the Karakoram Highway.

Syed Tariq Fatemi, Special Assistant to the Prime Minister,
Karachi, February 2015[4]

Fascinatingly, however, different metaphorical conventions have emerged for maritime connections, past and present. For those countries looking to be part of China's oceanic ambitions, references to the "ancient" Silk Road are made in speeches and official documents as a story of "hubs" and "nodes." It is a terminology that helps countries like Greece, Oman, Singapore, and Sri Lanka to signal their strategic value in a transoceanic network of deep-water ports and container shipping terminals. In many cases, this diplomatic rhetoric is a fresh iteration of previous strategies. For Sri Lanka, for example, allusions to peaceful oceans and friendship speak to policies and a rivalry among great powers that stretches back to the Cold War. Over the course of the 1960s, the United States and Soviet Union developed submarine ballistic missiles, and as the nuclear arms race continued to escalate it was evident that the Indian Ocean was becoming strategically critical to both sides.[5] The Arabian Sea was particularly attractive to the US naval fleet, a location from which its nuclear submarines could reach Soviet industrial centers. And across the Indian Ocean region more broadly, cruise missiles were deployed, nuclear storage facilities built, and missile testing sites operationalized. There was also the distinct possibility of a resource war at a time when British naval power was fast diminishing and international relations across Asia and the Middle East were defined by mistrust, instability, and periods of outright hostility.[6] The nuclear ambitions of those countries within the region, most immediately India, further complicated any consensus on demilitarization. In 1964, Sri Lanka tabled a proposal for a nuclear-free Indian Ocean at the Second Summit of the Non-Aligned Movement held in Cairo. Faced with strategic disadvantages in the region, the USSR presented similar ideas to the UN, proposals that were rejected by the United States. By the time the non-aligned movement met again in Lusaka in 1970, the discussion had evolved into a "peace zone" concept, with Sri Lanka leading a UN resolution a year later for the Indian Ocean to be declared "for all time a zone of peace." From there, Commonwealth meetings drew up action plans for an Indian Ocean community, hoping to reverse increasing militarization.[7]

Spykman's theory of the "Rimland" and subsequent strategies of containment had drawn attention to the importance of coastal regions, including those of the Indian Ocean. And yet throughout the Cold War, the analysis of maritime regions was overshadowed by accounts of land-based conflicts and the need to prevent the spread of world-threatening ideologies.[8] It was noted earlier that the collapse of the Soviet Union placed a spotlight on the countries of Central Asia. By contrast, little attention was given to the Indian Ocean as a geopolitically sensitive region at this time, in large part because of unrivaled US naval power stretching from the Persian Gulf to the South China Sea and Pacific beyond. This began to change once India and China sought greater regional influence and paid more attention to their maritime trade and security interests. Since then, freedom of navigation, resource rights, and overseas port investments have become sources of tension for a region that has an ever-growing number of stakeholders and a weak multilateral architecture capable of mediating competing interests. By the late 2000s, more than 40 percent of the world's conflicts were taking place in countries bordering the Indian Ocean.[9] Sri Lanka, however, was beginning to turn a corner as a 26-year-long civil war came to an end with the defeat of the LTTE, commonly known as the Tamil Tigers. The cessation of violence and transition toward a more politically stable environment yielded a social and economic recovery buttressed by a dramatic influx of foreign investment. Successive postwar governments aimed to position the country as a trade and logistics hub in a fast-growing transcontinental shipping industry.

The Winds of Peace

The launch of Belt and Road cemented Sri Lanka as one of the key nodes of the 21st Century Maritime Silk Route Economic Belt. Early deals worth more than US $3 billion for the development of ports in Colombo and Hambantota raised eyebrows around the world, with such projects seen as likely "debt traps" for the country. Indeed, as Colombo struggled to repay the loans, renegotiations in 2017 involved Beijing leasing the Hambantota Port for a 99-year term, raising further accusations of neo-imperialism.[10] Belt and Road had clearly upped the stakes in maritime geopolitics, with New Delhi, Tokyo, and Washington expressing their concerns over the situation in Sri Lanka, as well as China's equally secretive port deals in Pakistan (Gwadar), Myanmar (Kyaukphyu), Malaysia (Melaka), and Kenya (Lamu). Acutely aware of both its vulnerability and advantageous location in the geopolitics of a multipolar Indian Ocean, the Sri Lankan government refloated the idea of a maritime zone of peace.[11] In a situation reminiscent of their Cold War non-alignment, this time Sri Lanka framed such a strategy around a peaceful maritime silk road, along which, it was proclaimed, traders moved and worked in harmony and friendship:

> Sri Lanka has been known to the travelers of the ancient world as a hub in the Indian Ocean, who identified the country with many names like Lanka, Serendib and Ceylon . . . . The people of Sri Lanka, as islanders, since ancient times, have been influenced by several waves of external interactions that led to the exchange, not only of goods but also ideas and knowledge with travelers and traders passing through or visitors from lands close and far. . . . As a result, Sri Lanka is a multi-ethnic and multi-cultural nation. Sri Lanka benefited from the message of the Buddha who lived and taught in Northern India. Arab traders brought with them the teachings of Prophet Mohammed. It is believed that Guru Nanak, the founder of the Sikh religion, visited Sri Lanka in 1511. . . . It is clear that the world needs peaceful oceans to sustain its benefits in the ever growing blue economy. . . . Sri Lanka has the benefit of the vast ocean around us over which we enjoy exclusive economic rights. The country is also situated on the world's busiest shipping lane. This is both an opportunity and a challenge for our nation, which is situated right in the middle of the Orient between East and West. . . .
>
> Sri Lanka takes the security of sea lanes and maritime security in the oceans around us, seriously. We are eager to work with the maritime

powers of the Indian Ocean and beyond, to make our oceans secure for unimpeded commerce and peaceful navigation. We are determined, as it is in our interest, to work with the maritime powers of the region to ensure that the Indian Ocean is conflict free. We will therefore work with the maritime powers of the region with commitment to prevent conflict, combat terrorism and piracy and assist to harmonize geo-strategic complexities.

Prasad Kariyawasam, Ambassador to the United States,
Hawaii, February 2016[12]

Similarly, in late 2018 the Sri Lankan analyst Menik Wakkumbura stated that the island's fortunate location on the "maritime silk route," combined with its commitment to the "openness of the maritime domain," meant that it was well placed to develop a maritime policy that navigated the "global power shifts" of our time.[13] Elsewhere, I have explained at length how Colombo and Beijing have developed a form of maritime heritage diplomacy centered around the fifteenth-century Ming dynasty admiral Zheng He. This involves glossing over violent battles and the kidnapping of the Sri Lankan king in favor of a more diplomatically expedient "memory" of friendship and harmonious trade.[14] Interestingly, in the wake of Belt and Road, India developed its own maritime metaphors for regional diplomacy. Project Mausam utilized Indian Ocean monsoon histories as a framework for building trade and security alliances across the region. Etymologically derived from the Arabic word for season, mausam also carries connotations of monsoon and as such operates as a metaphor for the trade winds that shaped so much of India's dealings with its regional neighbors. Some years earlier, Robert Kaplan had evoked similar imagery for his own analysis of the growing significance of the Indian Ocean to international affairs, arguing in his book Monsoon that the region "already forms center-stage for the challenges of the twenty-first century."[15]

In an effort to build Mausam into a regional architecture, more than 50 partner countries were approached. Interestingly, within India itself the Ministry of Culture played a key role in the concept's development, utilizing expertise from the National Museum, the Indira Gandhi National Centre for the Arts, and the Archaeological Survey of India. For a brief period, this was rebranded as the Cotton Route.[16] Similarly oriented around the littoral states of the Indian Ocean, this strategic policy expanded on Mausam to include the "continental gateways" of Iran and South Africa, linking India to resources in Russia and the African continent, respectively.[17] In summarizing the significance of the two initiatives in a report for the National Maritime Foundation, a Delhi-based think tank, Adwita Rai noted: "At face value these initiatives can be best described as policy initiatives to revive ancient maritime linkages and exemplify India's involvement. However, as it is unfolding they can also be seen as initiatives to complement India's strategic vision from 'Look East' to 'Act East'. India under the new government has been actively pursuing its vision of 'Act East' and these initiatives have given robust thrust to its ambition. With the increasing power play and drifting focus to the east, it can be seen as India's initiatives to strengthen its position by merging strategic, economic and cultural thought."[18]

Confecting India's foreign policy via such themes stretches as far back as independence. Both Gandhi and Nehru were committed to seeing the revival of Indian civilization after the ignominies suffered under colonial rule. In his capacity as the country's first prime minister, Nehru favored a concept of civilizational unity rooted in the geographies of the Indus Valley over a politics of regional identities as the foundation for building the country's political and cultural identity in a postcolonial era. Since then, India's foreign policy debates have been oriented around tensions between a more pluralist, inclusive politics, as advocated by Nehru, and the more conservative politics of Hindu nationalism. In accounting for this in their book *India at the Global High Table*, Terisata Schaffer and Howard Schaffer note how these competing world views have been repeatedly grounded in two strategic icons from India's ancient past, Kautilya and Ashoka, and their contrasting philosophies regarding regional engagement and the exercising of power. It is this "ancient heritage," they suggest, that serves as the starting point for understanding India's foreign policy today. Five thousand years of history are the basis for an Indian exceptionalism that creates expectations and ambitions about India's place in the world and its regional supremacy.[19]

In 2016, India looked to expand its footprint in the future of regional security and trade by teaming up with the Abe government in Japan to co-lead the Asia Africa Growth Economic Corridor, a multilateral initiative oriented around the four pillars of development, infrastructure, institutional connectivity, and people-to-people partnerships. Increasing anxieties about China's growing regional influence, together with the need to repair bridges severely damaged by Donald Trump, led the Biden administration to vociferously declare its commitment to the alliance known as Quad, or the Quadrilateral Security Dialogue, between Australia, India, Japan, and the United States. Although in development for a decade or so, Debasish Roy Chowdhury noted in 2021 that the Quad continued to suffer from a "confusing alliance logic, foundational contradictions and deliberate ambiguity."[20] Paralleling this has been another geopolitical concept with a much stronger pedigree, the Indo-Pacific. Viewed by the US as a "containment" strategy for China, the Indo-Pacific has become a regional architecture straddling multiple sectors, including trade, cybersecurity, and military collaboratives, among others. Interestingly, in 2020 Rory Medcalf, an Australian exponent of the project, attempted to strengthen the concept's credibility by framing it in geocultural terms, albeit in painfully contrived ways:

> The precursors of the Indo-Pacific in this geopolitical sense also go back thousands of years, to a proto-economy of regional maritime trade and migration before recorded history. This was followed by the spread of Hinduism and Islam to Southeast Asia, Buddhism to China, Japan and Korea, Chinese tributary relations to Southeast Asia and briefly the Indian Ocean, and European colonialism and consequent pan-Asian resistance across so much of the map. The contours of the Indo-Pacific were there all along in the cartography of exploration. From the 1400s to the mid-20th century, the typical map titled 'Asia' caught the sweep of the Indo-Pacific—the two oceans, India, Southeast Asia, China and beyond—in a single frame. A fresh appraisal explains how the age of empires broke then bound then broke the region again, concluding with the clash of America and Japan in the Indo-Pacific war that ended in 1945.[21]

Together then, these examples from Australia, China, India, and Sri Lanka illustrate the ongoing importance of harnessing ideas about history and geography. In an era when power in international affairs is secured through the building of networks and multisector modes of connectivity, we see such countries formulate their foreign policy and regional architecture interests less in terms of centers and rims and instead nurture concepts oriented around regional flows, mobilities, and geographically expansive and culturally open pasts.

Conclusion

As I noted in the introduction to this section, mixing, or, to be more precise, overlaying, metaphors has its pitfalls. Laruelle argues that the conflation of crossroads and cores means that places such as Afghanistan are now seen as regions where routes "converged" rather than "passed through." Afghanistan, she points out, has historically been a transit area rather than "being the heart of a network," as now suggested by some political analysts and foreign policymakers.[22] Clinton's framework made the geographies of the Silk Road largely synonymous with Mackinder's Heartland, with little reflection as to how these terms have been constructed and understood at different moments in time.[23] Elsewhere though, the distinction between the two is critical to foreign policy. For Russia, Eurasia and the Heartland metaphor remain the most strategically significant concepts, as they place Moscow at the "center" of world affairs and make Central Asia the periphery.[24] This also disavows China's Silk Road "revival" ambitions of being the geocultural and geopolitical heart of the region. For some, Belt and Road constitutes a significant step toward the creation of a "new great game" in Asia.[25] Interestingly though, with many analysts holding expertise in particular regions or sectors, claims of nineteenth-century throwbacks have tended to be separated by land and sea.[26] As academic commentary on Belt and Road flourished in the 2010s, much of it focused on the countries of Central Asia, reflecting the ongoing hold of the Heartland and Great Game in the analysis of Eurasia as a space, or indeed concept, of international relations and geopolitics.[27] Eurasianists, as Nicola Contessi points out, also continue to identify with post-Soviet Russia as their scope of analysis.[28] But as we have seen here, Belt and Road brings the Indian Ocean and Mediterranean as well as the East and South China Seas into the picture, greatly expanding the geographies of power accumulation and competition across land and sea.

China's so-called Silk Roads of the twenty-first century fundamentally challenge assumptions about the Heartland and Great Game: how they are thought about and where they might be located. It demands an intellectual remapping of Eurasia as a geopolitical space, something Chris Hann has called for.[29] Recalling Ivie's analysis on the importance of language, such adjustments will no doubt happen over time as the discourse of the Silk Roads creates a new architecture of analysis and calls into being new realities. The different strands of Parts Three and Four show how the co-opting of the Silk Road within the contexts of international aid, diplomacy, and cooperation has long been imbued with both colonizing and decolonizing qualities. It is evident that the pendulum on this has swung back and forth, depending on which agency, individual, or organization invokes the term and to what end they deploy it within the politics of the moment. But as the Silk Road has entered the world of foreign policy, Belt and Road has taken its themes of peace, exchange, and friendship—all of which formed in quite different contexts—and migrated them across to a world where connectivity holds ever greater geopolitical significance.

PART FIVE
CONCLUSION

11

Silk Road Futures

Given the analysis of the previous chapter, we might postulate whether we are heading toward a future wherein "who rules the Silk Roads commands Eurasia; who rules Eurasia commands the World." It would be unwise, however, to formulate an argument around such a proposition at a time when the landscape of international affairs is described as increasingly multipolar and simultaneously dividing into the types of blocs and alliances familiar to the Cold War era. That said, it does offer an interesting provocation to tease out some of the threads running through the previous chapters. The book opened with the question of how to conceptualize the Silk Road, or indeed Silk Roads, and the answer offered here has spanned across 10 chapters. We know it is a narrative of historical connectivity and dialogue. But I have unpacked this to reveal how these themes have been imbued with certain ideas and values: intercultural dialogue and cosmopolitanism; peace, tolerance, and harmony; geopolitical ambition and state power; civilizational grandeur; and adventure and discovery.

In their juxtaposition, these do not easily sit alongside one another. But it is a combination, I would suggest, that means the Silk Road will continue to stabilize as an important and compelling geocultural and geostrategic concept. This assertion is based on the momentum that has gathered around the term since 2013, and that China's Silk Road "revival" commitment will remain in place for the foreseeable future given the political work this idea is doing both domestically and internationally. It is a situation that raises important questions concerning how we approach the Silk Road as a domain of intellectual enquiry and knowledge production, and it is this issue that I want to tackle in this final chapter.[1] Since the 1990s, there has been a steady growth in Silk Road studies centers around the world (see Appendix B). Those in the West have approached it in normative terms, focusing on land-based histories of connection, mobility, and transmission, invariably in relation to locations in Central Asia, including northwest China.[2] More recently, however, Silk Road centers have opened across a number of Belt and Road

The Silk Road. Tim Winter, Oxford University Press. © Oxford University Press 2022.
DOI: 10.1093/oso/9780197605059.003.0011

partner countries dedicated to logistics, infrastructure, foreign policy, and so forth.[3] Beyond sharing the same branding nomenclature, it is a bifurcation that means such academic pursuits have little in common. It also suggests that few, if any, higher education institutions in the West have come to realize the multifarious ways the Silk Road now needs to be addressed: as a concept of strategy; development; and as a space of complex social and cultural affairs, a situation that may change, of course, over time.

Recalling the point that Silk Road discourses evolve at the intersection of popular culture, political events, and expert commentary, we see that same dynamic continues today through their adoption for a Chinese foreign policy spanning continents and oceans. In the Silk Road, Belt and Road nexus, we see the past and future continually folded back on one another. Separating the former into "old" and "new" misses this back-and-forth and the phenomena that arise from it. Clearly, the Silk Road is no longer merely the domain of historical fields such as archaeology, numismatics, or philology. Given that the term is highly malleable and amenable to metaphorical invocation and thus now finds traction across a number of disciplines beyond history, challenging questions arise regarding its analytical purchase. With such issues yet to be properly debated, it is unclear whether the study of the Silk Roads will continue to fragment across disciplines or perhaps consolidate into a multi- or interdisciplinary "field," one that takes up the task of finding coherence and a meaningful intellectual base.

Silk Road Internationalism

It would be overly ambitious to try and resolve these questions here, but to briefly venture down such pathways I return to the theme of internationalism as an example of how we might analytically move between the past and future in ways that develop a critical disposition toward the Silk Roads as a productive space of inquiry. We have seen the different ways the term evolved as a discourse of internationalism in the twentieth century, both in terms of the narratives of history that have formed around it and the ways in which the Silk Roads have been put to service by those with internationalist ambitions in the present. Belt and Road has added a new and important chapter to this dynamic. To be clear, in co-opting the Silk Roads for branding Belt and Road, China not only takes a depiction of transregional, transoceanic histories and begins to mold them to its own vision, it also picks up a well-established policy architecture of internationalism in the attempt to build more "harmonious" futures. Here, then, I want to consider these two themes to illustrate how we can better understand the broader significance of the Silk Roads going forward.

China adopts the Silk Roads to internationalize its vision of peace, harmony, mutual respect, and solidarity and to promote the idea that dialogue helps to build a more stable international order. Such developments can be understood through the lens of cultural internationalism, as developed through the work of Akira Iriye.[4] Iriye's arguments are rooted in the events of the late-nineteenth century, specifically the activities of those committed to developing an "international community." As Mark Mazower notes, internationalists saw their task as countering the forces of nineteenth-century nationalism and rescuing "the mission of empire from its darker, dirtier side."[5] In certain key ways, this paralleled the developments discussed in Chapter 2 in that efforts to establish institutions across Europe were fueled by powerful notions of progress built around scientific knowledge and a belief in the universalism of the region's governmental, cultural, and intellectual traditions. There is a reasonably well-developed literature on the theme of internationalism, which explains how the structures of aristocratic diplomacy created under the Concert of Europe offered a blueprint for the international organizations that would follow, namely the League of Nations and the United Nations.[6] Iriye focuses on the networks and institutions built within the fields of science, education, the arts, and humanities and sees this cultural internationalism in world-ordering terms, such that it is read alongside the political world order that formed around the Westphalian system and imperial rule and an economic order based on international flows of capital. Crucially here, he pins the cultural to conceptualizations prevalent in nineteenth-century Europe and their associations with discourses of civilization. This means that culture is understood in a significantly broader sense than it is today. We also need to remember that debates about civilization carried a duality of meaning. The term circulated in ways that spoke to both the interpretations about antiquity discussed in Chapter 2 and what it meant to be a modern civilized society in the nineteenth century. The resulting tying of culture to certain moral and political ideals led to claims that those states deemed "fully" civilized were ones that promoted and nurtured science, education, artistic endeavors, and scholarly pursuits in ways that created new forms of citizenry. This extended to harnessing science and the humanities to curate and safeguard the past as history and heritage.

As Iriye notes, with the concept of race increasingly discredited by the end of the nineteenth century, civilization was seen as more eternal and immutable. Notwithstanding Spengler's influential depiction of the West as entering its "winter" and the devastating events of World War I, internationalists were committed to their values becoming the bedrock of an international society. The task of promoting them outside Europe against a backdrop of militarized nationalism and imperial rivalry was significant and one that was taken up by the League of Nations, primarily through its Committee on Intellectual Cooperation.[7] This of course provided the foundations for the creation of UNESCO after World War II, which has mobilized science, education, and culture for the promotion of peace and international stability ever since. But as Iriye reminds us, the UN constitutes only a small part of this cultural internationalism, and his account points to the dramatic growth of nongovernmental organizations in this space over the course of the twentieth century. By the 1990s, the international structures of cooperation built up across a number of domains were thus significant contributors to a post–Cold War global order and discourses of global governance. Of course, this does not mean to say that these networks and associations and their internationalist ideals have sat outside or been free from the strategic interests of powerful nations, far from it. In fact, we need to tie this history of internationalism to the geoculture of the liberal world order as outlined by Immanuel Wallerstein. To recall such arguments from Chapter 1, for Wallerstein this involved the exporting of European epistemologies and ideals with a confidence of their universal value. And in a similar vein, Duncan Bell traces the thinkers, ideas, and movements that formed part of the project to reorder the world around liberalism. Although there were multiple views of what a liberal, democratic world should look like, by the beginning of the twentieth century Anglo-American versions of liberalism came to be reimagined in ways that pushed its origins further back, enabling its advocates to claim that its values were those of Western modernity.[8]

The question of the degree to which such modes of analysis are applicable for understanding developments today is far from easy to answer. China's ambitions to secure influence internationally clearly have very little to do with the promotion of liberalism or free-market capitalism.[9] Equally significant, the problems of drawing clear distinctions between state and nonstate actors when analyzing China further clouds assertions around internationalist versus state ambition.[10] In putting such questions to one side, the comparative I want to draw here involves the convergence of particular state ambitions, civilizational discourses, and modes of cultural internationalism that have world-ordering possibilities.

Today, peace, harmony, trust, and mutual respect are the mainstays of China's diplomatic discourse for "reviving" the Silk Roads for the twenty-first century. Part Three situated this within the broader trajectory the Silk Road has followed since the 1950s. The two chapters explained how a geocultural imaginary of routes has been deployed at different moments by organizations in an effort to counter the hegemony of "rooted" pasts associated with the territorial nation. I argued that these two elements, nationalism and internationalism, cohabit the forms of Silk Road cultural and heritage diplomacy that China has now set in motion, as an array of actors advance one of the key pillars of Belt and Road. In developing such forms of cooperation, China signals its commitment to safeguarding and "preserving" history and culture as a modern "civilized state" in line with the cultural internationalism discussed above, but it does so in ways that decouple culture and development from human rights discourses and the demands for governance reform that have characterized Western aid in recent decades.

But it is also worth noting that geocultural concepts have the capacity to accommodate shifts in the discourses of global governance and international cooperation as new priorities and paradigms arise. This was exemplified by COVID-19. As various observers suggested, the pandemic led to a shift in Beijing's ambitions for Belt and Road, with greater emphasis placed on the Digital Silk Road and the building of "soft infrastructures" of cooperation across fields such as health, medicine, education, science, and culture. Most explicitly though, China's Health Silk Road builds on decades of medical diplomacy, enabling it to proclaim international leadership in public health via medical advisory services, vaccine rollouts, and mask diplomacy. Zou Dongxin argues that China's approach responds to "general failures of neoliberalism" and that "principles like equity and state-sponsored care" strongly align with the World Health Organization's core goal of Health for All, as enshrined in the Alma-Ata Declaration of 1978.[11] By mid-2020, such programs were integrated into CIDCA, the China International Development Cooperation Agency, established just two years earlier. Foreign policy calculations mean that China's contributions to a global Health for All are primarily oriented around South–South cooperation, with much of their COVID-19 aid targeting countries in Africa, the Middle East, and Southeast Asia. As Emma Mawdsley notes, South–South partnerships are often framed by "powerful discourses of empathy and solidarity, shaped by Third World-ist, socialist, non-aligned and colonial/ post-colonial positionalities" and have evolved through a dynamic where "geopolitical marginalisation enabled the stitching together of an attractive claim to a specific moral purpose while achieving joint economic and diplomatic advancement."[12]

In introducing a report on ASEAN-China cooperation for COVID-19, Chaw Chaw Sein ruminated on whether "China will accelerate the BRI to be a healthy Silk Road rather than a bumpy road."[13] For Ngeow Chow-Bing, addressing the needs of public health education and medical infrastructure in these regions is also about "packaging its participation in regional and global health governance as an illustration of how the Health Silk Road is contributing to the betterment of humanity; reinforcing BRI with important public health infrastructure; and enlarging its role in global medical supply chain and investment."[14] Of course, COVID-19 vaccine and public health diplomacy have become important vectors for assessing today's great power rivalries, as Russia, India, and the United States all look to compete with China in building alliances and friends through the delivery of public goods.[15] It is highly likely that this will remain a theater of competition over the longer term, as the need for digital tools to monitor contact tracing and build public health and quarantining digital infrastructures gives new legitimacy to the international roll-out of state-led surveillance technologies. In the case of China, this means we are likely to see significant overlaps between the ambitions established for the Digital Silk Road and Health Silk Road architectures of Belt and Road.

Post-pandemic public health exemplifies how Silk Road internationalism enables China to align with the norms and values of global governance as they continue to evolve and, at the same time, introduce new language and ideas into these domains. There is a small body of research that highlights China's growing impact on the UN system.[16] One pertinent example here is UNESCO, to which China has become the largest financial contributor at 15.5 percent of total budget in 2020 and funds more than 19 percent of its world heritage program.[17] Today, UNESCO's stated goal for its multilateral Silk Road platform is to promote "mutual understanding, intercultural dialogue, reconciliation and cooperation among nations and people sharing the Silk Roads shared heritage."[18] But this is also couched within the larger framework of the UN's 17 Sustainable Development Goals (SDGs).[19] As a result, the Silk Road is not only put to work in the promotion of peace, justice, and strong institutions, it is now also harnessed to reduce inequality and to promote gender equity and youth education, as well as to give coherence to the conservation of land-based and underwater habitats endangered by climate change and human intervention.[20] Since the launch of BRI, the United Nations World Tourism Organization and United Nations Alliance of Civilizations have also adopted Silk Road initiatives oriented toward the SDGs. By nestling conferences, exhibitions, and media projects about civilizational values within such architectures of cooperation, China is able to proclaim that the country has certain qualities as a "civilizational state," which enables it to provide leadership in global affairs.

This all suggests that the couching of civilization discourses within a Silk Road diplomacy architecture raises important questions about historical parallels and departures. China's attempt to resuscitate the term within international affairs—and shift it away from a language of a clashing East and West—has not received the attention it warrants in the analysis of Belt and Road.[21] Tackling this question does not mean seeking to pin down what constitutes civilization as an empirical entity or sociohistorical category but interpreting how the term circulates and acts as a vehicle to normalize particular ideas and values. Through its Silk Road discourses of intercivilizational and intercultural, Chinese diplomacy directly speaks to notions of sovereignty and territorial integrity, which remain central concerns for many of those Belt and Road partner countries that have endured colonialism, invasions, and sanctions. Such memories and experiences shape the ways in which non-Western countries engage with, and thus mold, the internationalism of the UN. China's promises to revive Silk Road partnerships in the Middle East, South Asia, and the Mediterranean include citations of historical humiliation and the prospect of restored dignities and economic security through win-win cooperation. A language of "shared pasts" and "shared destiny" represents China's attempt to build solidarities of South-South cooperation, wherein the dignity and pride harnessed in civilizational discourses and material cultures that showcase grandeur also build affinities across borders.[22] As I explained in *Geocultural Power* and revisit later, this has led to new forms of cultural-sector cooperation across the geographies of Belt and Road. Such themes also ran through presentations by delegates from Egypt, Greece, Iran, Pakistan, and others during the Dialogue of Asian Civilizations conference in 2019. We thus might situate such developments within the pan-Asianist discourses seen in Chapter 4 to consider the degree to which twenty-first-century Silk Road multilateralism constitutes a platform for their revival.

It also remains unclear whether China's leadership in this space forms part of a larger ambition to work within existing architectures of global governance or to undermine and degrade their influence. As Scott Kennedy notes, understanding China's motivations for influencing the procedures and norms of global governance and cooperation is a key challenge for political scientists. To date, much of the evidence informing such debates has come from China's engagement with the International Monetary Fund (IMF), World Trade Organization (WTO), Internet governance, and, more recently, the World Health Organization (WHO).[23] For Kennedy then, China's ascension to the inner circle of the WTO in 2008 marked the country's "arrival as a global governance insider."[24] Of course, no simple label can be applied to account for the complex forces running through this landscape, which stem from, and result in, various combinations of both liberal and illiberal values.

All this takes place in a context of deteriorating US–China relations and the resurgence of populist and nationalist movements in different parts of the world. Much like the internationalism of the twentieth century, cooperation in science, education, health, the humanities, and the arts plays out in relation to competitive state power and the resultant alliances that form in the quest to secure influence over regions. Political commentary in the West often portrays China as becoming increasingly "isolated" internationally. But for those tracking Belt and Road, the reality is evidently much more complicated. I would suggest, then, that while the concept of the Silk Road continues to gain currency at a global level, China's Silk Road internationalism is likely to increasingly align with the geographies and alliances of Belt and Road. It is a situation that raises fascinating questions about Beijing's proclamations to foster dialogue between East and West, between civilizations, and between those in the Global South. Political theorists tend to label these aspects of foreign policy as soft power. But the scale and cross-sectorial scope of Belt and Road mean that the political and material consequences of these geocultural imaginaries of cooperation will only become manifest over time. For example, we saw earlier that civilizational tropes in the nineteenth century were coupled with ideas about liberal democracy and its export. China's decoupling of these in an age when connectivities are strategically forged across different sectors, including those in the digital domain, means accounts of soft power inadequately capture the major transitions that may be underway now. As we know, civilization also carries ideas of superiority and barbarism. It was apparent in the Orientalism of the eighteenth and nineteenth centuries and underpinned Huntington's analysis of the post–Cold War order as a clash of civilizations.[25] One way of formulating a field of critical Silk Road studies, then, is asking whether today's Silk Road internationalism introduces a new cultural politics into international affairs, wherein a state-led "dialogue of civilizations" forms part of a wider ambition to build those linkages that are captured by the term South–South, and what consequences this might hold geopolitically.

In effect then, as the distribution of power moves steadily eastward in the twenty-first century, we need to attend to the ways in which China's Silk Road internationalism advances some distinct world-ordering claims around the geocultural categories of East and West and civilization. To recall Wallerstein's arguments, geocultures need to be read as architectures for the setting of norms and advancing particular world views that are deployed to impose a sense of directionality on international affairs. And in this regard, something fascinating seems to be happening as imaginaries of East and West alter and shift again. In the long nineteenth century, European imperialists and internationalists alike contributed to ideas of a modern, industrialized, and enlightened West, one that found its Eastern Other in "the Orient" of Asia. During the Cold War, these geographies shifted to a Soviet East and capitalist West, whereby these categories were redefined in more politically explicit terms, such that East–West was first and foremost about ideological struggle and geopolitical blocs. Today, China's rise is increasingly viewed as the primary challenge to a liberal world order created in the vision of the United States after World War II. In the Western imaginary then, the East returns to East Asia. But in branding the Belt and Road Initiative as the "revival" of the Silk Roads for the twenty-first century, Chinese geopolitical ambition and cultural internationalism simultaneously put back into play a language of East and West oriented around Eurasia, which, from a Chinese perspective, decenters the US from world affairs and in world history.

At the Crossroads of History

Finally, then, I return to the issues that surround narratives of history and how they come to be forged in the context of geopolitics and in the project of building empires and nations. George Orwell's famous aphorism, "who controls the past controls the future; who controls the present controls the past," succinctly captures the importance of understanding why the past matters and why it continually remains a site of struggle.[26] The production

176 THE SILK ROAD

of history documented in this book is far less sinister than that portrayed by Orwell in 1984. Here, then, I have explored various reasons why past events spanning centuries and regions have come to be wrapped in nostalgia and the romantic appeal of encountering foreign cultures and undertaking arduous expeditions. This does not mean, however, that there are not far-reaching political consequences at play in such imaginings of history. The steady rise of populism and nationalism in multiple regions is yet another reminder of why it matters that we understand how the past is remade for and by the present and to what ends it is massaged and manipulated into particular forms by those who seek commercial and political gain. I have emphasized that the starting point for understanding the Silk Road in such terms is not to naturalize it as a framing of antiquity and premodern history. As we have seen at length, Silk Road imaginaries privilege certain themes and places over others, reduce complex events into particular motifs, and selectively reconstruct the past through routes and networks and the flows of a select group of cultural forms, material and nonmaterial. In other words, they reorder space and time, collapse and conceal, reveal and expand in equal measure. The consequences of this are manifold. There will remain divergent opinions concerning the merits of the term for academic analysis, and for those who do invoke it ideas continue to shift and thrive. The aim has not been to set aside the Silk Road as an approach to writing histories. I would suggest, however, that its seductive appeal stymies the all-important critiques required to both test and strengthen its merits as a concept and understand the political work it might be doing.[27]

In accounting for the biases in the historical record for Southeast Asia, James Scott makes the somewhat pithy observation that "the larger the pile of rubble you leave behind, the larger your place in the historical record! The more dispersed, mobile, egalitarian societies regardless of their sophistication and trading networks, and despite being often more populous, are relatively invisible in the historical record because they spread their debris more widely."[28] The themes explored here, notably the discussion that opened Chapter 2, illustrate why the assembling of history around different forms of material culture is more complex than Scott suggests. In broad terms, his observation holds true, but as Belt and Road gives new momentum to Silk Road histories of mobility and long-distance networks, this picture seems to be clouding in fascinating and significant ways. Since 2013, the funding opportunities and collaborations across disciplines and across borders around Silk Road histories have increased dramatically. But this is a highly complex space for archaeologists, anthropologists, conservators, and historians to occupy. One of the lessons of this book is that scholars have a limited capacity to shape the narrative. The Silk Roads offer a fascinating example of the porous boundaries between academia, public history, and heritage and between popular culture and policy. In the age of Belt and Road, how this occurs matters.

Chinese government directives for universities to internationalize have led to a rapid upturn in the number of humanities-based collaborations established in Belt and Road countries, a trend I anticipate will be long-term (see Figure 11.1). As we saw in the case of nineteenth-century Europe, structures of empire, together with post-Enlightenment modes of knowledge production, enabled Europeans to position themselves as the expert, and thus rightful, guardians of the past of others. Then as now, geocultural power arises from having the capacity to write, map, scan, and assemble geocultural histories into strategically expedient narratives and construct ways of knowing the other. As Chinese institutions increasingly look outward, the Silk Roads afford the construction of narratives at the scale of Eurasia, the foregrounding of routes and stories that connect Chinese culture and history to expansive geographies across land and sea and the ascribing of peace and harmony to these accounts of trade and exchange. Silk Road imaginaries of transmission and carriage open up a plethora of opportunities to rethink many of the accepted wisdoms about European, African, Asian, and even world history.[29] As such, they offer interesting ways to contest forms of Eurocentrism that remain prevalent today. They help to shift the lens away from Europe itself, casting a much wider gaze on world events through a prism of connection and exchange. Much-needed transcultural histories are brought into focus, themes that Eckhardt Fuchs argues continue to be overlooked by an epistemology of "non-Western" pasts that are inevitably indexed vis à vis the cultural and civilizational "center" of the West, Europe.[30] The Silk Roads also constitute geocultural imaginaries forged around modes of intraregional exchange that can transcend the methodological nationalism which too often pervades pre-national histories.

Interest in Silk Road histories in China may well lead to international scholarly collaborations that address themes that remain under-represented in Western scholarship.[31] Activating these Silk Road discourses within such a vast political economy of trade and capital investment holds real possibilities for rewriting world and regional histories, recalibrating discourses about East and West, centers and peripheries, declines and redemptions. Events

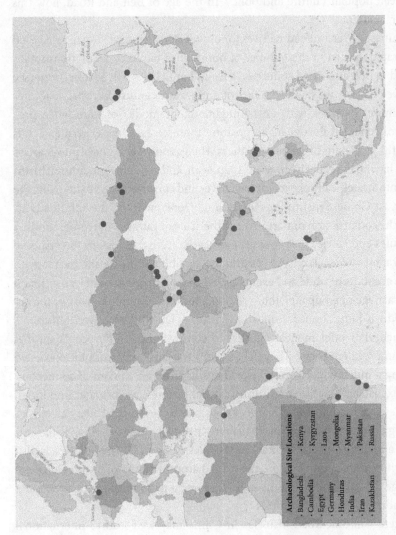

Archaeological Site Locations
- Bangladesh
- Cambodia
- Egypt
- Germany
- Honduras
- India
- Iran
- Kazakhstan
- Kenya
- Kyrgyzstan
- Laos
- Mongolia
- Myanmar
- Pakistan
- Russia

Figure 11.1 Location of Chinese land-based archaeology collaborations, with 28 of 36 launched post-2013. Modified from Storozum and Li, 2020.

Credit Line: Courtesy of Toyah Horman.

traced in Chapters 4 and 7—namely, Japan's approach to the Silk Road and UNESCO's Roads of Dialogue project—are important precedents in this regard. Together, they recrafted the geographies, timelines, and themes of the Silk Road in distinct ways, emphasizing in particular intra-Asian histories. Silk Road narratives can also be a platform for raising awareness of other little-known histories, such as, to cite one example, the Arab and Persian influences on Renaissance Italy and thus by implication on modern Western civilization. These shifts occur through forms of co-production via historians, art galleries, journalists, museums, tourism attractions, and so forth. In anticipating such possibilities, in no way do I imagine that we will see the consolidation of a single, universal Silk Road narrative. The analysis offered here testifies to how the Silk Road takes on particular inflections in different regions, and this pluralization will likely continue. Indeed, I suspect it is unlikely that Zhang Qian or Faxian, figures that dominate Chinese state media depictions, will be the central focus of European-made documentaries or dramas.

Here, then, in terms of the international dissemination of ideas about regional and world history, UNESCO's world heritage program has made a notable impact in recent decades. Plans to construct Maritime Silk Road transregional heritage routes, if successful, will give international visibility to intersecting land and maritime trade networks and likely contribute to new understandings about their relationship to histories of capitalism and the birth of the modern world, to use Chris Bayly's expression.[32] As Lincoln Paine reminds us, oceans and seas have been greatly neglected, and there is a need to better recognize non-European maritime pasts.[33] Maritime Silk Road heritage discourses encourage new ways of talking about the Indian Ocean region and the significance of pre-European forms of connectivity.[34] Over time, we may also see the Silk Road open up to new, more critical themes and become a platform upon which more difficult histories, such as slavery, piracy, plague, and empire, can be raised.

This is, of course, a road littered with potholes. As Svetlana Boym reminds us, "nostalgia speaks in riddles and puzzles, so one must face them in order not to become its next victim—or its next victimizer."[35] In this regard, I would suggest we look more carefully at the possible consequences of a Silk Road nostalgia that now circulates within academia, popular culture, and different domains of policy. The threads of analysis pursued here point to the need for also understanding how they co-produce each other and who might be the victims of the different forms of violence such intersections produce. Lazy observations lead to stereotypes, which, in turn, can lead to insinuations. Analyses built around a "return to Marco Polo's world" might be seductive but mislead in their reduction of complex events, both past and present. As I have highlighted in the book, narratives of history can be consequential for shaping contemporary events, whether it be great power strategies of the Cold War or the Palestinian struggle for statehood denied by Zionist interpretations of a landed past. Just like narratives of empire or nation, Silk Road histories are constructs that carry political consequences.

Today, China engages with sovereign nations, and it is highly unlikely that forging a Silk Road geocultural past will lead to independence movements or revolutions. The geocultural politics that we need to attend to today is about routes, corridors, and what Franck Billé calls "auratic geographies."[36] But within this, familiar questions remain highly pertinent. As we saw in the opening two chapters, nations need narratives, and states seek to assert control over them for governmental purposes. Zomia and Turkestan are among the examples of culturally identifiable regions spanning large areas that receive much less attention in international research collaboratives and cultural policy settings because they do not align with modern-day nation-state forms of representation and institutional support. Turkestan also exemplifies the geopolitical or ideological factors at play that steer governments away from bestowing legitimacy on certain historical geographies. It occupies a politically complicated space within a Silk Road revival discourse as governments in Central Asia and China actively move to suppress certain histories, given the work they can do in bolstering claims of autonomy or succession.

Given that China's use of civilization continues to exhibit notions of progress and moral value, it would be reasonable to assume that hierarchies and the language of centers and peripheries will stabilize within depictions of connectivity and transmission, such that new norms about backwardness and peripheries enter circulation. Such possibilities lie within the idea of a Maritime Silk Road. Today, there is little consensus as to what the term actually refers to. And yet since 2013, *National Geographic* and CCTV documentaries, World Tourism Organization reports, children's cartoons, and a plethora of journalistic stories and academic studies are steadily normalizing the idea of a route and history of connectivity centered around China. Various cities along China's southern coast now self-identify as the "starting point" of a Maritime Silk Road that heads south and westward. This represents a politically significant departure from the geography laid out by UNESCO in the

1990s, where focus was given to understanding maritime connections between China, Japan, and the Korean peninsula. Three decades later, regional
tensions and competition, together with a more confident China, all mean
that there are forces at play that reduce complex histories to a single blue
line connecting Quanzhou and Guangzhou to Southeast Asia and beyond.
With Belt and Road dramatically increasing the funding sources available to
Chinese institutions, it is highly likely that narratives of seafaring, trade, and
cultural exchange will become Sino-civilizational discourses over the longer
term.[37]

The introduction of Sinocentric narratives of connectivity and civilization
is perhaps most charged for regions where borders and cultural sovereignties
are contested, in some cases through violence. Indeed, I would argue that the
idea of "reviving" the Silk Roads for the twenty-first century adds a new layer
of complexity to international cultural politics in regions where artifacts, cultural practices, and archaeological sites are already enmeshed in the memory
politics of colonialism, war, and nationalism. In a world of Silk Road cooperation, that which is celebrated as "shared" is inevitably a small, carefully
selected, carefully curated part of conjoined pasts. Interestingly, the diplomatic capacities of shared heritage discourses often find fertile ground where
there is, in reality, little shared history. Less in common reduces the risk of
political entanglement. Studies of Kashmiri traditional architecture, for example, rarely become the subject of collaboration for India and Pakistan. In
contrast, China and Greece can confidently assert that they not only share
civilizational values but that the great architectural achievements of East and
West were somehow conjoined by the Silk Road. Of course, this does not
preclude proximate connections. Buddhism has become a productive space
for developing partnerships in the Himalayan region. Today, both China and
India collaborate with their regional neighbors, most notably Nepal, in the
preservation and study of Buddhist sites. The associations Buddhism and the
Silk Road hold with peace and harmony ensure that research and engagement programs support the broader diplomatic and strategic ambitions of
both countries.

The strong emphasis Silk Road historiography places on itinerant objects
tends to normalize overly deterministic commodity-chain histories, mon-
olithic ideas about core-periphery zones of trade, or accounts that fet-
ishize trade over religion, language, disease, and so forth. Through the Silk
Roads, we are seeing diffusion theories familiar to the nineteenth century
regain currency. To cite one example, the Maritime Silk Road is a geocultural

imaginary that affords scholarly interpretations of Chinese ceramics found in Kenya, Sarawak, or Syria that privilege unidirectional histories of connection. But, of course, attending Silk Road conferences in different countries soon reveals that the story takes on very different inflections among communities of scholars. Indian, Chinese, and Iranian experts, for example, invariably talk of their own cultures and civilizations as lying at the "heart" of Silk Road exchange.

What might seem a casual observation warrants closer attention. Two themes are pertinent here: the dynamics of research funding, which often privilege studies of national significance; and the prevalence of intellectual paradigms that construct self-centric narratives of routes and diffusion. Chapter 2 explained the latter in the context of colonial historiographies of civilization and East and West. I would argue that such patterns continue to shape Silk Road discourses today. Italian academies tend to privilege Marco Polo, and Chinese researchers approach the Silk Road as the transmission and movement of Chinese culture or the influence of external elements on Chinese society.[38] Likewise, Korean scholars working on maritime histories will often look at forms of migration, trade, or religious exchange that have occurred both into and outward from Korea. I note such dispositions not so much as a critique but in order to highlight their influence on the way international or transregional histories are studied and funded and why locations, people, and histories come to be eclipsed over time. Such questions become particularly interesting in the context of international collaborations, and I would suggest that a combination of factors, including prestige, funding, and asymmetries in expertise between institutions and countries, all have a bearing on which narratives receive attention and support over others and why overly nostalgic accounts of cultural diffusion enter circulation. For the Maritime Silk Road, for example, it is unlikely that Cambodian, Thai, or Vietnamese histories will gain the same visibility as the historical events and developments of the region's more powerful countries.

I cite these examples to suggest that a historical narrative of mobility and connection requires the same forms of debate and critical attention as those that have developed around national, imperial, and world history. I would suggest that this extends to a more rigorous discussion about the merits and implications of the Silk Road as a concept for museology practice and public heritage. What is the responsibility of scholars when media or heritage depictions pacify Zheng He's seven voyages of the fifteenth century and make them synonymous with the Maritime Silk Road? Equally, we are confronted with the challenge of unpacking the new ways in which states are using history and heritage to exercise power over regions and population groups. How, for example, do declarations about civilizational dialogue and cultural internationalism relate to the violence inflicted on minorities at home in China, India, Myanmar, Turkey, and elsewhere? In what way might a more critical Silk Road studies shine a light on such forms of state violence?

In other words, I am advocating for a path followed by other domains of scholarship and policy, where an initial emphasis on the study of a subject matter in normative ways opens up to more critical debates about the assumptions and epistemologies of the field. I have endeavored to show the Silk Roads as an artifact for and of history. Along the way, I have also argued that it is a narrative for and of internationalism. Looking forward, there is a need to build forms of international dialogue that more fully grapple with the increasing significance and the influence the Silk Roads carry across multiple sectors and regions. The starting point for this book was the lack of understanding about their history. The aim, then, has been to disentangle some threads, unfurl some sails, and chart some fresh directions as new routes for the Silk Road continue to be discovered.

APPENDIX A

Silk Road Exhibitions

The list below shows the momentum that gathered over the course of the twentieth century around formal exhibitions on the Silk Road and Central Asia. This list is indicative and is not intended to be a comprehensive reference. It draws on a list compiled by Helen Wang from the British Museum.

1910–1912	Twenty-five prints from Stein's second expedition to Dunhuang, British Museum's Prints and Drawings Gallery, London.
1914	*Wonders of the East: Stein Exhibition in the British Museum Extension*, The Joseph E. Hotung Gallery, British Museum, London.
1914–1916	Public exhibition of items collected during Ōtani Kozui expedition, Villa Nirakusō, Kobe.
1916–1938	Public exhibition of items collected during Ōtani Kozui expedition, Seoul.
1917	Public exhibition of items collected during Ōtani Kozui expedition, Exhibition Hall of Mongolian and Manchurian Products (currently Lüshan Museum), Dalian.
1919	Public exhibition of items collected during Sergei Fyodorovich Oldenburg expedition, Russian Museum, St Petersburg.
1928	Public exhibition of items collected during Albert Grünwedel and Albert von Le Coq expeditions, Ethnology Museum, Berlin.
1935–1936	*Royal Academy's International Exhibition of Chinese Art*, Royal Academy of Arts, London (items borrowed from Palace Museum, Beijing; Paul Pelliot acted as advisor).
1935	Public exhibition of items collected during Sergei Fyodorovich Oldenburg's first expedition, permanent display, State Hermitage, St Petersburg.
1947	Public exhibition of items collected by Paul Pelliot from Central Asia, Musée Guimet, Paris.
1974	Those artifacts from Central Asia collected during the Ōtani expeditions returned to display, National Museum of Korea, Seoul.
1976–1977	Special exhibition of Central Asia collection, State Hermitage, St Petersburg.
1988	*The Grand Exhibition of Silk Road Civilizations*, Nara.
1990	*Caves of the Thousand Buddhas: Chinese Art from the Silk Route*, British Museum, London.
1991	Special exhibition of Central Asian material from Museum für Indische Kunst, Berlin, National Museum of Korea, Seoul.
1992	*The Crossroads of Asia: Transformation in Image and Symbol in the Art of Ancient Afghanistan and Pakistan*, Fitzwilliam Museum, University of Cambridge, Cambridge.
1993	*Silk Road Coins: The Hirayama Collection*. A special loan exhibition from Japan, British Museum, London.

1994	*In Search of Sinbad: The Maritime Silk Route*, Musée de la Marine, Paris.
1994	*Eastern Roots of the Ancient Hungarian Culture*, National Hungarian Museum, Budapest.
1995–1996	*Sérinde, terre de Bouddha: Dix siècles d'art sur la route de la soie*, Galeries nationales du Grand Palais, Paris.
1996	*Les Arts de l'Asie Centrale. La collection Pelliot au Musée Guimet*, Musée Guimet, Paris.
1996	*Gateway to the Silk Road—Relics from the Han to the Tang Dynasties from Xi'an, China*, City Art Centre, Edinburgh.
1996	*The Heirs of the Silk Roads: Uzbekistan*, Berlin World Cultures Centre.
1997	*From Persepolis to the Punjab: Coins and the Exploration of the East*, British Museum, London.
1998	*The Lotus Sutra and Its World: Buddhist Manuscripts of the Silk Road*. Collections borrowed from Institute of Oriental Manuscripts of the Russian Academy of Sciences, Institute of Oriental Philosophy, Tokyo.
2000	*Mannerheim in Central Asia, 1906–1908*, Museum of Cultures, Helsinki.
2000	*Dunhuang: Jinian Dunhuang Cangjingdong Faxian Yi Bai Zhounian*, Museum of History, Beijing.
2001	*L'Asie des Steppes d'Alexandre le Grand à Gengis Khan*, Musée Guimet, Paris.
2001	*Fabulous Creatures from the Desert Sands: Central Asian Textiles from 2000 Years Ago*, Abegg-Stiftung, Riggisberg.
2001	*Monks and Merchants: Silk Road Treasures from Northwest China, 4th–7th Century*, The Asia Society Museum, New York.
2001	Small exhibition of photographs taken by Aurel Stein, British Museum Clore Education Centre, London.
2002	Documentary exhibition hosted in conjunction with the Turfan Revisited—The First Century of Research into the Arts and Cultures of the Silk Road Conference, Berlin Brandenburg Academy of Sciences and Humanities, Berlin.
2002	Smithsonian Folklife Festival, *The Silk Road: Connecting Cultures, Celebrating Trust*, Smithsonian Institute, Washington DC.
2003	*Seoyeok misul (Arts of Central Asia)*, National Museum of Korea, Seoul.
2004	*The Silk Road: Trade, Travel, War and Faith*, British Library, London.
2004	The Hirayama Ikuo Silk Road Museum opens in Yamanashi, Japan.
2005	Central Asian collection placed on permanent display, National Museum of Korea, Seoul.
2007	*The Silk Road and the Search for the Secrets of Silk*, The John Rylands Library, Manchester.
2007	*Origins of the Silk Roads: Sensational New finds from Xinjiang, China*, Martin-Gropius-Bau, Berlin.
2008	Two online exhibitions, *Hidden Treasures of the Silk Road* and *Fascinated by the Orient: Aurel Stein, 1862–1943*, Library of Hungarian Academy of Sciences and University Museum and Art Gallery of the University of Hong Kong.
2008	*Western Eyes: An Exhibition of Historical Photographs of China taken by European Photographers, 1860–1930*, National Library of China, Beijing.
2008	Exhibition of Central Asian Collection of the Lüshun Museum, Aomori Museum of Art, Aomori.

2008	*Caves of the Thousand Buddhas: Russian Expeditions to Central Asia at the End of XIX–Beginning of XX Centuries*, Asiatic Museum, St Petersburg.
2009	*Cultural Exchange along the Northern Silk Road*, Museum für Asiatische Kunst, Berlin.
2009	Full-size replicas of the Dunhuang Caves, produced by the Dunhuang Academy, put on display at Museum für Asiatische Kunst, Berlin.
2009	*On the Trail of Texts on the Silk Road: Russian Expedition Discoveries of Manuscripts in Central Asia*, Kyoto National Museum, Kyoto.
2009	*The Silk Road: A Journey through Life and Death*, Musées royaux d'Art et d'Historie, Brussels.
2010	*Traveling the Silk Road: Ancient Pathway to the Modern Word*, American Museum of Natural History, New York.
2010	*The Great Game: Archaeology and Politics in the Age of Colonialism*, Ruhr Museum, Essen.
2010	*Art of Dunhuang*, Yanhuang Art Gallery, Beijing.
2011	*Secrets of the Silk Road*, Penn Museum, Philadelphia.
2011	*Documenting Dunhuang: Historical Records from the late Qing and Republican Periods*, Dunhuang Academy, Dunhuang.
2011	*Images and Sacred Texts: Buddhism across Asia*, British Museum, London.
2012	*The Road Travelled by Buddhism*, Ryukoku Museum, Kyoto.
2012	*On the Silk Road and the High Seas: Chinese Ceramics, Culture and Commerce*, University of Mississippi Museum, Oxford, Mississippi.
2012	*Travelling the Silk Road: Ancient Pathway to the Modern World*, National Museum of Australia, Canberra.
2012	*Following the Footsteps of Grünwedel*, Museum für Asiatische Kunst, Berlin.
2012	*Silk Road of the Eastern Seas*, Vietnam National Museum of History, Hanoi.
2012	*Buddhism along the Silk Road—5th-8th Century*, Metropolitan Museum of Art, New York.
2012	*The Colours of Dunhuang: The Magical Door Opening to the Silk Road*, Tophane-i Amire Culture and Art Center, Istanbul.
2013	*Dunhuang: Buddhist Art at the Gateway of the Silk Road*, China Institute Gallery, New York.
2013	*The Technological Preservation of the Caves and Cultural Heritage of Dunhuang*, Dunhuang Academy, Dunhuang.
2013	*The Culture and Art of Central Asia*, permanent collection of the Central Asian collections opened at the State Hermitage, St Petersburg.
2013	*Aurel Stein: A Hundred Years On*, produced by the British Library, Royal Geographical Society, and the University of Nottingham, hosted at the British Library, London.
2013	*Expedition Silk Road: Treasures from the Hermitage*, Hermitage Amsterdam, Amsterdam.
2014–2015	*The Diamond Sutra and Early Printing*, British Library, London.
2014	*China Maritime Silk Road Antiques Photo Exhibition*, hosted at the United Nations headquarters, New York, and organized by the permanent mission of the People's Republic of China and the Fujian Provincial People's Government.
2015	*Buddhist Art in Asia: India, Southeast Asia, Central Asia and Tibet*, Gwangju National Museum, Gwangju.

2015   *Fascinated by the Orient: Life and Works of Sir Aurel Stein*, Indira Gandhi National Centre for the Arts, New Delhi.

2015   *Silks from the Silk Road: Origins, Transmissions and Exchange*, China National Silk Museum, Hangzhou.

2016   *Cave Temples of Dunhuang: Buddhist Art on China's Silk Road*, Getty Center, Los Angeles.

2016   *Tang—Art from the Silk Road Capital*, Art Gallery NSW, Sydney.

2016   *The Ruins of Koco: Traces of Wooden Architecture on the Ancient Silk Road*, Museum für Asiatische Kunst, Berlin.

2016   *The Soul of Silk Road*, Chengdu Museum, Chengdu.

2017   *The Silk Road and the World's Civilisations*, Beijing Art Biennale, National Art Museum of China, Beijing.

2017   *Silk Road Legacy Radiating from Chang'an*, Shaanxi History Museum, Shaanxi.

2018   British Museum lent Central Asian material for the exhibition *Threads of Devotion*, Nara National Museum, Nara.

2018   British Museum lent Central Asian material for the exhibition *The Glory of Korea*, National Museum of Korea, Seoul.

2018   *Hungarians on the Silk Road*, the Pallas Athene Innovation and Geopolitical Foundation, the Library of the Hungarian Academy of Sciences, and the Dunhuang Academy, hosted at the Library of the Hungarian Academy of Sciences, Budapest.

2019   *Life along the Silk Road: 13 Stories during the Great Era*, State Hermitage, China National Silk Museum, the Institute of Archaeology Xinjiang, and the Dunhuang Research Academy, hosted at the China National Silk Museum, Hangzhou.

2019–2020   *Buddhism*, British Library, London.

2019   *Return from the East: Silk, Spices and Precious Stones*, Musée d'Arts de Nantes, Nantes.

2019   *Sharing a Common Future: Exhibition of Treasures from National Museums along the Silk Road*, National Museum of China, Beijing.

2019   *The Route of the Sea: Nanhai Shipwreck Maritime Trade in the Southern Song Dynasty*, Guangdong Provincial Museum, Guangzhou.

2019   *Cultural Exchanges along the Silk Road: Art Treasures from the Tubo Period*, Dunhuang Research Institute, Dunhuang.

2019   *Fusion of Colour: A Special Exhibition on the Civilizations of the Silk Road*, Sackler Museum of Archaeology and Art, Peking University, Beijing.

2020   *The Silk Roads: Before and after Richthofen*, China National Silk Museum, Hangzhou.

2021   The Humboldt Forum in Berlin, including the new Asian Art Galleries that are made up of collections from the now-dismantled Museum für Asiatische Kunst and the Ethnological Museum. As part of this new space, a partial reconstruction of the "Cave of the Sixteen Sword Bearers," material brought back from the German expeditions to Turfan, will be put on display—the first time they can be viewed in a unified composition in more than a hundred years.

Silk Road Associations and Networks

List of Silk Road–related associations and networks established 2002–2021. This list is indicative and is not intended to be a comprehensive reference.

1996	Central Asia-Caucasus Institute, Silk Road Program established 2002, John Hopkins University
2010	Association for Central Asian Civilizations and Silk Road Studies
2013	Silk Routes Partnership for Migration
	Global Silk Road University Consortium
2014	Silk Road Fund
	Silk Road Economic Development Research Center, Hong Kong
	Silk Road Universities Network
	Silk Road Cities Alliance
2015	Silk Road Law School Alliance
	University Alliance of the Silk Road
	International Association for the Study of Silk Road Textiles
	Maritime Silk Road Society
	Culture Committee, Silk Road Chamber of International Commerce
	New Silk Road Friends Association
	Silk Road Think Tank Association
2016	Alliance of the Silk Road Business Schools
	Silk Road Forensic Consortium
	Silk Road International League of Theatres
	Maritime-Continental Silk Road Cities Alliance
	Silk Road Urban Alliance
	Silk Road International Association
2017	Silk Road Grand Award Association
	Music Education Alliance across the Silk Road
	Oxford University Silk Road Society
	Alliance of Silk Road Business Schools
2018	Silk Road International Library Alliance
	Silk Road Museum Alliance
	Swiss-China World Silk Association
	Heritage Alliance of the New Silk Road
2019	Maritime Silk Road Port Cooperation Mechanism
	New Silk Road Network
	Air Silk Road Airport and Urban International Alliance

Notes

The Silk Road

1. "The Silk Road," *Morning Bulletin*, May 15, 1943, 3.

Chapter 1

1. Susan Whitfield, *Silk Roads: Peoples, Cultures, Landscapes* (Berkeley: University of California, 2019). In 2007, Whitfield also published; Susan Whitfield, "Was There a Silk Road?," *Asian Medicine* 3 (2007): 201–13.
2. For a discussion about Carl Ritter's use of the term, see Matthias Mertens, "Did Richthofen Really Coin 'The Silk Road'?," *The Silk Road* 17 (2019): 1–9. For a detailed account of Richthofen's depiction of the Silk Road, see Tamara Chin, "The Invention of the Silk Road, 1877," *Critical Inquiry* 40, no. 1 (2013): 194–219; and Daniel Waugh, "Richthofen's 'Silk Roads': Towards the Archaeology of a Concept," *Silk Road* 5, no. 1 (2007): 1–10.
3. The full title of this five-part volume was *China: The Results of My Travels and the Studies Based Thereon, 1877–1912* (in German, *China, Ergebnisse Eigner Reisen Un Darauf Gegründeter Studien*).
4. Eric Hobsbawm, *Nations and Nationalism since 1780: Programme, Myth, Reality* (Cambridge: Cambridge University Press, 1992), 10, Kindle.
5. Hobsbawm, *Nations and Nationalism since 1780*, 15.
6. See, for example, the interesting discussion on walls, including China's Great Wall, by William Callahan. William Callahan, "The Politics of Walls: Barriers, Flows, and the Sublime," *Review of International Studies* 44, no. 3 (2019): 456–81.
7. Andre Gunder Frank, "On the Silk Road: An 'Academic' Travelogue," *Economic and Political Weekly* 25, no. 46 (1990): 2536–39.
8. As Ernest Renan noted, "getting its history wrong is part of being a nation." Cited in Hobsbawm, *Nations and Nationalism since 1780*, 18.
9. Lynn Hunt, *Writing History in the Global Era* (New York: W.W. Norton & Company, 2015), Kindle.
10. To cite one example, Olstein suggests that the history of globalization has set out to track "the processes that transformed the globe into a single interconnected unit in which external contacts, flows, and networks have a predominant impact on world societies." Diego Olstein, *Thinking History Globally* (London: Palgrave Macmillan, 2015), 25, Kindle.

11. Alexander Maxwell, "Introduction, Bridges and Bulwarks: A Historiographic Overview of East-West Discourses," in *The East-West Discourse: Symbolic Geographic and its Consequences*, ed. Alexander Maxwell (Bern: Peter Land, 2011), 1–32.

12. Francis Fukuyama, "The End of History?," *National Interest* no. 16 (1989): 3–18.

13. See, e.g., Thomas L. Friedman, *The World Is Flat: A Brief History of the Twenty-First Century* (New York: Farrar, Straus and Giroux, 2005); and David Harvey, *The Condition of Postmodernity: An Enquiry into the Origins of Cultural Change* (Malden: Blackwell, 1990).

14. Valerie Hansen, *The Silk Road: A New History with Documents* (Oxford: Oxford University Press, 2017), Chapter 5.

15. Susan Whitfield, *Life along the Silk Road* (Berkeley: University of California Press, 2015).

16. Hansen, *Silk Road.*

17. In 2017, a group of international experts gathered in London for a workshop to conceptualize the Maritime Silk Road for the purposes of UNESCO World Heritage designation. Much of the discussion centered around disagreements in periodization, chronology, and the designation of meaningful regions.

18. Peter Frankopan, *The Silk Roads: A New History of the World* (New York: Vintage Books, 2017).

19. See Christopher Beckwith, *Empires of the Silk Road: A History of Central Eurasia from the Bronze Age to the Present* (Princeton: Princeton University Press, 2009); and Xinru Liu, *The Silk Road in World History* (Oxford: Oxford University Press, 2010).

20. Marie Thorsten, "Silk Road Nostalgia and Imagined Global Community," *Comparative American Studies: An International Journal* 3, no. 3 (2005): 301–17. See also James Millward, *The Silk Road: A Very Short Introduction* (Oxford: Oxford University Press, 2013), Kindle; Daniel Waugh, "The Silk Roads in History," *Expedition* 52, no. 3 (2010): 9–22; and Khodadad Rezakhani, "The Road That Never Was: The Silk Road and Trans-Eurasian Exchange," *Comparative Studies of South Asia, Africa and the Middle East* 30, no. 3 (2010): 420–33.

21. Rezakhani, "The Road That Never Was," 420.

22. Ulf Hannerz, *Writing Future Worlds: An Anthropologist Explores Global Scenarios* (Cham: Palgrave Macmillan, 2016), loc. 149 of 6635, Kindle.

23. Ulf Hannerz, "Geocultural Scenarios," in *Frontiers of Sociology*, ed. Peter Hedstrom and Bjorn Wittrock (Leiden: Brill, 2009), 276.

24. Issac Kamola, *Making the World Global: U.S. Universities and the Production of the Global Imaginary* (Durham: Duke University Press, 2019); and Merje Kuus, *Geopolitics and Expertise: Knowledge and Authority in European Diplomacy* (Chichester: Wiley Blackwell, 2014).

25. Ernest Cassirer, *The Philosophy of the Enlightenment* (Boston: Beacon Press, 1955), quoted in Immanuel Wallerstein and Peter Philips, "National and World Identities and the Interstate System," in *Geopolitics and Geoculture: Essays on the Changing World-System*, ed. Immanuel Wallerstein (Cambridge: Cambridge University Press, 1991), 144.

26. Immanuel Wallerstein, *European Universalism: The Rhetoric of Power* (New York: New Press, 2006).

27. Gurminder Bhambra, *Connected Sociologies* (London: Bloomsbury, 2014); and Walter Mignolo, "Globalization and the Geopolitics of Knowledge," *Nepantia: Views from the South* 4 (2003): 97–119.

Chapter 2

1. Eric Hobsbawm and Terence Ranger, *The Invention of Tradition* (Cambridge: Cambridge University Press, 1983).

2. Yannis Hamilakis, *The Nation and Its Ruins: Antiquity, Archaeology, and National Imagination in Greece* (Oxford: Oxford University Press, 2007), 58.

3. Hamilakis, *The Nation and Its Ruins*, 63.

4. See Mikhail M. Bakhtin, "The Epic and the Novel: Towards a Methodology for the Study in the Novel," in *The Dialogic Imagination, Four Essays by Mikhail Bakhtin*, ed. Michael Holquist (Austin: University of Texas Press, 1981); and Paul Connerton, *How Societies Remember* (Cambridge: Cambridge University Press, 1989), 56–57.

5. For a detailed discussion of such transitions in relation to the emergence of the concept of civilization in Europe, see Johann Arnason, "The Rediscovery of Civilizations," in *Civilizations in Dispute: Historical Questions and Theoretical Traditions*, ed. Johann Arnason (Leiden: Brill, 2003). Osterhammel's *Unfabling the East* also discusses the transitions in European knowledge about Asia during this period and how historians of more recent times have interpreted the intellectual construction of "Asia." See Jürgen Osterhammel, *Unfabling the East: The Enlightenment's Encounter with Asia* (Princeton: Princeton University Press, 2018).

6. See Bruce Trigger, *A History of Archaeological Thought* (Cambridge: Cambridge University Press, 1989); Elizabeth Errington and Vesta Curtis, "The British and Archaeology in Nineteenth-Century Persia," in *From Persepolis to the Punjab: Exploring Ancient Iran, Afghanistan and Pakistan*, ed. Elizabeth Errington and Vesta Curtis (London: British Museum Press, 2007), 166–78; Elizabeth Errington and Vesta Curtis, "The Explorers and Collectors," in *From Persepolis to the Punjab: Exploring Ancient Iran, Afghanistan and Pakistan*, ed. Elizabeth Errington and Vesta Curtis (London: British Museum Press, 2007), 3–16; and Tim Winter, "Heritage and Nationalism: An Unbreachable Couple?," in *The Palgrave Handbook of Contemporary Heritage Research*, ed. Steve Watson and Emma Waterton (London: Palgrave Macmillan, 2015), 331–45.

7. John Hobson, *The Eastern Origins of Western Civilization* (Cambridge: Cambridge University Press, 2004), 23.

8. See Jürgen Osterhammel, *The Transformation of the World: A Global History of the Nineteenth Century* (Princeton: Princeton University Press, 2014).

9. See Astrid Swenson and Peter Mandler, ed., *From Plunder to Preservation: Britain and the Heritage of the Empire*, c. 1800–1940 (Oxford: Oxford University Press,

2013); and Benjamin Porter, "Near Eastern Archaeology: Imperial Pasts, Postcolonial Presents, and the Possibilities of a Decolonized Future," in *Handbook of Postcolonial Archaeology*, ed. Jane Lydon and Uzma Z. Rizvi (Oxford: Routledge, 2016), 53.

10. Eric Cline, *Biblical Archaeology: A Very Short Introduction* (Oxford: Oxford University Press, 2009), loc. 372 of 2485, Kindle.

11. Nadia Abu El Haj, *Facts on the Ground: Archaeological Practice and Territorial Self-Fashioning in Israeli Society* (Chicago: University of Chicago Press, 2001).

12. For further details, see Thomas Davis, *Shifting Sands: The Rise and Fall of Biblical Archaeology* (Oxford: Oxford University Press, 2004), Kindle.

13. Justin M. Jacobs, *The Compensations of Plunder: How China Lost Its Treasures* (Chicago: University of Chicago Press, 2020), 6, Kindle.

14. See, e.g., Brian Fagan, *Return to Babylon: Travelers, Archaeologists, and Monuments in Mesopotamia* (Boulder: University of Colorado Press, 2007).

15. Osterhammel, *Unfabling the East*, 29; Eckhardt Fuchs, "Introduction: Provincializing Europe," in *Across Cultural Borders: Historiography in Global Perspective*, ed. Eckhardt Fuchs and Benedikt Stuchtey (Lanham: Rowman & Littlefield Publishers, 2002), Kindle.

16. Maya Jasanoff, *Edge of Empire: Conquest and Collecting in the East, 1750–1850* (New York: Harper Perennial, 2005).

17. Bernard S. Cohn, *Colonialism and its Forms of Knowledge: The British in India* (Princeton: Princeton University Press, 1996), 80.

18. Tony Bennett, "The Exhibitionary Complex," *New Formations* no. 4 (1988): 73–102.

19. Stefan Berger, "National Museums in between Nationalism, Imperialism and Regionalism, 1750–1914," in *National Museums and Nation-Building in Europe 1750–2010: Moblization and Legitimacy, Continuity and Change*, ed. Peter Aronsson and Gabriella Elgenius (London: Routledge, 2015), 16.

20. See Prasenjit Duara, "The Discourse of Civilization and Pan-Asianism," *Journal of World History* 12, no. 1 (2001): 100–08.

21. Suzanne Marchand notes that the sweeping arc Said constructs inadequately accounts for the decade-by-decade changes that occurred in Oriental Studies across Europe and the bearing they had on new forms of knowledge and respect for regions of study. See Edward Said, *Orientalism* (Harmondsworth: Penguin Books, 1994); and Suzanne Marchand, introduction to *German Orientalism in the Age of Empire: Religion, Race, and Scholarship* (Cambridge: Cambridge University Press, 2010), xvii–xxxiv.

22. See Geoffrey C. Gunn, *Overcoming Ptolmey: The Revelation of an Asian World Region* (Lanham: Lexington Books, 2018), Kindle.

23. Daniel Waugh, "The Making of Chinese Central Asia," *Central Asia Survey* 26, no. 2 (2007): 242.

24. Gunn, *Overcoming Ptolmey*.

25. Claudius Ptolemy, *Geography of Claudius Ptolemy*, trans. Edward Luther Stevenson (New York: Cosimo Classics, 2011), quoted in Gunn, *Overcoming Ptolmey*, loc. 131 of 8281.

26. Gunn, *Overcoming Ptolmey*, loc. 159 of 8281.

27. Gunn, *Overcoming Ptolmey*, loc. 403 of 8281.

28. Marchand, *German Orientalism in the Age of Empire*, 155.
29. Marchand, *German Orientalism in the Age of Empire*, 154.
30. Marchand, *German Orientalism in the Age of Empire*, 154.
31. Marchand, *German Orientalism in the Age of Empire*, 154.
32. Tamara Chin, "The Invention of the Silk Road, 1877," *Critical Inquiry* 40, no. 1 (2013): 194–219.
33. Chin, "Invention of the Silk Road, 1877," 201.
34. Ferdinand von Richthofen, "The Ancient Silk-Traders' Route across Central Asia," *Geographical Magazine* 5 (1878a): 10–14; and Ferdinand von Richthofen, "The Ancient Silk-Traders' Route across Central Asia," *Popular Science Monthly: Supplement* nos. 7–12 (1878b): 378–83.
35. For further details on the construction of the Trans-Caspian Railway, see W.E. Wheeler, "The Control of Land Routes: Russian Railways in Central Asia," *Journal of the Royal Central Asian Society* 21, no. 4 (1934): 585–608.
36. Wheeler, "Control of Land Routes," 605.
37. In the early nineteenth century, the threat posed by Russia only seemed to increase as treaties signed in Turkmenchay and Adrianople in 1828 and 1829, respectively, signaled the possibility of Russian protectorates in Persia and Turkey. For further details, see Edward Ingram, "Great Britain's Great Game: An Introduction," *International History Review* 2, no. 2 (1980): 162.
38. Ingram, "Great Britain's Great Game," 166.
39. See Peter Hopkirk, *The Great Game: On Service in High Asia* (London: John Murray, 2006); and Karl E. Meyer and Shareen Blair Brysac, *Tournament of Shadows: The Great Game and the Race for Empire in Central Asia* (New York: Basic Books, 1999).
40. Suzanne Marchand argues that throughout the eighteenth and nineteenth centuries German Orientalists often cast lonely figures, given little recognition by an educational system and by a public that showed little interest in Asian civilizations. Marchand, *German Orientalism in the Age of Empires*, 102–56.

Chapter 3

1. Russell-Smith has argued that this expedition informed Aurel Stein's decision to set off in search of the caves nearly three decades later. See Lilla Russell-Smith, "Hungarian Explorers in Dunhuang," *Journal of the Royal Asiatic Society* 10, no. 3 (2000): 341.
2. Peter Hopkirk, *Foreign Devils on the Silk Road: The Search for the Lost Treasures of Central Asia* (London: John Murray, 1980), loc. 608 of 3743, Kindle.
3. Justin M. Jacobs, *The Compensations of Plunder: How China Lost Its Treasures* (Chicago: University of Chicago Press, 2020), 7, Kindle.
4. Hopkirk, *Foreign Devils on the Silk Road*, locs. 837–41 of 3743.
5. Hopkirk, *Foreign Devils on the Silk Road*, loc. 986 of 3743.
6. Justin Jacobs, "Cultural Thieves or Political Liabilities? How Chinese Officials Viewed Foreign Archaeologists in Xinjiang, 1893–1914," *Silk Road* 10 (2012): 117; and Jacobs, *Compensations of Plunder*.

7. Vsevolod Ivanovich Roborovskiy, for example, conducted pioneering archaeological work in the Turfan region between 1893 and 1895. See Nile Green, ed., "Introduction: Writing, Travel, and the Global History of Central Asia," in *Writing Travel in Central Asian History*, ed. Nile Green (Bloomington: Indiana University Press, 2014), 24, Kindle.

8. Karl E. Meyer and Shareen Blair Brysac, *Tournament of Shadows: The Great Game and the Race for Empire in Central Asia* (New York: Basic Books, 1999), 360–63.

9. Justin Jacobs, "Nationalist China's 'Great Game': Leveraging Foreign Explorers in Xinjiang, 1927–1935," *Journal of Asian Studies* 73, no. 1 (2014): 45.

10. Jacobs, "Cultural Thieves or Political Liabilities?," 121.

11. Hermann Kreutzmann, "Geographical Research in Chinese Central Asia: Aims and Ambitions of International Explorers in the 19th and 20th Centuries," *Die Erde* 138, no. 4 (2007): 369.

12. Meyer and Brysac, *Tournament of Shadows*, 111–36.

13. Suzanne Marchand, *German Orientalism in the Age of Empire: Religion, Race, and Scholarship* (Cambridge: Cambridge University Press, 2010), 417.

14. For further details, see Marchand, *German Orientalism in the Age of Empire*, 419.

15. Marchand, *German Orientalism in the Age of Empire*, 424.

16. Susan Whitfield, "Scholarly Respect in an Age of Political Rivalry," in *Russian Expeditions to Central Asia at the Turn of the 20th Century*, ed. Irina F. Popova (St Petersburg: Rossiiskaia Akademia Nauk, Instiut vostochnykh rukopisei rossijskoi Akademii nauk, 2008), 203–19.

17. Simone-Christiane Raschmann, "The Berlin-Turfan Collection," Staatsbibliothek zu Berlin, accessed November 30, 2018, https://staatsbibliothek-berlin.de/die-staatsbib liothek/abteilungen/orient/aufgaben-profil/veroeffentlichungen/berlin-turfan-col lection/.

18. Ingo Strauch, "Priority and Exclusiveness: Russians and Germans at the Northern Silk Road (Materials From the Turfan-Akten)," *Etudes de Lettres* 2–3 (2014): 147–50.

19. Strauch, "Priority and Exclusiveness."

20. Valerie Hansen, *The Silk Road: A New History with Documents* (Oxford: Oxford University Press, 2017); and Frances Wood, *The Silk Road: Two Thousand Years in the Heart of Asia* (Berkeley: University of California Press, 2002).

21. Selçuk Esenbel, introduction to *Japan on the Silk Road: Encounters and Perspectives of Politics and Culture in Eurasia*, ed. Selçuk Esenbel (Leiden: Brill, 2018), 7–8.

22. For further details, see Catrin Kost, "'Yours Ever So Sincerely': Albert von le Coq Seen through His Correspondence with Aurel Stein," in *Sir Aurel Stein, Colleagues and Collections*, ed. Helen Wang (London: British Museum, 2012), 1–9.

23. Meyer and Brysac, *Tournament of Shadows*, 371.

24. Prasenjit Duara, "The Discourse of Civilization and Pan-Asianism," *Journal of World History* 12, no. 1 (2001): 103.

25. Leo Klejn, *Soviet Archaeology: Schools, Trends and History* (Oxford: Oxford University Press, 2012), 3–12.

26. V. Bulkin, Leo Klejn, and G.S. Lebedev, "Attainments and Problems of Soviet Archaeology," *World Archaeology* 13, no. 3 (1982): 272–95.

27. Klejn, *Soviet Archaeology*, 13–49, 135–42.

28. Pavel Dolukhanov, "Archaeology and Nationalism in Totalitarian and Post-totalitarian Russia," in *Nationalism and Archaeology: Scottish Archaeological Forum*, ed. John Atkinson, Iain Banks, and Jerry O'Sullivan (Glasgow: Cruithne Press, 1996), 200–13.

29. Bulkin, Klejn, and Lebedev, "Attainments and Problems of Soviet Archaeology," 276.

30. The content of the Soviet nationalities policy was formulated for the Twelfth Party Congress in April 1923. A resolution passed by the Central Committee modified the policy a few months later. See Terry Martin, *The Affirmative Action Empire: Nations and Nationalism in the Soviet Union, 1923–1939* (Ithaca: Cornell University Press, 2017), Kindle.

31. Martin, *Affirmative Action Empire*, loc. 470 of 820.

32. Francine Hirsch, *Empire of Nations: Ethnographic Knowledge and the Making of the Soviet Union* (Ithaca: Cornell University Press, 2014), Kindle.

33. Oksana Sarkisova, *Screening Soviet Nationalities: Kulturfilms from the Far North to Central Asia* (London: I.B. Tauris, 2017), loc. 502 of 6343, Kindle.

34. Sarkisova, *Screening Soviet Nationalities*, loc. 3356 of 6343.

35. Sarkisova, *Screening Soviet Nationalities*, loc. 3501 of 6343.

36. Jacobs, "Cultural Thieves or Political Liabilities?," 117.

37. Jacobs, "Nationalist China's 'Great Game,'" 51.

38. This trip also features in other accounts of this period's archaeology. See, e.g., Hopkirk, *Foreign Devils on the Silk Road*; and Helen Wang, "Sir Aurel Stein," in *From Persepolis to the Punjab: Exploring Ancient Iran, Afghanistan and Pakistan*, ed. Elizabeth Errington and Vesta Curtis (London: British Museum Press, 2007), 227–34.

39. For a detailed account of this process, see James Leibold, *Reconfiguring Chinese Nationalism: How the Qing Frontier and its Indigenes Became Chinese* (New York: Palgrave Macmillan, 2007), Kindle.

40. Justin Jacobs, "Confronting Indiana Jones: Chinese Nationalism, Historical Imperialism and the Criminalisation of Aurel Stein and the Raiders of Dunhuang, 1899–1944," in *China on the Margins*, ed. Sherman Cochran and Paul Pickowicz (Ithaca: Cornell University East Asia Program, 2010), 65–90.

41. Jacobs, "Confronting Indiana Jones," 82.

42. Daniel Waugh, "The Silk Roads in History," *Expedition* 52, no. 3 (2010): 13–14.

43. Hedin also used the term for a set of recommendations to the Chinese government. His *Plan for the Revival of the Silk Road* included proposals for new air and rail transport corridors linking Europe to Asia. The report was drafted to help advance the interests of Lufthansa and the German government, among others. See Sven Hedin, *The Silk Road* (London: George Routledge and Sons, 1938), 229–31. See also Tamara Chin, "The Invention of the Silk Road, 1877," *Critical Inquiry* 40, no. 1 (2013): 194–219.

44. Daniel Waugh, "Richthofen's 'Silk Roads': Towards the Archaeology of a Concept," *Silk Road* 5, no. 1 (2007): 7.

Chapter 4

1. For further details, see Johann Arnason, *Social Theory and Japanese Experience: The Dual Civilization* (London: Kegan Paul, 1997); and Prasenjit Duara, "The Discourse of Civilization and Pan-Asianism," *Journal of World History* 12, no. 1 (2001): 99–130. The most comprehensive account of Japan's reconstructed relationship with the outside world comes from S.N. Eisenstadt, *Japanese Civilization: A Comparative View* (Chicago: University of Chicago Press, 1996).

2. Duara, "Discourse of Civilization and Pan-Asianism."

3. Mark Ravina, *To Stand with the Nations of the World: Japan's Meiji Restoration in World History* (Oxford: Oxford University Press, 2017), Kindle.

4. See Johann Arnason, "The Southeast Asian Labyrinth: Historical and Comparative Perspectives," *Thesis Eleven* no. 50 (1997): 99–122; and Jeremy C.A. Smith, *Debating Civilisations: Interrogating Civilisational Analysis in a Global Age* (Manchester: Manchester University Press, 2017), Kindle.

5. Smith, *Debating Civilisations*, 176–80.

6. Christopher Harding, *Japan Story: In Search of a Nation, 1850 to the Present* (London: Allen Lane, 2018).

7. Justin Jacobs, "Confronting Indiana Jones: Chinese Nationalism, Historical Imperialism and the Criminalisation of Aurel Stein and the Raiders of Dunhuang, 1899–1944," in *China on the Margins*, ed. Sherman Cochran and Paul Pickowicz (Ithaca: Cornell University East Asia Program, 2010), 82.

8. See Duara, "Discourse of Civilization and Pan-Asianism," 103.

9. Hyung Il Pai, *Heritage Management in Korea and Japan: The Politics of Antiquity and Identity* (Seattle: University of Washington Press, 2013), 83.

10. Okakura Kazuko, *The Ideals of the East with Special Reference to the Art of Japan* (Rutland: Charles E. Tuttle Co., 1970), locs. 204–15 of 1902, Kindle.

11. Stefan Tanaka explains the concept in the following ways: "the terms *tōyō* and *tōyōshi* present difficulties in translation, for they were a manifestation of the ambiguity of Japan's view of itself and position in the world. On the one hand, *tōyōshi*, which developed to fill the void of the Enlightenment's 'world histories' and supplement Western history (*seiyōshi*), can be seen simply as Japanese oriental studies (a contradictory appellation in itself)." Stefan Tanaka, *Japan's Orient: Rendering Pasts into History* (Berkeley: University of California Press, 1993), locs. 170–72 of 4192, Kindle.

12. See Tanaka, *Japan's Orient*, loc. 936 of 4192.

13. See De-Min Tao, "Shiratori Kurakichi: 1865–1943," in *Encyclopedia of Historians and Historical Writing*, ed. Kelly Boyd, vol. 1 (London: Fitzroy Dearborn Publishers, 1999), 1090.

14. Tanaka, *Japan's Orient*, locs. 1139–52 of 4192.

15. Tanaka, *Japan's Orient*, loc. 1235 of 4192.

16. Tanaka, *Japan's Orient*, locs. 1143–47 of 4192.

17. For further details, see Koji Mizoguchi, "Nation-State, Circularity and Paradox," in *Archaeology, Society and Identity in Modern Japan*, ed. Koji Mizoguchi (Cambridge: Cambridge University Press, 2006), 55–120.

18. Mizoguchi, "Nation-State, Circularity and Paradox."

19. Duara, "Discourse of Civilization and Pan-Asianism," 110. Also see Christopher Szpilman, "Western and Central Asia in the Eyes of the Japanese Radical Right," in *Japan on the Silk Road: Encounters and Perspectives of Politics and Culture in Eurasia*, ed. Selçuk Esenbel (Leiden: Brill, 2018), 48–68.

20. Jeremy A. Yellen, *The Greater East Asia Co-Prosperity Sphere: When Total Empire Met Total War* (Ithaca: Cornell University Press, 2019), 15, 24, Kindle.

21. Ōtani later served as the 22nd patriarch of the Honpa Honganji, a branch of the Jōdo Shinshū sect, and the chief abbot of its head temple, the Nishi Honganji in Kyoto. For further details, see Erdal Küçükyalçin, "Ōtani Kozui and his Vision of Asia: From Villa Nirakusō to 'The Rise of Asia' Project," in *Japan on the Silk Road: Encounters and Perspectives of Politics and Culture in Eurasia*, ed. Selçuk Esenbel (Leiden: Brill, 2018), 181–98; and Brij Tankha, "Exploring Asia, Reforming Japan: Ōtani and Itō Chūta," in *Japan on the Silk Road: Encounters and Perspectives of Politics and Culture in Eurasia*, ed. Selçuk Esenbel (Leiden: Brill, 2018), 156–80.

22. See Imre Galambos, "Japanese 'Spies' Along the Silk Road: British Suspicions Regarding the Second Ōtani Expedition (1908–09)," *Japanese Religions* 35, nos. 1–2 (2010): 33–61; Imre Galambos, "Japanese Exploration of Central Asia: The Ōtani Expeditions and Their British Connections," *Bulletin of SOAS* 75, no. 1 (2012): 113–34; and Imre Galambos, "Buddhist Relics from the Western Regions: Japanese Archaeological Exploration of Central Asia," in *Writing Travel in Central Asian History*, ed. Nile Green (Bloomington: Indiana University Press, 2014), 152–69, Kindle.

23. For a more detailed discussion of this trip and the construction of his villa in Kobe, see Tankha, "Exploring Asia, Reforming Japan," 168.

24. Tankha, "Exploring Asia, Reforming Japan."

25. Research for Peter Hopkirk's work was undertaken in the archives of London at Kew and the political and secret files kept in the India Office Library.

26. Galambos, "Japanese 'Spies' along the Silk Road," 33–61.

27. Galambos, "Buddhist Relics from the Western Regions," 152–69.

28. Galambos, "Buddhist Relics from the Western Regions," 166.

29. Sven Saaler and Christopher Szpilman, eds, *Pan-Asianism: A Documentary History Vol 1, 1850–1920* (Lanham: Rowman & Littlefield, 2011).

30. Tansen Sen, *Buddhism, Diplomacy and Trade: The Realignment of India-China Relations, 600–1400* (Lanham: Rowman & Littlefield, 2016), 8, Kindle.

31. Mark Ravinder Frost, "Handing Back History: Britain's Imperial Heritage State in Colonial Sri Lanka and South Asia, 1870–1920" (Keynote Address, National Symposium of Historical Studies, University of Sri Lanka, Colombo, January 31, 2018).

32. For a detailed account of the intersection between pan-Asianism and pan-Islamism, see Cemil Aydin, *The Politics of Anti-Westernism in Asia: Visions of World Order in Pan-Islamic and Pan-Asian Thought* (New York: Columbia University Press, 2007), Kindle.

33. Aydin, *Politics of Anti-Westernism in Asia*.

34. Aydin, *Politics of Anti-Westernism in Asia*.

35. Ali Merthan Dündar, "The Effects of the Russo-Japanese War on Turkic Nations: Japan and Japanese in Folk Songs, Elegies and Poems," in *Japan on the Silk Road: Encounters and Perspectives of Politics and Culture in Eurasia*, ed. Selçuk Esenbel (Leiden: Brill, 2018), 199–227.

36. Selçuk Esenbel, "Introduction," in *Japan on the Silk Road: Encounters and Perspectives of Politics and Culture in Eurasia*, ed. Selçuk Esenbel (Leiden: Brill, 2018), 33.

37. Hyung Il Pai, "Resurrecting the Ruins of Japan's Mythical Homelands: Colonial Archaeological Surveys in the Korean Peninsula and Heritage Tourism," in *The Handbook of Post-colonialism and Archaeology*, ed. Jane Lydon and Uzma Z. Rizvi (Walnut Creek: Left Coast Press, 2010), 93–112.

38. Hyung Il Pai, *Heritage Management in Korea and Japan*, 88.

39. Judith Snodgrass, *Presenting Japanese Buddhism to the West: Orientalism, Occidentalism, and the Columbian Exposition* (Chapel Hill: University of North Carolina Press, 2003).

40. See *Chau Ju-Kua: His Work on the Chinese and Arab Trade in the Twelfth and Thirteenth Centuries, Entitled Chu-fan-chī*, trans. Friedrich Hirt and W.W. Rockhill (St Petersburg: Imperial Academy of Sciences, 1911).

41. Matsuda Hisao, "General Survey: The Development of Researches in the History of the Intercourse Between East and West in Japan," in *Research in Japan in History of Eastern and Western Cultural Contacts: Its Development and Present Situation*, ed. Japanese National Commission for UNESCO (Tokyo: Japanese National Commission for UNESCO, 1957), 1–18.

42. See Kwa Chong-Guan, ed., introduction to *Early Southeast Asia Viewed from India: An Anthology of Articles from the "Journal of the Greater India Society"* (Delhi: Manohar, 2013).

43. Studies by members of the society confirmed the diffusion of India's religions and languages by merchants and other seafarers over a number of centuries. See Kwa Chong-Guan, *Early Southeast Asia Viewed from India*.

Part Two

1. Bruno Latour, "Visualisation and Cognition: Drawing Things Together," in *Knowledge and Society Studies in the Sociology of Culture Past and Present*, ed. H. Kuklick, vol. 6 (Stamford: JAI Press, 1986), 1–40.

2. Abū Zayad Al-Sīrāfī, *Accounts of China and India*, trans. Tim Mackintosh-Smith (New York: New York University Press, 2017).

3. Valerie Hansen, *The Silk Road: A New Documentary History to 1400* (Oxford: Oxford University Press, 2016).

4. See Susan Whitfield, *Life along the Silk Road* (Berkeley: University of California Press, 2015).

5. Somewhat problematically, Marco Polo has also become the benchmark by which others are judged and historically located. Ibn Battuta, Xuanzang, and Rabban Bar

Sauma, for example, are among the great scholar-travelers from outside the West who are often referred to as the "Marco Polo of the East."

6. See Hu Ying, "'Would That I Were Marco Polo': The Travel Writing of Shan Shili (1856–1943)," in *Traditions of East Asian Travel*, ed. Joshua A. Fogel (New York: Berghahn Books, 2006), 144–66.

Chapter 5

1. Hellmut de Terra, "On the World's Highest Plateaus," *National Geographic Magazine*, March 1931, 319.
2. Nile Green, ed., *Writing Travel in Central Asian History* (Bloomington: Indiana University Press, 2014), Kindle.
3. See Green, *Writing Travel in Central Asian History*.
4. Nile Green, ed., "Introduction: Writing, Travel, and the Global History of Central Asia," in *Writing Travel in Central Asian History*, ed. Nile Green (Bloomington: Indiana University Press, 2014), 26, Kindle.
5. Karl Baedeker, *Russia, with Teheran, Port Arthur, and Peking; Handbook for Travellers* (Leipzig: Karl Baedeker, 1914).
6. See Frederick Bohrer, *Photography and Archaeology* (London: Reaktion Books, 2011); and Rosalind C. Morris, ed., *Photographies East: The Camera and Its Histories in East and Southeast Asia* (Durham: Duke University Press, 2009).
7. Nigel Cliff, introduction to *The Travels: Marco Polo*, by Marco Polo, trans. Nigel Cliff (London: Penguin Books, 2015), xxxix.
8. John Larner, *Marco Polo and the Discovery of the World* (New Haven: Yale University Press, 1999), 181.
9. See James L. Hevia, "The Photography Complex: Exposing Boxer-Era China (1900–1901), Making Civilisation," in *Photographies East: The Camera and Its Histories in East and Southeast Asia*, ed. Rosalind C. Morris (Durham: Duke University Press, 2009), 79–119. See also Martin Heidegger, "The Age of the World Picture," in *The Question Concerning Technology, and Other Essays*, trans. William Lovitt (New York: Garland Publishing, 1977), 115–54; Maria Pelizzari, *Traces of India: Photography, Architecture, and the Politics of Representation, 1850–1900* (Montreal: Canadian Centre for Architecture and Yale Center for British Art, 2003); and Timothy Mitchell, *Colonising Egypt* (Berkeley: University of California Press, 1988).
10. William J. Morden, "By Coolie and Caravan across Central Asia," *National Geographic Magazine*, October 1927, 369.
11. J.R. Hildebrand, "The World's Greatest Overland Explorer," *National Geographic Magazine*, November 1928, 508.
12. Hildebrand, "World's Greatest Overland Explorer," 522.
13. In 2018, National Geographic acknowledged that for decades the magazine had reproduced racist stereotypes, particularly through its photography. For further details, see Susan Goldberg, "For Decades, Our Coverage Was Racist. To Rise above Our Past, We Must Acknowledge It," *National Geographic*, last modified March 12,

2018, https://www.nationalgeographic.com/magazine/2018/04/from-the-editor-race-racism-history/.

14. See, e.g., Frederick Simpich, "Manchuria, Promised Land of Asia," *National Geographic Magazine*, October 1929.

15. See A. Gayamov, "Soviet Music," *Soviet Travel*, 3, 1933, 8–11; and Boris Olenin, "Sukhum-Kaleh, City of Joy," *Soviet Travel*, 3, 1933, 15–17.

16. Elena Sudakova, ed., *See USSR: Intourist Posters and the Marketing of the Soviet Union* (London: GRAD Publishing, 2013), 77.

17. In Sweden and Germany, the films were shown under the titles of *Med Sven Hedin i Österled* and *Mit Sven Hedin durch Asiens Wüsten*, respectively. For a full-length version of the film, see S.L. James, "Swedish Mission Project," Internet Archive, uploaded September 29, 2009, video, 1:41:16, https://archive.org/details/swedish-mission-proj ect/sven-hedin-1928-expedition-through-the-gobi.avi.

18. de Terra, "On the World's Highest Plateaus."

19. de Terra, "On the World's Highest Plateaus," 363.

20. Walter Bosshard, *Hazards of Asia's Highlands & Deserts* (London: Figurehead, 1932).

21. Bosshard, *Hazards of Asia's Highlands & Deserts*, 87.

22. For detailed first-hand accounts of the expedition, see W. Pedro, "Mongolia, Kansu, and Sinkiang as Seen by a Member of the Haardt-Citroën Expedition," *Journal of the Royal Asiatic Central Asian Society* 20, no. 2 (1933): 205–19; and Joseph Hackin, "In Persia and Afghanistan with the Citroën Trans-Asiatic Expedition," *Geographical Journal* 83, no. 5 (1934): 353–61.

23. For a detailed explanation of this, see L.V.S. Blacker, "La Croisière Jaune," *Geographical Journal* 81, no. 1 (1933): 54–55.

24. "Scientists to Span Asia in Great Tour," *New York Times*, November 21, 1930, 22.

25. "Hear Radio from Asia: Amateurs Up-State Receive Haardt Expedition's Messages," *New York Times*, September 10, 1931, 22.

26. Georges-Marie Haardt, "The Trans-Asiatic Expedition Starts," *National Geographic Magazine*, June 1931, 782.

27. Haardt, "Trans-Asiatic Expedition Starts," 782.

28. "Haardt Scientific Expedition," *Gnowangerup Star and Tambellup-Ongerup Gazette*, September 3, 1932, 3.

29. "Across Asia," *Times* (London), March 16, 1931, 11.

30. Hmc62100, "Citroën la Croisière jaune part 1," uploaded March 25, 2011, YouTube video, 8:16, https://www.youtube.com/watch?v=6jzGQ-Te8b0&t=17s.

31. "The Screen; At the 55th Street Playhouse," *New York Times*, November 18, 1936.

32. Georges Le Fèvre, *An Eastern Odyssey* (Boston: Little Brown, 1935).

33. Edward Murray, "With the Nomads of Central Asia," *National Geographic Magazine*, January 1936.

34. The *National Geographic Magazine* depiction of the journey contrasts with the more scholarly account offered by Joseph Hackin in a talk to the Royal Geographic Society in November 1933. Hackin makes no reference to Marco Polo in an account that gave particular attention to the ethnography and geography of Afghanistan. See Hackin, "In Persia and Afghanistan with the Citroën Trans-Asiatic Expedition."

35. Murray, "With the Nomads of Central Asia," 50.

36. Ella Maillart, *Oasis Interdites: de Pékin au Cachemire* (Paris: Grasset, 1937); and Peter Fleming, *News from Tartary: An Epic Journey across Central Asia* (London: Tauris Parke Paperbacks, 2001), locs. 2127–29 of 5078, Kindle.

37. Fleming, *News from Tartary*, locs. 375–90 of 5078.

38. See, e.g., Daniel Waugh, "Silk Roads in History," *Expedition* 52, no. 3 (2010): 9–22; and Tamara Chin "The Invention of the Silk Road, 1877," *Critical Inquiry* 40, no. 1 (2013): 194–219.

39. Sven Hedin, *The Silk Road* (London: George Routledge and Sons, 1938), 228.

40. Amilcare Iannucci and John Tulk, "From Alterity to Holism: Cinematic Depictions of Marco Polo and His Travels," in *Marco Polo and the Encounter of East and West*, ed. Suzanne Conklin Akbari and Amilcare Ianucci (Toronto: University of Toronto, 2008), 210.

41. Iannucci and Tulk, "From Alterity to Holism," 211.

42. Suzanne Akbari, "Introduction: East, West, and In-between," in *Marco Polo and the Encounter of East and West*, ed. Suzanne Akbari and Amilcare Iannucci (Toronto: University of Toronto Press, 2008), 3–20.

43. See Lawrence Copley Thaw and Margaret S. Thaw, "Along the Old Silk Routes: A Motor Caravan with Air-Conditioned Trailer Retraces Ancient Roads from Paris across Europe and Half of Asia to Delhi," *National Geographic Magazine*, December 1940, 453–86.

44. Thaw and Thaw, "Along the Old Silk Routes," 453.

45. Travelfilmarchive, "From New Lands to Old, 1938," uploaded June 24, 2014, YouTube video, 25:15, https://www.youtube.com/watch?v=95BCZ9J2qq0.

Chapter 6

1. Milton J. Clark, "How the Kazakhs Fled to Freedom," *National Geographic Magazine*, November 1954, 621, 642.

2. William O. Douglas, "Journey to Outer Mongolia," *National Geographic Magazine*, March 1962, 289.

3. Douglas, "Journey to Outer Mongolia," 345.

4. See, e.g., Harrison E. Salisbury, "Centuries Roll Back in Central Asia to Life as in Genghis Khan's Day," *New York Times*, October 3, 1953; and Harrison E. Salisbury, "Mongolian Communist Line Vies with Genghis Khan's Tradition," *New York Times*, August 5, 1959.

5. For examples of this field of scholarship, see Greg Barnhisel, *Cold War Modernists: Art, Literature, and American Cultural Diplomacy* (New York: Columbia University Press, 2015); Beatriz Colomina, Annmarie Brennan and Jeannie Kim, eds., *Cold War Hothouses: Inventing Postwar Culture, from Cockpit to Playboy* (New York: Princeton Architectural Press, 2004); and Jessica C.E. Gienow-Hecht, ed., *Music and International History in the Twentieth Century* (New York: Berghann Books, 2015).

6. Luce Boulnois, *The Silk Road* (London: George Allen and Unwin, 1966).

7. Jan Myrdal, *The Silk Road: A Journey from the High Pamirs and Ili through Sinkiang and Kansu* (London: Victor Gollancz, 1980), 7.

8. Robert Collins, *East to Cathay: The Silk Road* (New York: McGraw-Hill Book Company, 1986).

9. Nile Green, "From the Silk Road to the Railroad (and Back): The Means and Meanings of the Iranian Encounter with China," *Iranian Studies* 48, no. 2 (2015): 165–92.

10. Directed by Denys de la Patellière, Raoul Lévy, and Noël Howard, the film was made as a co-production between Afghanistan, Egypt, France, Italy, and Yugoslavia.

11. Amilcare Iannucci and John Tulk, "From Alterity to Holism: Cinematic Depictions of Marco Polo and His Travels," in *Marco Polo and the Encounter of East and West*, ed. Suzanne Conklin Akbari and Amilcare Iannucci (Toronto: University of Toronto Press, 2008), 216.

12. For an overview of the film, see Brendan Davis, "Movie Review: Marco Polo (1975)," Celestial Pictures, last modified November 2, 2018, http://shawbrothersuniverse. com/movie-review-marco-polo-1975/.

13. Iannucci and Tulk, "From Alterity to Holism," 225.

14. Iannucci and Tulk, "From Alterity to Holism," 228.

15. Iannucci and Tulk, "From Alterity to Holism," 232.

16. See Dan Edwards, "Looking at/Looking in Antonioni's 'Chung Kuo, China': A Critical Reflection across Three Viewings," *Senses of Cinema*, last modified March 2015, http://sensesofcinema.com/2015/feature-articles/looking-at-looking-in-antonionis-chung-kuo-cina-a-critical-reflection-across-three-viewings/.

17. For further details, see: Susan Sontag, *On Photography* (London: Allen Lane, 1978).

18. In 1974, the Chinese newspaper *Renminh Ribao* published articles denouncing the film, with a subsequent English version published by Foreign Language Press a few months later under the title: "A Vicious Motive, Despicable Tricks—A Criticism of Antonioni's Anti-China Film 'China.'"

19. Umberto Eco, "De Interpretatione or the Difficulty of Being Marco Polo (On the Occasion of Antonioni's China Film)," trans. Christine Leefeldt, *Film Quarterly* 30, no. 4 (1977): 9.

20. Karl Schoenberger, "Exposition Celebrating Ancient Route Opens Today: Japan's 'Silk Road Fever' Hits All-Time High," *Los Angeles Times*, April 24, 1988, http://articles. latimes.com/1988-04-24/news/mn-2704_1_silk-road-series.

21. Schoenberger, "Exposition Celebrating Ancient Route Opens Today."

22. Che Muqi, *The Silk Road: Past and Present* (Beijing: Foreign Language Press, 1989), 4.

23. Che Muqi, *Silk Road*, 144.

24. Yu Quiyu, *A Bittersweet Journey through Culture* (New York: CN Times Books Inc., 2015), locs. 1273–83 of 5330, Kindle.

25. See, e.g., Lynn Salmon, "China—A Trip along the Silk Road (Part 1 of 3)," *A Trip along the Silk Roads—1991* (blog), *Does Something Smell Fishy*, Spring 1991, https:// www.thesalmons.org/lynn/china.html.

26. John King, *Karakoram Highway: The High Road to China* (Melbourne: Lonely Planet, 1989), 61.

27. David Hatcher Childress, *Lost Cities of China, Central Asia & India* (Kempton: Adventures Unlimited Press, 1998), loc. 3965 of 5229, Kindle.

28. Colin Thubron, *The Lost Heart of Asia* (London: Vintage Books, 1994); and William Dalrymple, *In Xanadu: A Quest* (New York: Harper Collins Publishers, 1989).

29. Childress, *Lost Cities of China, Central Asia & India*, loc. 3965 of 5229.

30. See "All Aboard for Russia," *Times* (London), January 9, 1993, 86; and Anne McElvoy, "The Silver Track to Tashkent," *Times* (London), January 1, 1994, 31.

31. See David Airey and Myra Shackley, "Tourism Development in Uzbekistan," *Tourism Management* 18, no. 4 (1997): 199–208.

32. "Samarkand to Bukhara," *Times* (London), February 20, 1993, 34; and Mike Gerrard, "Smooth Passage on the Old Silk Route," *Times* (London), May 6, 1995, 20.

33. See Jennifer Cody, "Tracking Travel: Focus on Japan," *Wall Street Journal*, June 7, 1994, B1.

34. In 1996, for example, the UNWTO cohosted a conference in Xi'an on tourism development in the region, including visa reforms for Silk Road itineraries. See David Churchill, "Plea to Open Silk Road to China and the East," *Times* (London), August 8, 1996, 20.

35. Cynthia Werner, "The New Silk Road: Mediators and Tourism Development in Central Asia," *Ethnology* 42, no. 2 (2003): 141–59.

36. Erica Marat, "Nation Branding in Central Asia: A New Campaign to Present Ideas about the State and the Nation," *Europe-Asia Studies* 61, no. 7 (2009): 1128.

37. This formed part of an advertisement placed in the *Economist* in December 2008. See "Country Advertisement of Kazakhstan," *Economist*, December 13, 2008, cited in Marat, "Nation Branding in Central Asia," 1129.

38. Marat, "Nation Branding in Central Asia," 1129.

39. See Airey and Shackley, "Tourism Development in Uzbekistan," 199–208; and William V. Gillen, "'Switzerland of Central Asia' Targets Tourism," *Washington Report on Middle East Affairs* 16, no. 2 (1997): 67.

40. For further details of this project, see Michael Barry Lane and Ronald Lewock, eds, *Rebuilding the Silk Road: Cultural Tourism and Revival of Heritage in Uzbekistan* (Paris: UNDP-UNESCO, 1996).

41. This was followed by the Khiva Declaration on Tourism and the Preservation of Cultural Heritage (1999); The Bukhara Declaration on Silk Road Tourism (2002); Astana Declaration (2009); and Shiraz Declaration (2010). See "Technical Cooperation and Silk Road Declarations," UNWTO, accessed December 7, 2018, https://www.unwto.org/declarations-silk-road.

42. UNWTO, "Summary of Silk Road Activities 1993–2011," UNWTO Silk Road Programme, accessed December 14, 2018, http://.silkroad.unwto.org/sites/all/files/docpdf/summaryofactivities1993-2011.pdf (site discontinued).

43. Werner, "The New Silk Road."

44. See Cynthia Beall and Melvyn Goldstein, "Past Becomes Future for Mongolian Nomads," *National Geographic Magazine*, May 1993; and Mike Edwards, "Sons of Genghis: The Great Khans," *National Geographic Magazine*, February 1997. See also Mike Edwards, "The Adventures of Marco Polo: Part I," *National Geographic Magazine*, May 2001; Mike Edwards, "The Adventures of Marco Polo: Part II," *National Geographic Magazine*, June 2001; and Mike Edwards, "The Adventures of Marco Polo: Part III," *National Geographic Magazine*, July 2001.

45. See, e.g., Frances Wood, *The Silk Road: Two Thousand Years in the Heart of Asia* (Berkeley: University of California Press, 2002); and Joyce Morgan and Conrad Walters, *Journeys on the Silk Road* (Guilford: Lyons Press, 2012).

46. UNWTO, *Western Silk Road Roadmap* (Madrid: UNWTO, 2018), 14–15. See also UNWTO, *The Potential of the Western Silk Road—Working Paper* (Madrid: UNWTO, 2017).

47. Tony Bennett, *Pasts beyond Memory: Evolution, Museums, Colonialism* (London: Routledge, 2004); Tony Bennett, *Museums, Power, Knowledge: Selected Essays* (London: Routledge, 2018); Jiat-Hwee Chang, *A Genealogy of Tropical Architecture* (London: Routledge, 2016); and Claire Lyons, John Papadopoulos, Lindsey Stewart, and Andrew Szegedy-Maszak, *Antiquity and Photography: Early Views of Ancient Mediterranean Sites* (Los Angeles: The J. Paul Getty Museum, 2005).

Part Three

1. Samuel P. Huntington, "The Clash of Civilizations?" *Foreign Affairs*, Summer 1993, https://www.foreignaffairs.com/articles/united-states/1993-06-01/clash-civilizations.

2. For an overview of the growth in civilization as a concept from the 1980s onward, see Johann Arnason, "Introduction: Domains and Perspectives of Civilizational Analysis," *European Journal of Social Theory* 13, no. 1 (2010): 5–13; and Edward Tiryakian, "Civilisational Analysis: Renovating the Sociological Tradition," in *Rethinking Civilizational Analysis*, ed. Saïd Amir Arjomand and Edward Tiryakian (London: SAGE Publications, 2010), 30–47.

Chapter 7

1. See Robert C. Hildebrand, *Dumbarton Oaks: The Origins of the United Nations and the Search for Postwar Security* (Chapel Hill: University of North Carolina Press, 1990), 25.

2. For a lengthy discussion of this issue, see Robert J. McMahon, ed., *The Cold War in the Third World* (Oxford: Oxford University Press, 2013), Kindle.

3. Elena Kuzmina, *The Prehistory of the Silk Road*, ed. Victor H. Mair (Philadelphia: University of Pennsylvania, 2008), 5–6.

4. See, e.g., Brian M. Fagan, *Return to Babylon: Travelers, Archaeologists, and Monuments in Mesopotamia* (Boulder: University of Colorado Press, 2007); Tapati Guha-Thakurta, *Monuments, Objects, Histories: Institutions of Art in Colonial and Postcolonial India* (New York: Columbia University Press, 2004); and Maurizio Peleggi, *Thailand: The Worldly Kingdom* (London: Reaktion, 2007).

5. Michael Clarke, *Xinjiang and China's Rise in Central Asia—A History* (London: Routledge, 2011), 7. See also Dru C. Gladney, *Dislocating China: Reflections on*

Muslims, Minorities, and Other Subaltern Subjects (London: University of Chicago Press, 2004).

6. William Preston Jr, "The History of U.S.-UNESCO Relations," in *Hope & Folly: The United States and UNESCO 1945–1985,* ed. William Preston Jr, Edward Herman, and Herbert Schiller (Minneapolis: University of Minnesota Press, 1989), 48.

7. Preston Jr, "The History of U.S.-UNESCO Relations," 51.

8. See Seng Tan and Amitav Acharya, eds, *Bandung Revisited: The Legacy of the 1955 Asian-African Conference for International Order* (Singapore: NUS Press, 2008).

9. Laura Wong, "Relocating East and West: UNESCO's Major Project on the Mutual Appreciation of Eastern and Western Cultural Values," *Journal of World History* 19, no. 3 (2008): 349–74.

10. Wong, "Relocating East and West," 349.

11. Japanese National Commission for UNESCO, ed., *Research in Japan in History of Eastern and Western Cultural Contacts: Its Development and Present Situation* (Tokyo: Japanese National Commission for UNESCO, 1957).

12. Matsuda Hisao, "General Survey: The Development of Researches in the History of the Intercourse between East and West in Japan," in *Research in Japan in History of Eastern and Western Cultural Contacts: Its Development and Present Situation,* ed. Japanese National Commission for UNESCO (Tokyo: Japanese National Commission for UNESCO, 1957), 7.

13. Matsuda, "General Survey," 3.

14. Matsuda, "General Survey," 8.

15. Mori Masao, "The Steppe Route," in *Research in Japan in History of Eastern and Western Cultural Contacts: Its Development and Present Situation,* ed. Japanese National Commission for UNESCO (Tokyo: Japanese National Commission for UNESCO, 1957), 19–34.

16. Matsuda Hisao, "The Central Asia in Ancient Times," in *Research in Japan in History of Eastern and Western Cultural Contacts: Its Development and Present Situation,* ed. Japanese National Commission for UNESCO (Tokyo: Japanese National Commission for UNESCO, 1957), 39.

17. Matsuda, "Central Asia in Ancient Times," 39.

18. These included Haneda Tōru and Ishida Mikinosuke. See Matsuda, "General Survey," 4.

19. See, e.g., Abe Takeo, "The Uigur History," in *Research in Japan in History of Eastern and Western Cultural Contacts: Its Development and Present Situation,* ed. Japanese National Commission for UNESCO (Tokyo: Japanese National Commission for UNESCO, 1957), 49–54.

20. Writing more than four decades later, Vadime Elisseeff also noted that Japanese scholarship on the Oasis Route shed new light on the history of the Tarim Basin in northwest China, stating that "its relationships with its neighbours: the north-south routes showed that, in addition to east-west flows, there were transverse currents which brought Turks and Tibetans into greater contact with others." Vadime Elisseeff, *The Silk Roads: Highways of Culture and Commerce* (New York: Berghahn Books, 2000), 13.

21. Matsuda Hisao and Fujieda Akira, "Editor's Notes," in *Research in Japan in History of Eastern and Western Cultural Contacts: Its Development and Present Situation*, ed. Japanese National Commission for UNESCO (Tokyo: Japanese National Commission for UNESCO, 1957), 3–4.

22. Ann Sherif, *Japan's Cold War: Media, Literature, and the Law* (New York: Columbia University Press, 2009), Kindle.

23. See Giles Scott-Smith and Charlotte A. Lerg, eds, *Campaigning Culture and the Global Cold War: The Journals of the Congress for Cultural Freedom* (London: Palgrave Macmillan, 2017), Kindle.

24. Preston Jr, "The History of U.S.-UNESCO Relations," 72.

25. Makoto Iokibe, "Introduction: Japanese Diplomacy from Prewar to Postwar," in *The Diplomatic History of Postwar Japan*, ed. Makoto Iokibe, trans. Robert D. Eldridge (Oxford: Routledge, 2011), loc. 214 of 456, Kindle.

26. For a detailed account of this period and the shifting diplomatic strategies of Japan toward China and the Soviet Union, see Sayuri Guthrie-Shimizu, "Japan, the United States, and the Cold War, 1945–1960," in *The Cambridge History of the Cold War*, ed. Melvyn P. Leffler and Odd Arne Westad, vol. 1, *Origins* (Cambridge: Cambridge University Press, 2010), 244–65, Kindle.

27. For further details of the association, see "Min-On Concert Association—Who We Are," Min-On Concert Association, accessed December 3, 2018, http://www.min-on.org/index.php/about-min-on/who-we-are.

28. Available at "Silk Road Series: A Series of 'Musical Voyages along the Silk Road,'" Min-On Concert Association, accessed December 3, 2018, http://www.min-on.org/index.php/cultural-exchange/silk-road-series.

29. "Silk Road Series: A Series of 'Musical Voyages along the Silk Road.'"

30. See Nagasawa Kazutoshi, "Silk Road Studies in Japan: Its History and Present Situation," *International Seminar for UNESCO Integral Study of the Silk Roads: Roads of Dialogue* (Osaka: UNESCO, 1988), 1–5, https://fr.unesco.org/silkroad/node/8892.

31. Boria Majumdar and Nalin Mehta, "Hybridity and Subversion: The Olympic Flame in India," in *Bearing Light: Flame Relays and the Struggle for the Olympic Movement*, ed. John J. MacAloon (Oxford: Routledge, 2013), 179, Kindle.

32. Majumdar and Mehta, "Hybridity and Subversion," 171.

33. "Japan Air Lines," *Times* (London), October 3, 1962, 3.

34. In an article marking the opening of the exhibition, the *Los Angeles Times* put the cost at US $82 million. See Karl Schoenberger, "Exposition Celebrating Ancient Route Opens Today: Japan's 'Silk Road Fever' Hits All-Time High," *Los Angeles Times*, April 24, 1988, http://articles.latimes.com/1988-04-24/news/mn-2704_1_silk-road-series.

35. See Schoenberger, "Exposition Celebrating Ancient Route Opens Today."

36. Silk Road Exposition, ed., "Explanation," in *The Sea Route: The Grand Exhibition of Silk Road Civilizations* (Nara: Nara National Museum, 1988), 150–222.

37. Egami Namio, "The Silk Road and Japan," in *The Sea Route: The Grand Exhibition of Silk Road Civilizations*, ed. Silk Road Exposition (Nara: Nara National Museum, 1988), 14.

38. Nagasawa observes that a number of young Japanese scholars were critical of this trend because it demoted Central Asia to merely being a point of transition and that, instead, "Silk Road history should be researched from the inside." See Nagasawa, "Silk Road Studies in Japan," 13.

39. Schoenberger, "Exposition Celebrating Ancient Route Opens Today," 2.

40. Silk Road Exposition, ed., *The Oasis and Steppe Routes: The Grand Exhibition of Silk Road Civilizations* (Nara: Nara National Museum, 1988), 9.

41. Silk Road Exposition, *Oasis and Steppe Routes*, 7.

42. Silk Road Exposition, *The Route of Buddhist Art: The Grand Exhibition of Silk Road Civilizations* (Nara: Nara National Museum, 1988), 13.

43. See, e.g., Japan International Cooperation Agency, "60 Years of Japanese ODA," *JICA's World*, January 2014, 1–16.

44. Ran Zwigenberg, *Hiroshima: The Origins of Global Memory Culture* (Cambridge: Cambridge University Press, 2014).

Chapter 8

1. For further details, see Jiang Zemin, "Full Text of Jiang's Speech to Saudi Eminent Persons" (Speech, Prince's Residence, Riyadh, Saudi Arabia, November 3, 1993), http://en.people.cn/features/Sixnation/txt/19991103A103.html.

2. See Karl Schoenberger, "Exposition Celebrating Ancient Route Opens Today: Japan's 'Silk Road Fever' Hits All-time High," *Los Angeles Times*, April 24, 1988, http://artic les.latimes.com/1988-04-24/news/mn-2704_1_silk-road-series.

3. UNESCO, "Rediscovering the Silk Roads," *UNESCO Courier*, November 1988, 12–15.

4. See Marie-Thérèse Bobot, "In Memoriam: Vadime Elisseeff (1918–2002)," *Arts Asiatiques* 57 (2002): 229–31.

5. Max Cerrans, "Vadime Elisseeff: A Taste for Universality," *UNESCO Sources*, September 1990, 5.

6. For further details, see Vadime Elisseeff, "The Roads of Dialogue," *Integral Study of the Silk Roads: Roads of Dialogue Newsletter*, October 1989, 1.

7. For further details of the project's aims and scope, see John Lawton, ed., *The Integral Study of the Silk Roads: Roads of Dialogue* (Paris: UNESCO, 2008). For a more detailed breakdown of the scholarship that fed into the program, see Vadime Elisseeff, *The Silk Roads: Highways of Culture and Commerce* (New York: Berghahn Books, 2000), 17.

8. See Elisseeff, *Silk Roads*.

9. UNESCO, "Project News 1990/1991," *Integral Study of the Silk Roads: Roads of Dialogue Newsletter*, Spring 1989, 6–7.

10. Federico Mayor, cited in Sun Yifu, *From Venice to Osaka—A Voyage into Ancient Chinese Civilisation: UNESCO Retraces the Maritime Silk Route* (Beijing: China Pictorial Publishing Press, 1992), 3.

11. Sun Yifu, *From Venice to Osaka*, 18.

12. François-Bernard Huyghe, "The Kingdom of Silla and the Treasures of Nara," *UNESCO Courier*, July 1991, 44.

13. Sun Yifu, *From Venice to Osaka*, 230–31.

14. Young-pil Kwon, "The Otani Collection," *Orientations* 20, no. 3 (1989): 53–63.

15. See Huyghe, "Kingdom of Silla and the Treasures of Nara," 46.

16. Huyghe, "Kingdom of Silla and the Treasures of Nara," 46.

17. Huyghe, "Kingdom of Silla and the Treasures of Nara," 45.

18. Sun Yifu, *From Venice to Osaka*, 245, 251.

19. François-Bernard Huyghe, "The Return of the Fulk al-Salamah," *UNESCO Courier*, August/September 1991, 80.

20. A number of research institutes were established during the program. They included a center dedicated to nomadic cultures in Ulaanbaatar, Mongolia, and the International Institute for Central Asian Studies in Samarkand. Institutes dedicated to Silk Road studies were also opened in China, Sri Lanka, and Japan. For an overview of these centers and institutes, see UNESCO, *Integral Study of the Silk Roads: Roads of Dialogue Newsletter*, 1995; and John Lawton, *Integral Study of the Silk Roads*.

21. For further details, see UNESCO, "Hirayama Fellowships," *Integral Study of the Silk Roads: Roads of Dialogue Newsletter*, 1995, 2–4.

22. The project was oriented around three key audiences, "academics, young people and the general public." Doudou Diène, "Foreword," in *Bibliographical Database—The Silk Roads: Roads of Dialogue*, ed. UNESCO, vol. 1 (Brussels: LORETO a.s.l.b., 1997), ii.

23. John Noble Wilford, "New Finds Suggest Even Earlier Trade on Fabled Silk Road," *New York Times*, March 16, 1993, https://www.nytimes.com/1993/03/16/science/new-finds-suggest-even-earlier-trade-on-fabled-silk-road.html#whats-next.

24. Wilford, "New Finds Suggest Even Earlier Trade on Fabled Silk Road."

25. At this time Diène was UNESCO's director for intercultural projects. See Diène, "Foreword," i.

26. Federico Mayor, "Preface of the Director-General of UNESCO," in *Integral Study of the Silk Roads: Roads of Dialogue*, ed. John Lawton (Paris: UNESCO, 2008), 3.

27. To be added to the World Heritage List, a site must reach a threshold of "Outstanding Universal Value."

28. For further details, see "The International Dunhuang Project: The Silk Road Online," British Library, accessed June 18, 2018, http://idp.bl.uk.

29. See Tim Winter, "Heritage Diplomacy," *International Journal of Heritage Studies* 21, no. 10 (2015): 997–1015.

30. Edward Wastnidge, *Diplomacy and Reform in Iran: Foreign Policy under Khatami* (London: I.B. Tauris, 2016).

31. For a comprehensive elaboration of the project's ambitions and commentaries on these, see UNESCO and United Nations, *Dialogue among Civilisations; The Round Table on the Eve of the United Nations Millennium Summit* (Paris: UNESCO, 2001).

32. See Evgeniy Kiy, "State Hermitage Museum," *Arts Asiatiques* 69 (2014): 173–76; and Olga Lundysheva and Anna Turanskaya, "Old Uyghur Fragments in the Serindia Collection: Provenance, Acquisition, Processing," *Written Monuments of the Orient* 6, no. 2.12 (2020): 43–64.

33. See Caren Dreyer, "The 'Turfan Files' in the Museum of Asian Art, Berlin," *The Silk Road* 18 (2020): 73–80.

34. For a detailed account of the housing of the Ōtani collection, see Ji Young Park, "Vestige of an Empire. Treasure of the Nation: Presenting the Ōtani Collection in China, Japan and Korea," in *Toward the Future: Museums and Art History in East Asia*, ed. Suzuki Hiroyuki and Akiyama Akira (Tokyo: Japanese Committee for CIHA, Comité International de l'Histoire de l'Art, and the Otsuka Museum of Art, 2020), 120–29. See also Kim Haewon, "A History of the Central Asian Collection at the National Museum of Korea," *The International Journal of Korean Art and Archaeology* 4 (2010):160–72.

35. See Éva Apor and Helen Wang, eds, *Catalogue of the Collections of Sir Aurel Stein in the Library of the Hungarian Academy of Sciences* (Budapest: Library of the Hungarian Academy of Sciences, 2002); and Helen Wang, ed., *Sir Aurel Stein, Colleagues and Collections* (London: British Museum, 2012).

36. Constance Chen, "Empire of Artifacts: U.S. Epistemological Colonialism in 1920s China," *Verge: Studies in Global Asias* 7, no. 1 (2021): 170–96.

37. Nathalie Monnet, "Two Inseparable Names, Dunhuang and Paul Pelliot," *The Institute of Oriental Philosophy Journal* 27 (2017): 57–60.

38. Cole Roskam, "Situating Chinese Architecture within 'A Century of Progress': The Chinese Pavilion, the Bendix Golden Temple, and the 1933 Chicago World's Fair," *Journal of the Society of Architectural Historians* 73, no. 3 (2014): 354.

39. For further details of this program, see Joseph Ting, *The Maritime Silk Route: 2000 Years of the South China Sea* (Hong Kong: Urban Council, 1996).

40. For further details, see " 'Sharing a Common Future': National Museum of China Exhibition 2019," Silk Road Futures, accessed December 2, 2019, https://www.silk roadfutures.net/sharing-a-common-future.

41. Xi Jinping, "Speech by H.E. Xi Jinping President of the People's Republic of China at UNESCO Headquarters" (Speech, UNESCO Headquarters, Paris, France, March 28, 2014), https://www.fmprc.gov.cn/mfa_eng/wjdt_665385/zyjh_665391/t1142560.shtml.

42. Ding Wei, "Jointly Building the Belt and Road in Cultural Areas" (Speech, Tianqiao Performing Arts Center, Beijing, China, October 21, 2016), http://www.srilt.org/en/symposium/27.html (site discontinued).

43. See Rana Mitter, *China's Good War: How World War II Is Shaping a New Nationalism* (Cambridge: Belknap Press, 2020); Tim Winter, "Geocultural Power: China's Belt and Road Initiative," *Geopolitics* (2020), doi.org/10.1080/14650045.2020.1718656; and Yang Yang, "Producing Multiple Imaginations of the Silk Road in Xi'an, China's Urban Development," *International Journal of Cultural Policy* 26, no. 6 (2020): 854–66.

44. Maria Carrai, "Chinese Political Nostalgia and Xi Jinping's Dream of Great Rejuvenation," *International Journal of Asian Studies* 18, no. 1 (2021): 7–25. See also James Millward, "We Need a New Approach to Teaching Modern Chinese History: We Have Lazily Repeated False Narratives for Too Long," *James A. Millward* (blog), October 9, 2020, https://jimmillward.medium.com/we-need-a-new-appro ach-to-teaching-modern-chinese-history-we-have-lazily-repeated-false-d24983bd7 ef2; Wang Gungwu, *China Reconnects: Joining a Deep-Rooted Past to a New World Order* (New Jersey: World Scientific, 2019); and Yujie Zhu and Christina Maags, *Heritage Politics in China: The Power of the Past* (London: Routledge, 2020).

45. CCTV English, "National Treasure, Season 2, Episode 1," uploaded July 26, 2019, YouTube video, 1:39:57, https://www.youtube.com/watch?v=J2LNHmC_67Q.

46. Afshin Majlesi, "Tehran Hosts Sino-Iranian Friendship Conference as Ancient Silk Road Backs to Life," *Tehran Times*, October 24, 2016, https://www.tehrantimes.com/news/407630/Tehran-hosts-Sino-Iranian-friendship-conference-as-ancient-Silk.

47. UNESCO and Republic of Korea Funds-in-Trust-Project, *Support for the Preparation for the World Heritage Serial Nomination of the Silk Roads in South Asia* (Paris: UNESCO, 2016), http://unesdoc.unesco.org/images/0024/002460/2460 96e.pdf.

48. UNESCO Kazakhstan, "At UNESCO, Kazakhstan's President Nazarbayev Calls for Intercultural Dialogue to Counter Extremism," UNESCO Kazakhstan, accessed July 18, 2018, http://www.unesco.kz/new/en/unesco/news/2998 (site discontinued).

49. UNESCO Kazakhstan, "UNESCO and 'The Centre for the Rapprochement of Cultures' in Kazakhstan Have Defined an Action Plan for the Intercultural Dialogue," UNESCO Kazakhstan, last modified August 5, 2016, http://en.unesco.kz/the-first-scientific-and-methodological-meeting-of-the-council-of-the-state-museum-of-the.

50. Vladislav Inozemtsev, "Why Kazakhstan Holds the Keys to the Global Economy," *The Independent* (UK), November 10, 2015, http://www.independent.co.uk/voices/why-kazakhstan-holds-the-keys-to-the-global-economy-a6727391.html; Matthew Kiernan, "Silk Road Key to China's Next Move," *Huffington Post*, August 31, 2015, http://www.huffingtonpost.com/matthew-j-kiernan/silk-road-key-to-china-n_b_8068318.html; and AKIPress, "Kazakh-Chinese Business Council Sign Deals Worth $10bn," Eurasian Business Briefing, last modified December 15, 2015, http://www.eurasianbusinessbriefing.com/10bn-worth-of-deals-signed-at-kazak-chinese-business-council/ (site discontinued).

51. See, e.g., "'The Silk Road Concert' Promoting Dialogue among Cultures Kicks-off at Palais des Nations, Co-organized by UNAOC and Fundación Onuart," United Nations Alliance of Civilizations, last modified October 16, 2017, https://www.unaoc.org/2017/10/the-silk-road-concert-promoting-dialogue-among-cultures; and "Al-Nasser Remarks at the High Level Symposium on the Synergies along the Silk Road for the 2030 Agenda for Sustainable Development," United Nations Alliance of Civilizations, last modified March 28, 2016, https://www.unaoc.org/2016/03/al-nasser-remarks-at-the-high-level-symposium.

52. Andrew Scobell, "Whither China's 21st Century Trajectory?," in *Routledge Handbook of Asian Security Studies*, ed. Sumit Ganguly, Andrew Scobell, and Joseph Liow Chin Long (London: Routledge, 2018), loc. 948 of 14784, Kindle.

Part Four

1. Robert Kaplan, *The Return of Marco Polo's World: War, Strategy, and American Interests in the Twenty-first Century* (New York: Penguin Random House, 2018).

2. Laurence Bergreen, *Marco Polo: From Venice to Xanadu* (New York: Knopf, 2007), quoted in Kaplan, *The Return of Marco Polo's World*, 11.

3. Kaplan, *Return of Marco Polo's World*, 12.
4. Kaplan, *Return of Marco Polo's World*, 11.
5. Kaplan, *Return of Marco Polo's World*, 11.
6. Martin J. Medhurst, Robert L. Ivie, Philip Wander, and Robert L. Scott, *Cold War Rhetoric: Strategy, Metaphor, and Ideology* (East Lansing: Michigan State University Press, 1997).

Chapter 9

1. A detailed description of Kaye's deployment of the term and its subsequent usage by others is offered by Seymour Becker, "The 'Great Game': The History of an Evocative Phrase," *Asian Affairs* 43, no. 1 (2012): 61–80.
2. This expression has been used by numerous authors over the course of the twentieth century. See, e.g., W.E. Wheeler, "The Control of Land Routes: Russian Railways in Central Asia," *Journal of the Royal Central Asian Society* 21, no. 4 (1934): 585–608.
3. See Sarah O'Hara, "Great Game or Grubby Game? The Struggle for Control of the Caspian," *Geopolitics* 9, no. 1 (2004): 138–60.
4. The article was published in the *Geographical Journal* in April the same year. See Halford Mackinder, "The Geographical Pivot of History," *Geographical Journal* 23, no. 4 (1904): 421–37.
5. Halford J. Mackinder, *Democratic Ideals and Reality: A Study in the Politics of Reconstruction*, rev. ed. (1919; repr., London: H. Holt, 1944), 113.
6. See Joseph J. Thorndike Jr, "Geopolitics: The Lurid Career of a Scientific System which a Briton Invented, the Germans Used and Americans Need to Study," *Life*, December 21, 1942, 106–15.
7. For further details, see Donald W. Meinig, "Heartland and Rimland in Eurasian History," *Western Political Quarterly* 9, no. 3 (1956): 553–69.
8. See Alfred Thayer Mahan, *The Influence of Sea Power upon History; 1660–1783* (Boston: Little, Brown and Co., 1890).
9. Nicholas J. Spykman, *The Geography of Peace* (New York: Harcourt & Brace, 1944), 43, quoted in Christopher J. Fettweis, "Sir Halford Mackinder, Geopolitics, and Policymaking in the 21st Century," *Parameters* 30, no. 2 (2000): 61.
10. For a more detailed account of Spykman's ideas and their impact, see Colin S. Gray, "Nicholas John Spykman, the Balance of Power, and International Order," *Journal of Strategic Studies* 38, no. 6 (2015): 873–97.
11. Meinig, "Heartland and Rimland in Eurasian History," 555.
12. Thorndike Jr, "Geopolitics," 109.
13. Meinig, "Heartland and Rimland in Eurasian History," 556.
14. Mackinder, "The Geographical Pivot of History," 434–36.
15. Lamb differentiates between the two as frontiers being zones and borders as clear divisions between sovereignties. On pages 4–7, he offers a more detailed explanation of this distinction and its historical usage in policy-making. See Alastair Lamb, *Asia Frontiers: Studies in a Continuing Problem* (London: Pall Mall Press, 1968), 4–7.

16. Lamb, *Asia Frontiers*, 16–17.

17. Lamb, *Asia Frontiers*, 35.

18. Robert McMahon similarly noted the prevalence of the "domino theory" within US policies toward the Third World, whereby similarities between countries and an inability to make individual decisions were among the assumptions held by strategists. See Andrew J. Rotter, "Culture, the Cold War, and the Third World," in *The Cold War in the Third World*, ed. Robert J. McMahon (New York: Oxford University Press, 2013), 170, Kindle.

19. Robert L. Ivie, "Metaphor and the Rhetorical Invention of Cold War 'Idealists,'" *Communications Monographs* 54, no. 2 (1987): 170.

20. See, e.g., Ian Cuthbertson, "The New 'Great Game,'" *World Policy Journal* 11, no. 4 (1995): 31–43; and Alexander Cooley, *Great Games, Local Rules: The New Great Power Contest in Central Asia* (New York: Oxford University Press, 2012).

21. See Matthew Edwards, "The New Great Game and the New Great Gamers: Disciples of Kipling and Mackinder," *Central Asian Survey* 22, no. 1 (2003): 83–102.

22. Bassin and Aksenov offer an interesting overview of the emergence of geopolitical theory in the post-Soviet period. See Mark Bassin and Konstantin E. Aksenov, "Mackinder and the Heartland Theory in Post-Soviet Geopolitical Discourse," *Geopolitics* 11 (2006): 99–118.

23. See Andrei Tsygankov, "Uses of Eurasia: The Kremlin, the Eurasian Union, and the Izborsky Club," in *Eurasia 2.0: Russian Geopolitics in the Age of New Media*, ed. Mark Bassin and Mikhail Suslov (Lanham: Rowman & Littlefield, 2016), 65.

24. See also Andrei Tsygankov, "Mastering Space in Eurasia: Russia's Geopolitical Thinking after the Soviet Break-up," *Communist and Post-Communist Studies* 36 (2003): 101–27.

25. As Clowes explains, the idea of the Heartland enabled Russian military and political strengths with coastal power. Edith W. Clowes, *Russia on the Edge: Imagined Geographies and Post-Soviet Identity* (Ithaca: Cornell University, 2011), x–xv.

26. In their article "Mackinder and the Heartland Theory in Post-Soviet Geopolitical Discourse," Mark Bassin and Konstantin Aksenov make a very similar argument in their analysis of the "strategic and civilizational" challenges Russian bureaucrats and public intellectuals faced in the post-Soviet era. See Bassin and Aksenov, "Mackinder and the Heartland Theory in Post-Soviet Geopolitical Discourse," 99–118.

27. See Dmitry V. Shlapentokh, "Eurasianism: Past and Present," *Communist and Post-Communist Studies* 30, no. 2 (1997): 129.

28. Mark Bassin, "Re-imagining World Spaces: The New Relevance of Eurasia," Humanities Futures: Franklin Humanities Institute, last modified April 24, 2015, https://humanitiesfutures.org/papers/re-imagining-world-spaces-new-relevance-eurasia/.

29. Shlapentokh, "Eurasianism: Past and Present," 129. See also Mark Bassin, "Eurasianism 'Classical' and 'Neo': The Lines of Continuity," *Slavic Eurasian Studies* no. 17 (2008): 279–94.

30. Bassin, "Eurasianism 'Classical' and 'Neo,'" 286.

31. See Clowes, *Russia on the Edge*, xiv. Nick Megoran also traces the influence Mackinder's ideas had on analysts in Russia, the United States, and Uzbekistan in the post–Cold War period. See Nick Megoran, "Revisiting the 'Pivot': The Influence of Halford Mackinder on Analysis of Uzbekistan's International Relations," *Geographical Journal* 170, no. 4 (2004): 347–58.

32. Zbigniew Brzezinski, "The Grand Chessboard: US Geostrategy for Eurasia," *Harvard International Review* 20, no. 1 (1998): 48–53.

33. See, e.g., Edwards, "New Great Game and the New Great Gamers," 83–102; and Megoran, "Revisiting the 'Pivot,'" 347–58.

34. See, e.g., Nicola Contessi, "Central Eurasia and the New Great Game: Players, Moves, Outcomes, and Scholarship," *Asian Security* 9, no. 3 (2013): 231–41; Tom Harper, "Towards an Asian Eurasia: Mackinder's Heartland Theory and the Return of China to Eurasia," *Cambridge Journal of Eurasian Studies* 1 (2017): 1–27; and Petar Kurečić, "The New Great Game: Rivalry of Geostrategies and Geoeconomics in Central Asia," *Hrvatski Geografski Glasnik* 72, no. 1 (2010): 21–48.

35. Alexander Maxwell, "Introduction, Bridges and Bulwarks: A Historiographic Overview of East-West Discourses," in *The East-West Discourse: Symbolic Geographic and its Consequences*, ed. Alexander Maxwell (Bern: Peter Land, 2011).

36. Yanik suggests that by the early 2000s the discourse had evolved from Turkey "bridging continents" to "bridging civilisations." See Lerna K. Yanik, "The Metamorphis of Metaphors of Vision: 'Bridging' Turkey's Location, Role and Identity after the End of the Cold War," *Geopolitics* 14, no. 3 (2009): 538–39.

37. For a detailed account of this, see Emre Erşen, "The Evolution of 'Eurasia' as a Geopolitical Concept in Post-Cold War Turkey," *Geopolitics* 18 (2013): 24–44.

38. Marlene Laruelle, "The US Silk Road: Geopolitical Imaginary or the Repackaging of Strategic Interests?," *Eurasian Geography and Economics* 56, no. 4 (2015): 360–75.

39. Kent Calder, *The New Continentalism: Energy and Twenty-First-Century Eurasian Geopolitics* (New Haven: Yale University Press, 2012).

40. Nadège Rolland, *China's Eurasian Century? Political and Strategic Implications of the Belt and Road Initiative* (Seattle: National Bureau of Asian Research, 2017), 9.

41. Dennis Mootz, "Stamps and Propaganda," *Journal of the History Teachers' Association of NSW* December (2016): 30.

42. Hashimoto Ryutaro, "Address to the Japan Association of Corporate Executives" (Speech, Japan Association of Corporate Executives, Tokyo, Japan, July 24, 1997), www.Japan.kantei.go.jp/0731douyuukai.html (site discontinued), quoted in Timur Dadabaev, "'Silk Road' as Foreign Policy Discourse: The Construction of Chinese, Japanese and Korean Engagement Strategies in Central Asia," *Journal of Eurasian Studies* 9 (2018): 35.

43. For an alternative account of this period of Japanese foreign policy in Central Asia, see Laruelle, "The US Silk Road"; and Timur Dadabaev, "Engagement and Contestation: The Entangled Imagery of the Silk Road," *Cambridge Journal of Eurasian Studies* 2 (2018): 1–14.

44. Christopher Len divides Japan's post-Soviet engagement with Central Asia into a series of stages, culminating with the Arc of Freedom and Prosperity Initiative. For further

details, see Christopher Len, "Understanding Japan's Central Asian Engagement," in *Japan's Silk Road Diplomacy: Paving the Road Ahead*, ed. Christopher Len, Uyama Tomohiko, and Hirose Tetsuya (Washington, DC: Central Asia-Caucasus Institute and Silk Road Studies Program, 2008), 31–46.

45. For further details, see Laruelle, "US Silk Road," 360–75; and Dadabaev, "Engagement and Contestation," 1–14.

46. Rachel Brown, "Where Will the New Silk Road Lead? The Effects of Chinese Investment and Migration in Xinjiang and Central Asia," *Columbia University Journal of Politics and Society* 26 (2016): 72–74.

47. For further details, see Michael Clarke, "The Belt and Road Initiative: China's New Grand Strategy?," *Asia Policy* 24 (2017): 71–79.

48. "H.R. 2867 - 105th Congress: Silk Road Strategy Act of 1997," GovTrack, accessed June 26, 2018, https://www.govtrack.us/congress/bills/105/hr2867.

49. S. Frederick Starr, "Introduction," in *The New Silk Roads: Transport and Trade in Greater Central Asia*, ed. S. Frederick Starr (Washington, DC: Central Asia-Caucasus Institute, 2007), 5.

50. Hillary Rodham Clinton, "Secretary of State Hillary Rodham Clinton Speaks on India and the United States: A Vision for the 21st century" (Speech, Anna Centenary Library, Chennai, India, July 20, 2011), https://2009-2017.state.gov/secretary/2009 2013clinton/rm/2011/07/168840.htm, quoted in Laruelle, "US Silk Road," 363.

51. See Laruelle, "US Silk Road." Michael Clarke also offers a helpful overview of this period of US foreign policy in Central Asia. See Michael Clarke, "The Belt and Road Initiative: Exploring Beijing's Motivations and Challenges for its New Silk Road," *Strategic Analysis* 42, no. 2 (2018): 84–102.

52. Andrew C. Kuchins, "The Northern Distribution Network and the Modern Silk Road: Planning for Afghanistan's Future," Center for Strategic and International Studies, last modified December 17, 2009, https://www.csis.org/analysis/northern-distribution-network-and-modern-silk-road.

53. Christina Y. Lin, "China, Iran, and North Korea: A Triangular Strategic Alliance," Rubin Center—Research in International Affairs, last modified March 5, 2010, http://www.rubincenter.org/2010/03/lin-2010-03-05/ (site discontinued).

54. Melinda Liu, "Beijing's New High-Speed Rail Line," *Newsweek*, May 9, 2010, https://www.newsweek.com/beijings-new-high-speed-rail-line-70221.

55. Asian Development Bank, *The New Silk Road: Ten Years of the Central Asia Regional Economic Cooperation Program* (Manila: Asian Development Bank, 2011).

56. Patrick Byrne, "China and Turkey—Building a New Silk Road Together," *China.org. cn*, January 4, 2012, http://www.china.org.cn/opinion/2012-01/04/content_24322 020.htm.

57. Laruelle, "US Silk Road," 361.

58. Dadabaev, "Engagement and Contestation," 10; and Dadabaev, "'Silk Road' as Foreign Policy Discourse," 30–41.

59. Dadabaev, "Engagement and Contestation," 10.

60. Dadabaev, "Engagement and Contestation," 13.

Chapter 10

1. Wu Jianmin, "'One Belt and One Road,' Far-reaching Initiative," *China-US Focus*, March 26, 2015, http://www.chinausfocus.com/finance-economy/one-belt-and-one-road-far-reaching-initiative/.
2. Yang Jiechi, "Jointly Undertake the Great Initiatives with Confidence and Mutual Trust" (Speech, Boao Forum for Asia Annual Conference, Bo'ao, Hainan, April 10, 2014), http://www.fmprc.gov.cn/mfa_eng/wjdt_665385/zyjh_665391/t1145860.shtml.
3. David Arase, "China's Two Silk Roads Initiative: What It Means for Southeast Asia," *Southeast Asian Affairs* 2015, no. 1 (2015): 28. Russia's initial reluctance to be part of BRI and its subsequent embrace of the project is detailed by Sebastien Peyrouse, "The Evolution of Russia's Views on the Belt and Road Initiative," *Asia Policy* 24 (2017): 96–102.
4. Syed Tariq Fatemi, "Speech by Special Assistant to the Prime Minister Syed Tariq Fatemi at the Karachi Council of Foreign Relations" (Speech, Karachi Council on Foreign Relations, Islamabad, Pakistan, February 2, 2015), http://www.mofa.gov.pk/chile/pr-details.php?prID=2546 (site discontinued).
5. See Christian Bouchard and William Crumplin, "Neglected No Longer: The Indian Ocean at the Forefront of World Geopolitics and Global Geostrategy," *Journal of the Indian Ocean* 6, no. 1 (2010): 26–51.
6. For a lengthier discussion of this period, see Chandra Kumar, "The Indian Ocean: Arc of Crisis or Zone of Peace?," *International Affairs* 60, no. 2 (1984): 233–46.
7. B. Vivekanandan, "The Indian Ocean as a Zone of Peace: Problems and Prospects," *Asian Survey* 21, no. 12 (1981): 1237.
8. Bouchard and Crumplin, "Neglected No Longer," 27.
9. See Bouchard and Crumplin, "Neglected No Longer," 39; and Heidelberg Institute for International Conflict Research, *Conflict Barometer 2009: Crises - Wars - Coups d'État - Negotiations - Mediations - Peace Settlements* (Heidelberg: Heidelberg Institute for International Conflict Research, 2009).
10. Kai Schultz, "Sri Lanka, Struggling with Debt, Hands a Major Port to China," *New York Times*, December 12, 2017, https://www.nytimes.com/2017/12/12/world/asia/sri-lanka-china-port.html; and Kiran Stacey, "China Signs 99-Year Lease on Sri Lanka's Hambantota Port," *Financial Times*, December 11, 2017, https://www.ft.com/content/e150ef0c-de37-11e7-a8a4-0a1e63a52f9c.
11. See, e.g., Abhijit Singh, "Sri Lanka's Quest for Strategic Prominence in the Indian Ocean," *Diplomat*, December 9, 2016, https://thediplomat.com/2016/12/sri-lankas-quest-for-strategic-prominence-in-the-indian-ocean; and "Sri Lanka's PM Delivers 2017 Deakin Law Oration," Deakin University, last modified March 13, 2017, http://www.deakin.edu.au/about-deakin/news/articles/sri-lankas-pm-delivers-2017-deakin-law-oration.
12. Ambassador Prasad Kariyawasam, "Sri Lanka—A Hub in the Indian Ocean" (Speech, East West Center, Honolulu, Hawai'i, February 11, 2016), http://slembassyusa.org/embassy_press_releases/remarks-by-ambassador-prasad-kariyawasam-at-the-east-west-center-hawaii-sri-lanka-a-hub-in-the-indian-ocean/ (site discontinued).

13. Menik Wakkumbura, "SL's Maritime Affairs in Changing Indian Ocean," *Daily Mirror (Sri Lanka)*, October 11, 2018, http://www.dailymirror.lk/article/SL-s-Marit ime-Affairs-in-Changing-Indian-Ocean-156710.html.

14. See Tim Winter, *Geocultural Power: China's Quest to Revive the Silk Roads for the Twenty-First Century* (Chicago: University of Chicago Press, 2019), Chapter 4.

15. Robert D. Kaplan, *Monsoon: The Indian Ocean and the Future of American Power* (New York: Random House, 2010), 19.

16. For further details, see: Kumar Vikram, "Project Mausam Runs into Rough Weather," *New Indian Express*, January 22, 2017, http://www.newindianexpress.com/thesun daystandard/2017/jan/21/project-mausam-runs-into-rough-weather-1562182.html.

17. Andrew Korybko, "What Could India's 'Cotton Route' Look Like?," *Sputnik International*, March 29, 2015, http://sputniknews.com/columnists/20150329/102 0170021.html.

18. Adwita Rai, "Silk, Cotton and Cinnamon: Maritime Renaissance of the Indian Ocean," *International Fleet Review (IFR) Series* (New Delhi: National Maritime Foundation, 2016), http://maritimeindia.org/View%20Profile/636437227516774 253.pdf (site discontinued).

19. See Teresita Schaffer and Howard Schaffer, *India at the Global High Table: The Quest for Regional Primacy and Strategic Autonomy* (Uttar Pradesh: Harper Collins, 2016).

20. Debasish Roy Chowdhury, "Quad Is Key to Biden's Strategy in Asia, but the Four-Way Alliance Is Ambiguous and Contradictory," *Time*, March 18, 2021, https://time.com/ 5947674/quad-biden-china/.

21. Rory Medcalfe, *Contest for the Indo-Pacific: Why China Won't Map the Future* (Melbourne: Schwartz Books Pty. Limited, 2020), loc. 273 of 811, Kindle.

22. Marlene Laruelle, "The US Silk Road: Geopolitical Imaginary or the Repackaging of Strategic Interests?," *Eurasian Geography and Economics* 56, no. 4 (2015): 369.

23. Laruelle, "US Silk Road," 370.

24. In 2018, Bruno Maçães bizarrely declared the "dawn" of Eurasia had arrived, whereby the latter was not merely a term of geography but "a certain way of thinking about a new moment in political history." Bruno Maçães, *The Dawn of Eurasia: On the Trail of the New World Order* (London: Allen Lane, 2018), loc. 341 of 377, Kindle.

25. Andrew Sheng, "OBOR and EuroAsia's New Great Game," *China Report* 53, no. 2 (2017): 249.

26. Among the many examples that could be cited for this, see Chad Pillai, "The Great Game in the Indian Ocean: Strategic Partnership Opportunities for the U.S.," Center for International Maritime Security, last modified May 29, 2018, http://cim sec.org/great-game-indian-ocean-strategic-partnership-opportunities-u-s/36590; and Garima Mohan, "Great Game in the Indian Ocean," Carnegie India, last mod- ified June 11, 2018, https://carnegieindia.org/2018/06/11/great-game-in-ind ian-ocean-pub-76666.

27. Chris Hann, for example, states that "Eurasia as I use the word, is composed prima- rily of the landmass that is conventionally divided into the two continents of Asia and Europe." See Chris Hann, "A Concept of Eurasia," *Current Anthropology* 57, no. 1 (2016): 1–27; see also Abbott Gleason, "Eurasia: What Is It? Is It?," *Journal of Eurasian*

Studies 1 (2010): 26–32; and Xing Li and Wang Wan, "'The Silk Road Economic Belt' and the 'China Dream' Relationship: A Strategy or Tactic," *Sociology Study* 5, no. 3 (2015): 170–71.

28. See Nicola Contessi, "Central Eurasia and the New Great Game: Players, Moves, Outcomes, and Scholarship," *Asian Security* 9, no. 3 (2013): 231–41. Examples of Contessi's argument can be found in Victor A. Shnirelman, "To Make a Bridge: Eurasian Discourse in the Post-Soviet World," *Anthropology of East Europe Review* 27, no. 2 (2009): 68–85; and Paradorn Rangsimaporn, "Interpretations of Eurasianism: Justifying Russia's Role in East Asia," *Europe-Asia Studies* 58, no. 3 (2006): 371–89.

29. Hann, "A Concept of Eurasia," 1–27.

Chapter 11

1. For a discussion of Belt and Road studies as a domain of scholarship, see James Sidaway, Simon Rowedder, Chih Yuan Woon, and Weiqiang Lin, "Introduction: Research Agendas Raised by the Belt and Road Initiative," *EPC: Politics and Space* 38, no. 5 (2020): 795–847.

2. See, for example, "Associations and Networks," Silk Road Futures, accessed February 19, 2020, https://www.silkroadfutures.net/associations-and-networks.

3. "Associations and Networks," Silk Road Futures.

4. Akira Iriye, *Cultural Internationalism and World Order* (Baltimore: John Hopkins University Press, 1997).

5. Mark Mazower, *Governing the World: The History of an Idea* (London: Penguin Press, 2012), 72.

6. See Mazower, *Governing the World*; Hugo Dobson, "Global Governance and the Group of Seven/Eight," in *Global Governance and Japan: The Institutional Architecture*, ed. Glenn Hook and Hugo Dobson (London: Routledge, 2007), 23–39; and Glenda Sluga, *Internationalism in the Age of Nationalism* (Philadelphia: University of Pennsylvania Press, 2013).

7. Established in Geneva in 1922 and running through to 1946, the committee promoted international exchange between scientists, researchers, teachers, artists, and intellectuals and included such dignitaries as Henri Bergson, Marie Curie, and Albert Einstein, among others.

8. See Duncan Bell, *Reordering the World: Essays on Liberalism and Empire* (Princeton: Princeton University Press, 2016), Chapter 2.

9. See, e.g., Ziya Öniş and Mustafa Kutlay, "The New Age of Hybridity and Clash of Norms: China, BRICS, and Challenges of Global Governance in a Postliberal International Order," *Alternatives: Global, Local, Political* 45, no. 3 (2020): 123–42; and Jessica Chen Weiss and Jeremy Wallace, "Domestic Politics, China's Rise, and the Future of the Liberal International Order," *International Organization* 75, no. 2 (2021): 635–64.

10. See Shaun Lin, James Sidaway, and Chih Yuan Woon, "Reordering China, Respacing the World: Belt and Road Initiative (一带一路) as an Emergent Geopolitical Culture," *The Professional Geographer* 71, no. 3 (2019): 507–22.

11. Zou Dongxin, "PRC Medical Internationalism: From Cold War to COVID-19," ARI Scope, last modified January 21, 2021, https://ari.nus.edu.sg/ariscope/prc-medical-internationalism-from-cold-war-to-covid-19/.

12. Emma Mawdsley, "South–South Cooperation 3.0? Managing the Consequences of Success in the Decade Ahead," *Oxford Development Studies* 47, no. 3 (2019): 266.

13. Chaw Chaw Sein, "Background and Significance," in *Research Report on ASEAN-China Cooperation in the Fight against COVID-19*, ed. University of Yangon and NACAI Secretariat (Yangon: University of Yangon and NACAI Secretariat, 2020), 3, http://www.iis.fudan.edu.cn/_upload/article/files/e0/a2/2242e2114e8a9d43482b7f4ae2b0/7b8e2bac-5c27-4316-a92f-140c52e3c0ee.pdf#page=37.

14. Ngeow Chow-Bing, "COVID-19, Belt and Road Initiative and the Health Silk Road: Implications for Southeast Asia," in *Research Report on ASEAN-China Cooperation in the Fight against COVID-19*, ed. University of Yangon and NACAI Secretariat (Yangon: University of Yangon and NACAI Secretariat, 2020), 34, http://www.iis.fudan.edu.cn/_upload/article/files/e0/a2/2242e2114e8a9d43482b7f4ae2b0/7b8e2bac-5c27-4316-a92f-140c52e3c0ee.pdf#page=37.

15. See, e.g., Suisheng Zhao, "Why China's Vaccine Diplomacy Is Winning," East Asia Forum, last modified April 29, 2021, https://www.eastasiaforum.org/2021/04/29/why-chinas-vaccine-diplomacy-is-winning/; and Jennifer Hillman and Alex Tippett, "A Robust U.S. Response to China's Health Diplomacy Will Reap Domestic and Global Benefits," Council on Foreign Relations, last modified April 15, 2021, https://www.thinkglobalhealth.org/article/robust-us-response-chinas-health-diplomacy-will-reap-domestic-and-global-benefits.

16. Ted Piccone, *China's Long Game on Human Rights at the United Nations* (Washington, DC: Brookings Institute, 2018); and Mika-Matti Taskien, "On Building a Community of Shared Future for the United Nations: Analysis on China's Performance in the United Nations General Assembly 2013–2018" (master's thesis, University of Helsinki, 2020), https://helda.helsinki.fi/handle/10138/314319.

17. "Status of Contributions to the Regular Budget as at 17 December 2020," UNESCO, accessed December 19, 2020, http://www.unesco.org/new/en/member-states/mscontent/status-of-contributions/.

18. "The International Network for the Silk Roads Programme," UNESCO, accessed November 12, 2020, https://en.unesco.org/silkroad/international-network-silk-roads-programme.

19. Kearrin Sims et al., "Global Development," in *Routledge Handbook of Global Development*, ed. Kearrin Sims et al. (London: Routledge), Forthcoming.

20. H.E. Nassir Abdulaziz Al-Nasser, "Remarks by H.E. Nassir Abdulaziz Al-Nasser the High Representative for the United Nations Alliance of Civilizations" (Speech, High Level Symposium on the Synergies along the Silk Road for the 2030 Agenda for Sustainable Development, New York, March 28, 2016), https://www.unaoc.org/2016/03/al-nasser-remarks-at-the-high-level-symposium/; and "Youth Eyes on the

Silk Roads Photo Contest," UNESCO Youth Eyes on the Silk Roads Photo Contest, accessed December 18, 2020, https://unescosilkroadphotocontest.org/.

21. There are a small number of article-length studies that highlight some of the ways in which civilization has regained currency within Belt and Road diplomacy. See, e.g., Xie Laihui, "The Belt and Road Initiative and the Road Connecting Different Civilisations," in *Routledge Handbook of the Belt and Road*, ed. Cai Fang and Peter Nolan (London: Routledge, 2019), 165–70; Carolijn van Noort, *China's Communication of the Belt and Road Initiative: Silk Road and Infrastructure Narratives* (London: Routledge, 2021); and Juan Carlos Moreno Garcia, "Egyptology and Global History: Between Geocultural Power and the Crisis of Humanities," *Journal of Egyptian History* 13 (2020): 29–76.

22. For a discussion of solidarity and South–South cooperation, see Veit Bachmann, Rirhandu Mageza-Barthel, and Emma Mawdsley, "The Politics of Development Geographies: New Partners, Transdisciplinary Perspectives—A Conversation with Emma Mawdsley," *Erdkunde* 74, no. 3 (2020): 205–17.

23. See Shahar Hameiri and Lee Jones, "China Challenges Global Governance? Chinese International Development Finance and the AIIB," *International Affairs* 94, no. 3 (2018): 573–93; Yi Edward Yang, "China's Strategic Narratives in Global Governance Reform under Xi Jinping," *Journal of Contemporary China* 30, no. 128 (2021): 299–313; and Scott Kastner and Margaret Pearson, "China and Global Governance: Opportunistic Multilateralism," *Global Policy* 11, no. 1 (2020): 164–69.

24. Scott Kennedy, "Introduction: Learning to Be Insiders," in *Global Governance and China: The Dragon's Learning Curve*, ed. Scott Kennedy (London: Routledge, 2018), loc. 776 of 916, Kindle.

25. H. Köchler, "Civilization as an Instrument of World Order? The Role of the Civilizational Paradigm in the Absence of a Balance of Power" (Lecture, International Symposion on "Civilizations and World Orders," Istanbul, Turkey, May 13, 2006).

26. George Orwell, *Nineteen Eighty-Four* (London: Harvill Secker, 1949).

27. For an overview of why "history matters," see Lynn Hunt, *History: Why It Matters* (Cambridge: Polity, 2018); Lynn Hunt, *Writing History in the Global Era* (New York: W.W. Norton & Company, 2015), Kindle.

28. James C. Scott, *The Art of Not Being Governed: An Anarchist History of Upland Southeast Asia* (New Haven: Yale University Press, 2009), 33–34.

29. For a fascinating discussion of such issues, see Juan Carlos Moreno Garcia, "Egyptology and Global History: An Introduction," *Journal of Egyptian History* 13 (2020): 5–10; and Manuel Perez-Garcia and Lucio De Sousa, eds, *Global History and New Polycentric Approaches: Europe, Asia and the Americas in a World Network System* (Singapore: Palgrave Macmillan, 2018).

30. Eckhardt Fuchs, "Introduction: Provincializing Europe," in *Across Cultural Borders: Historiography in Global Perspective*, ed. Eckhardt Fuchs and Benedikt Stuchtey (Lanham: Rowman & Littlefield Publishers, 2002), locs. 83–497, Kindle.

31. See Xin Fan, *World History and National Identity in China: The Twentieth Century* (Cambridge: Cambridge University Press, 2021), Kindle.

32. See Christopher Bayly, *The Birth of the Modern World 1780–1914: Global Connections and Comparisons* (Oxford: Blackwell, 2012).

33. Lincoln Paine, *The Sea and Civilization: A Maritime History of the World* (London: Atlantic Books, 2014).

34. See Akita Shigeru, Liu Hong, and Momoki Shiro, eds, *Changing Dynamics: Mechanisms of Maritime Asia in Comparative Perspectives* (Singapore: Palgrave Macmillan, 2021).

35. Svetlana Boym, *The Future of Nostalgia* (New York: Basic Books, 2001), xvii.

36. Franck Billé, "Auratic Geographies: Buffers, Backyards Entanglements," *Geopolitics* (2021), https://doi.org/10.1080/14650045.2021.1881490.

37. See, for example, Manuel Perez-Garcia, *Global History with Chinese Characteristics: Autocratic States along the Silk Road in the Decline of the Spanish and Qing Empires 1680–1796* (Singapore: Palgrave Macmillan, 2021).

38. For example, the Centro di Ricerca Marco Polo, Centre for Global Europe-Asia Connections, https://www.unive.it/pag/36676.

Bibliography

A Trip along the Silk Roads—1991 (blog). *Does Something Smell Fishy.* https://www.the salmons.org/lynn/china.html.

Abe Takeo. "The Uigur History." In *Research in Japan in History of Eastern and Western Cultural Contacts: Its Development and Present Situation,* edited by Japanese National Commission for UNESCO, 49–54. Tokyo: Japanese National Commission for UNESCO, 1957.

Abu El Haj, Nadia. *Facts on the Ground: Archaeological Practice and Territorial Self-Fashioning in Israeli Society.* Chicago: University of Chicago Press, 2001.

Airey, David, and Myra Shackley. "Tourism Development in Uzbekistan." *Tourism Management* 18, no. 4 (1997): 199–208.

Akbari, Suzanne. "Introduction: East, West, and In-between." In *Marco Polo and the Encounter of East and West,* edited by Suzanne Akbari and Amilcare Iannucci, 3–20. Toronto: University of Toronto Press, 2008.

AKIPress. "Kazakh-Chinese Business Council Sign Deals Worth $10bn." Eurasian Business Briefing. Last modified December 15, 2015. http://www.eurasianbusinessbriefing.com/10bn-worth-of-deals-signed-at-kazak-chinese-business-council/ (site discontinued).

Akita Shigeru, Liu Hong, and Momoki Shiro, eds. *Changing Dynamics Mechanisms of Maritime Asia in Comparative Perspectives.* Singapore: Palgrave Macmillan, 2021.

Al-Nasser, H.E. Nassir Abdulaziz. "Remarks by H.E. Nassir Abdulaziz Al-Nasser the High Representative for the United Nations Alliance of Civilizations." Speech at the High Level Symposium on the Synergies along the Silk Road for the 2030 Agenda for Sustainable Development, New York, March 28, 2016. https://www.unaoc.org/2016/03/al-nasser-remarks-at-the-high-level-symposium/.

Al-Sīrāfī, Abū Zayad. *Accounts of China and India.* Translated by Tim Mackintosh-Smith. New York: New York University Press, 2017.

Apor, Éva, and Helen Wang, eds. *Catalogue of the Collections of Sir Aurel Stein in the Library of the Hungarian Academy of Sciences.* Budapest: Library of the Hungarian Academy of Sciences, 2002.

Arase, David. "China's Two Silk Roads Initiative: What It Means for Southeast Asia." *Southeast Asian Affairs* no. 1 (2015): 25–45.

Arnason, Johann. "Introduction: Domains and Perspectives of Civilizational Analysis." *European Journal of Social Theory* 13, no. 1 (2010): 5–13.

Arnason, Johann. "The Rediscovery of Civilizations." In *Civilizations in Dispute: Historical Questions and Theoretical Traditions,* edited by Johann Arnason, 1–65. Leiden: Brill, 2003.

Arnason, Johann. *Social Theory and Japanese Experience: The Dual Civilization.* London: Kegan Paul, 1997.

Arnason, Johann. "The Southeast Asian Labyrinth: Historical and Comparative Perspectives." *Thesis Eleven* no. 50 (1997): 99–122.

Asian Development Bank. *The New Silk Road: Ten Years of the Central Asia Regional Economic Cooperation Program*. Manila: Asian Development Bank, 2011.

Aydin, Cemil. *The Politics of Anti-Westernism in Asia: Visions of World Order in Pan-Islamic and Pan-Asian Thought*. New York: Columbia University Press, 2007. Kindle.

Bachmann, Veit, Rirhandu Mageza-Barthel, and Emma Mawdsley. "The Politics of Development Geographies: New Partners, Transdisciplinary Perspectives—A Conversation with Emma Mawdsley." *Erdkunde* 74, no. 3 (2020): 205–17.

Baedeker, Karl. *Russia, with Teheran, Port Arthur, and Peking; Handbook for Travellers*. Leipzig: Karl Baedeker, 1914.

Bakhtin, Mikhail M. "The Epic and the Novel: Towards a Methodology for the Study in the Novel." In *The Dialogic Imagination, Four Essays by Mikhail Bakhtin*, edited by Michael Holquist, 3–40. Austin: University of Texas Press, 1981.

Barnhisel, Greg. *Cold War Modernists: Art, Literature, and American Cultural Diplomacy*. New York: Columbia University Press, 2015.

Bassin, Mark. "Eurasianism 'Classical' and 'Neo': The Lines of Continuity." *Slavic Eurasian Studies* no. 17 (2008): 279–94.

Bassin, Mark. "Re-imagining World Spaces: The New Relevance of Eurasia." Humanities Futures: Franklin Humanities Institute. Last modified April 24, 2015. https://humanitiesfutures.org/papers/re-imagining-world-spaces-new-relevance-eurasia/.

Bassin, Mark, and Konstantin E. Aksenov. "Mackinder and the Heartland Theory in Post-Soviet Geopolitical Discourse." *Geopolitics* 11 (2006): 99–118.

Bayly, Christopher. *The Birth of the Modern World 1780–1914: Global Connections and Comparisons*. Oxford: Blackwell, 2012.

Beall, Cynthia, and Melvyn Goldstein. "Past Becomes Future for Mongolian Nomads." *National Geographic Magazine*, May 1993.

Becker, Seymour. "The 'Great Game': The History of an Evocative Phrase." *Asian Affairs* 43, no. 1 (2012): 61–80.

Beckwith, Christopher. *Empires of the Silk Road: A History of Central Eurasia from the Bronze Age to the Present*. Princeton: Princeton University Press, 2009.

Bell, Duncan. *Reordering the World: Essays on Liberalism and Empire*. Princeton: Princeton University Press, 2016.

Bennett, Tony. "The Exhibitionary Complex." *New Formations* no. 4 (1988): 73–102.

Bennett, Tony. *Museums, Power, Knowledge: Selected Essays*. London: Routledge, 2018.

Bennett, Tony. *Pasts beyond Memory: Evolution, Museums, Colonialism*. London: Routledge, 2004.

Berger, Stefan. "National Museums in between Nationalism, Imperialism and Regionalism, 1750–1914." In *National Museums and Nation-Building in Europe 1750–2010: Moblization and Legitimacy, Continuity and Change*, edited by Peter Aronsson and Gabriella Elgenius, 13–32. London: Routledge, 2015.

Bhambra, Gurminder. *Connected Sociologies*. London: Bloomsbury, 2014.

Billé, Franck. "Auratic Geographies: Buffers, Backyards, Entanglements." *Geopolitics* (2021). https://doi.org/10.1080/14650045.2021.1881490.

Blacker, L.V.S. "La Croisière Jaune." *Geographical Journal* 81, no. 1 (1933): 53–58.

Bobot, Marie-Thérèse. "In Memoriam: Vadime Elisseeff (1918–2002)." *Arts Asiatiques* 57 (2002): 229–31.

Bohrer, Frederick. *Photography and Archaeology*. London: Reaktion Books, 2011.

Bosshard, Walter. *Hazards of Asia's Highlands & Deserts*. London: Figurehead, 1932.

Bouchard, Christian, and William Crumplin. "Neglected No Longer: The Indian Ocean at the Forefront of World Geopolitics and Global Geostrategy." *Journal of the Indian Ocean Region* 6, no. 1 (2010): 26–51.

Boulnois, Luce. *The Silk Road*. London: George Allen and Unwin, 1966.

Boym, Svetlana. *The Future of Nostalgia*. New York: Basic Books, 2001.

British Library. "The International Dunhuang Project: The Silk Road Online." Accessed August 11, 2018. http://idp.bl.uk.

Brown, Rachel. "Where Will the New Silk Road Lead? The Effects of Chinese Investment and Migration in Xinjiang and Central Asia." *Columbia University Journal of Politics and Society* 26 (2016): 69–91.

Brzezinski, Zbigniew. "The Grand Chessboard: US Geostrategy for Eurasia." *Harvard International Review* 20, no. 1 (1998): 48–53.

Bulkin, V., Leo Klejn, and G.S. Lebedev. "Attainments and Problems of Soviet Archaeology." *World Archaeology* 13, no. 3 (1982): 272–95.

Byrne, Patrick. "China and Turkey—Building a New Silk Road Together." *China.org. cn*, January 4, 2012. http://www.china.org.cn/opinion/2012-01/04/content_24322 020.htm.

Calder, Kent. *The New Continentalism: Energy and Twenty-First-Century Eurasian Geopolitics*. New Haven: Yale University Press, 2012.

Callahan, William. "The Politics of Walls: Barriers, Flows, and the Sublime." *Review of International Studies* 44, no. 3 (2019): 456–81.

Carrai, Maria. "Chinese Political Nostalgia and Xi Jinping's Dream of Great Rejuvenation." *International Journal of Asian Studies* 18, no. 1 (2021): 7–25.

CCTV English. "National Treasure, Season 2, Episode 1." Uploaded July 26, 2019. YouTube video, 1:39:57. https://www.youtube.com/watch?v=J2LNHmC_67Q.

Cerrans, Max. "Vadime Elisseeff: A Taste for Universality." *UNESCO Sources*, September 1990.

Chang, Jiat-Hwee. *A Genealogy of Tropical Architecture*. London: Routledge, 2016.

Chau Ju-Kua: His Work on the Chinese and Arab Trade in the Twelfth and Thirteenth Centuries, Entitled Chu-fan-chï. Translated by Friedrich Hirt and W.W. Rockhill. St Petersburg: Imperial Academy of Sciences, 1911.

Chaw Chaw Sein. "Background and Significance." In *Research Report on ASEAN-China Cooperation in the Fight against COVID-19*, edited by University of Yangon and NACAI Secretariat, 2–4. Yangon: University of Yangon and NACAI Secretariat, 2020. http://www.iis.fudan.edu.cn/_upload/article/files/e0/a2/2242e2114e8a9d43482b7f4ae2b0/7b8e2bac-5c27-4316-a92f-140c52e3c0ee.pdf#page=37.

Che Muqi. *The Silk Road: Past and Present*. Beijing: Foreign Language Press, 1989.

Chen, Constance. "Empire of Artifacts: U.S. Epistemological Colonialism in 1920s China." *Verge: Studies in Global Asias* 7, no. 1 (2021): 170–96.

Chen Weiss, Jessica, and Jeremy Wallace. "Domestic Politics, China's Rise, and the Future of the Liberal International Order." *International Organization* 75, no. 2 (2021): 635–64.

Childress, David Hatcher. *Lost Cities of China, Central Asia & India*. Kempton: Adventures Unlimited Press, 1998. Kindle.

Chin, Tamara. "The Invention of the Silk Road, 1877." *Critical Inquiry* 40, no. 1 (2013): 194–219.

Chowdhury, Debasish Roy. "Quad Is Key to Biden's Strategy in Asia, but the Four-Way Alliance is Ambiguous and Contradictory." *Time*, March 18, 2021. https://time.com/5947674/quad-biden-china/.

Churchill, David. "Plea to Open Silk Road to China and the East." *Times* (London), August 8, 1996.

Clark, Milton J. "How the Kazakhs Fled to Freedom." *National Geographic Magazine*, November 1954.

Clarke, Michael. "The Belt and Road Initiative: China's New Grand Strategy?" *Asia Policy* 24 (2017): 71–79.

Clarke, Michael. "The Belt and Road Initiative: Exploring Beijing's Motivations and Challenges for its New Silk Road." *Strategic Analysis* 42, no. 2 (2018): 84–102.

Clarke, Michael. *Xinjiang and China's Rise in Central Asia—A History*. London: Routledge, 2011.

Cliff, Nigel. Introduction to *The Travels: Marco Polo*, by Marco Polo, xi–xlii. Translated by Nigel Cliff. London: Penguin Books, 2015.

Cline, Eric. *Biblical Archaeology: A Very Short Introduction*. Oxford: Oxford University Press, 2009. Kindle.

Clowes, Edith W. *Russia on the Edge: Imagined Geographies and Post-Soviet Identity*. Ithaca: Cornell University, 2011.

Cody, Jennifer. "Tracking Travel: Focus on Japan." *Wall Street Journal*, June 7, 1994.

Cohn, Bernard S. *Colonialism and Its Forms of Knowledge: The British in India*. Princeton: Princeton University Press, 1996.

Collins, Robert. *East to Cathay: The Silk Road*. New York: McGraw-Hill Book Company, 1986.

Colomina, Beatriz, Annmarie Brennan, and Jeannie Kim, eds. *Cold War Hothouses: Inventing Postwar Culture, from Cockpit to Playboy*. New York: Princeton Architectural Press, 2004.

Connerton, Paul. *How Societies Remember*. Cambridge: Cambridge University Press, 1989.

Contessi, Nicola. "Central Eurasia and the New Great Game: Players, Moves, Outcomes, and Scholarship." *Asian Security* 9, no. 3 (2013): 231–41.

Cooley, Alexander. *Great Games, Local Rules: The New Great Power Contest in Central Asia*. New York: Oxford University Press, 2012.

Cuthbertson, Ian. "The New 'Great Game.'" *World Policy Journal* 11, no. 4 (1995): 31–43.

Dadabaev, Timur. "Engagement and Contestation: The Entangled Imagery of the Silk Road." *Cambridge Journal of Eurasian Studies* 2 (2018): 1–14.

Dadabaev, Timur. "'Silk Road' as Foreign Policy Discourse: The Construction of Chinese, Japanese and Korean Engagement Strategies in Central Asia." *Journal of Eurasian Studies* 9 (2018): 30–41.

Dalrymple, William. *In Xanadu: A Quest*. New York: Harper Collins Publishers, 1989.

Davis, Brendan. "Movie Review: Marco Polo (1975)." Celestial Pictures. Last modified November 2, 2018. http://shawbrothersuniverse.com/movie-review-marco-polo-1975/.

Davis, Thomas. *Shifting Sands: The Rise and Fall of Biblical Archaeology*. Oxford: Oxford University Press, 2004. Kindle.

de Terra, Hellmut. "On the World's Highest Plateaus." *National Geographic Magazine*, March 1931.

Deakin University. "Sri Lanka's PM Delivers 2017 Deakin Law Oration." Last modified March 13, 2017. http://www.deakin.edu.au/about-deakin/news/articles/sri-lankas-pm-delivers-2017-deakin-law-oration.

Diène, Doudou. "Foreword." In *Bibliographical Database—The Silk Roads: Roads of Dialogue*, edited by UNESCO, vol. 1, i–iii. Brussels: LORETO a.s.l.b., 1997.

Ding Wei. "Jointly Building the Belt and Road in Cultural Areas." Speech at Symposium of the SRILT, Tianqiao Performing Arts Center, Beijing, China, October 21, 2016. http://www.srilt.org/en/symposium/27.html (site discontinued).

Dobson, Hugo. "Global Governance and the Group of Seven/Eight." In *Global Governance and Japan: The Institutional Architecture*, edited by Glenn Hook and Hugo Dobson, 23–39. London: Routledge, 2007.

Dolukhanov, Pavel. "Archaeology and Nationalism in Totalitarian and Post-Totalitarian Russia." In *Nationalism and Archaeology: Scottish Archaeological Forum*, edited by John Atkinson, Iain Banks, and Jerry O'Sullivan, 200–13. Glasgow: Cruithne Press, 1996.

Douglas, William O. "Journey to Outer Mongolia." *National Geographic Magazine*, March 1962.

Dreyer, Caren. "The 'Turfan Files' in the Museum of Asian Art, Berlin." *The Silk Road* 18 (2020): 73–80.

Duara, Prasenjit. "The Discourse of Civilization and Pan-Asianism." *Journal of World History* 12, no. 1 (2001): 99–130.

Dündar, Ali Merthan. "The Effects of the Russo-Japanese War on Turkic Nations: Japan and Japanese in Folk Songs, Elegies and Poems." In *Japan on the Silk Road: Encounters and Perspectives of Politics and Culture in Eurasia*, edited by Selçuk Esenbel, 199–227. Leiden: Brill, 2018.

Eco, Umberto. "De Interpretatione or the Difficulty of Being Marco Polo (On the Occasion of Antonioni's China film)." Translated by Christine Leefeldt. *Film Quarterly* 30, no. 4 (1977): 8–12.

Edwards, Dan. "Looking at/Looking in Antonioni's 'Chung Kuo, China': A Critical Reflection across Three Viewings." Senses of Cinema. Last modified March 2015. http://sensesofcinema.com/2015/feature-articles/looking-at-looking-in-antonionis-chung-kuo-cina-a-critical-reflection-across-three-viewings/.

Edwards, Matthew. "The New Great Game and the New Great Gamers: Disciples of Kipling and Mackinder." *Central Asian Survey* 22, no. 1 (2003): 83–102.

Edwards, Mike. "The Adventures of Marco Polo: Part I." *National Geographic Magazine*, May 2001.

Edwards, Mike. "The Adventures of Marco Polo: Part II." *National Geographic Magazine*, June 2001.

Edwards, Mike. "The Adventures of Marco Polo: Part III." *National Geographic Magazine*, July 2001.

Edwards, Mike. "Sons of Genghis: The Great Khans." *National Geographic Magazine*, February 1997.

Egami Namio. "The Silk Road and Japan." In *The Sea Route: The Grand Exhibition of Silk Road Civilizations*, edited by Silk Road Exposition, 10–20. Nara: Nara National Museum, 1988.

Eisenstadt, S.N. *Japanese Civilization: A Comparative View*. Chicago: University of Chicago Press, 1996.

Elisseeff, Vadime. "The Roads of Dialogue." *Integral Study of the Silk Roads: Roads of Dialogue Newsletter*, October 1989.

Elisseeff, Vadime. *The Silk Roads: Highways of Culture and Commerce*. New York: Berghahn Books, 2000.

Errington, Elizabeth, and Vesta Curtis. "The British and Archaeology in Nineteenth-Century Persia." In *From Persepolis to the Punjab: Exploring Ancient Iran, Afghanistan and Pakistan*, edited by Elizabeth Errington and Vesta Curtis, 166–78. London: British Museum Press, 2007.

Errington, Elizabeth, and Vesta Curtis. "The Explorers and Collectors." In *From Persepolis to the Punjab: Exploring Ancient Iran, Afghanistan and Pakistan*, edited by Elizabeth Errington and Vesta Curtis, 3–16. London: British Museum Press, 2007.

Erşen, Emre. "The Evolution of 'Eurasia' as a Geopolitical Concept in Post-Cold War Turkey." *Geopolitics* 18 (2013): 24–44.

Esenbel, Selçuk. "Introduction." In *Japan on the Silk Road: Encounters and Perspectives of Politics and Culture in Eurasia*, edited by Selçuk Esenbel, 1–34. Leiden: Brill, 2018.

Fagan, Brian M. *Return to Babylon: Travelers, Archaeologists, and Monuments in Mesopotamia.* Boulder: University of Colorado Press, 2007.

Fan, Xin. *World History and National Identity in China: The Twentieth Century.* Cambridge: Cambridge University Press, 2021. Kindle.

Fatemi, Syed Tariq. "Speech by Special Assistant to the Prime Minister Syed Tariq Fatemi at the Karachi Council of Foreign Relations." Speech at Karachi Council on Foreign Relations, Islamabad, Pakistan, February 2, 2015. http://www.mofa.gov.pk/chile/pr-details.php?prID=2546 (site discontinued).

Fettweis, Christopher J. "Sir Halford Mackinder, Geopolitics, and Policymaking in the 21st Century." *Parameters* 30, no. 2 (2000): 58–71.

Fleming, Peter. *News from Tartary: An Epic Journey across Central Asia.* London: Tauris Parke Paperbacks, 2001. Kindle.

Frank, Andre Gunder. "On the Silk Road: An 'Academic' Travelogue." *Economic and Political Weekly* 25, no. 46 (1990): 2536–39.

Frankopan, Peter. *The Silk Roads: A New History of the World.* New York: Vintage Books, 2017.

Friedman, Thomas, L. *The World Is Flat: A Brief History of the Twenty-First Century.* New York: Farrar, Straus and Giroux, 2005.

Frost, Mark Ravinder. "Handing Back History: Britain's Imperial Heritage State in Colonial Sri Lanka and South Asia, 1870–1920." Keynote address presented at National Symposium of Historical Studies, University of Sri Lanka, Colombo, January 31, 2018.

Fuchs, Eckhardt. "Introduction: Provincializing Europe." In *Across Cultural Borders: Historiography in Global Perspective*, edited by Eckhardt Fuchs and Benedikt Stuchtey, loc. 83–497. Lanham: Rowman & Littlefield Publishers, 2002. Kindle.

Fukuyama, Francis. "The End of History?" *National Interest* no. 16 (1989): 3–18.

Galambos, Imre. "Buddhist Relics from the Western Regions: Japanese Archaeological Exploration of Central Asia." In *Writing Travel in Central Asian History*, edited by Nile Green, 152–69. Bloomington: Indiana University Press, 2014. Kindle.

Galambos, Imre. "Japanese Exploration of Central Asia: The Ōtani Expeditions and Their British Connections." *Bulletin of SOAS* 75, no. 1 (2012): 113–34.

Galambos, Imre. "Japanese 'Spies' along the Silk Road: British Suspicions Regarding the Second Ōtani Expedition (1908–09)." *Japanese Religions* 35, nos. 1–2 (2010): 33–61.

Gayamov, A. "Soviet Music." *Soviet Travel* 3, 1933.

Gerrard, Mike. "Smooth Passage on the Old Silk Route." *Times* (London), May 6, 1995.

Gienow-Hecht, Jessica C.E., ed. *Music and International History in the Twentieth Century.* New York: Berghann Books, 2015.

Gladney, Dru C. *Dislocating China: Reflections on Muslims, Minorities, and Other Subaltern Subjects*. London: University of Chicago Press, 2004.

Gleason, Abbott. "Eurasia: What Is it? Is It?" *Journal of Eurasian Studies* 1 (2010): 26–32.

Gnowangerup Star and Tambellup-Ongerup Gazette. "Haardt Scientific Expedition." September 3, 1932.

Goldberg, Susan. "For Decades, Our Coverage Was Racist. To Rise above Our Past, We Must Acknowledge It." National Geographic. Last modified March 12, 2018. https://www.nationalgeographic.com/magazine/2018/04/from-the-editor-race-racism-history/.

GovTrack. "H.R. 2867 - 105th Congress: Silk Road Strategy Act of 1997." Accessed June 26, 2018. https://www.govtrack.us/congress/bills/105/hr2867.

Gray, Colin S. "Nicholas John Spykman, the Balance of Power, and International Order." *Journal of Strategic Studies* 38, no. 6 (2015): 873–97.

Green, Nile. "From the Silk Road to the Railroad (and Back): The Means and Meanings of the Iranian Encounter with China." *Iranian Studies* 48, no. 2 (2015): 165–92.

Green, Nile, ed. "Introduction: Writing, Travel, and the Global History of Central Asia." In *Writing Travel in Central Asian History*, edited by Nile Green, 1–40. Bloomington: Indiana University Press, 2014. Kindle.

Green, Nile, ed. *Writing Travel in Central Asian History*. Bloomington: Indiana University Press, 2014. Kindle.

Guha-Thakurta, Tapati. *Monuments, Objects, Histories: Institutions of Art in Colonial and Postcolonial India*. New York: Columbia University Press, 2004.

Gunn, Geoffrey C. *Overcoming Ptolmey: The Revelation of an Asian World Region*. Lanham: Lexington Books, 2018. Kindle.

Guthrie-Shimizu, Sayuri. "Japan, the United States, and the Cold War, 1945–1960." In *The Cambridge History of the Cold War*, edited by Melvyn P. Leffler and Odd Arne Westad, 244–65. Vol. 1 of *Origins*. Cambridge: Cambridge University Press, 2010. Kindle.

Haardt, Georges-Marie. "The Trans-Asiatic Expedition Starts." *National Geographic Magazine*, June 1931.

Hackin, Joseph. "In Persia and Afghanistan with the Citroën Trans-Asiatic Expedition." *Geographical Journal* 83, no. 5 (1934): 353–61.

Hameiri, Shahar, and Lee Jones. "China Challenges Global Governance? Chinese International Development Finance and the AIIB." *International Affairs* 94, no. 3 (2018): 573–93.

Hamilakis, Yannis. *The Nation and Its Ruins: Antiquity, Archaeology, and National Imagination in Greece*. Oxford: Oxford University Press, 2007.

Hann, Chris. "A Concept of Eurasia." *Current Anthropology* 57, no. 1 (2016): 1–27.

Hannerz, Ulf. "Geocultural Scenarios." In *Frontiers of Sociology*, edited by Peter Hedstrom and Bjorn Wittrock, 267–88. Leiden: Brill, 2009.

Hannerz, Ulf. *Writing Future Worlds: An Anthropologist Explores Global Scenarios*. Cham: Palgrave Macmillan, 2016. Kindle.

Hansen, Valerie. *The Silk Road: A New Documentary History to 1400*. Oxford: Oxford University Press, 2016.

Hansen, Valerie. *The Silk Road: A New History with Documents*. Oxford: Oxford University Press, 2017.

Harding, Christopher. *Japan Story: In Search of a Nation, 1850 to the Present*. London: Allen Lane, 2018.

Harper, Tom. "Towards an Asian Eurasia: Mackinder's Heartland Theory and the Return of China to Eurasia." *Cambridge Journal of Eurasian Studies* 1 (2017): 1–27.

Harvey, David. *The Condition of Postmodernity: An Enquiry into the Origins of Cultural Change*. Malden: Blackwell, 1990.

Hedin, Sven. *The Silk Road*. London: George Routledge and Sons, 1938.

Heidegger, Martin. "The Age of the World Picture." *The Question Concerning Technology, and Other Essays*, translated by William Lovitt, 115–54. New York: Garland Publishing, 1977.

Heidelberg Institute for International Conflict Research. *Conflict Barometer 2009: Crises - Wars - Coups d'État - Negotiations - Mediations - Peace Settlements*. Heidelberg: Heidelberg Institute for International Conflict Research, 2009.

Hevia, James L. "The Photography Complex: Exposing Boxer-Era China (1900–1901), Making Civilisation." In *Photographies East: The Camera and Its Histories in East and Southeast Asia*, edited by Rosalind C. Morris, 79–119. Durham: Duke University Press, 2009.

Hildebrand, J.R. "The World's Greatest Overland Explorer." *National Geographic Magazine*, November 1928.

Hildebrand, Robert C. *Dumbarton Oaks: The Origins of the United Nations and the Search for Postwar Security*. Chapel Hill: University of North Carolina Press, 1990.

Hillman, Jennifer, and Alex Tippett. "A Robust U.S. Response to China's Health Diplomacy Will Reap Domestic and Global Benefits." Council on Foreign Relations. Last modified April 15, 2021. https://www.thinkglobalhealth.org/article/robust-us-response-chinas-health-diplomacy-will-reap-domestic-and-global-benefits.

Hirsch, Francine. *Empire of Nations: Ethnographic Knowledge and the Making of the Soviet Union*. Ithaca: Cornell University Press, 2014. Kindle.

Hmc62100. "Citroën la Croisière jaune part 1." Uploaded March 25, 2011. YouTube video, 8:16. https://www.youtube.com/watch?v=6jzGQ-Te8b0&t=17s.

Hobsbawm, Eric. *Nations and Nationalism since 1780: Programme, Myth, Reality*. Cambridge: Cambridge University Press, 1992. Kindle.

Hobsbawm, Eric, and Terence Ranger. *The Invention of Tradition*. Cambridge: Cambridge University Press, 1983.

Hobson, John. *The Eastern Origins of Western Civilization*. Cambridge: Cambridge University Press, 2004.

Hopkirk, Peter. *Foreign Devils on the Silk Road: The Search for the Lost Treasures of Central Asia*. London: John Murray, 1980. Kindle.

Hopkirk, Peter. *The Great Game: On Service in High Asia*. London: John Murray, 2006.

Hunt, Lynn. *History: Why It Matters*. Cambridge: Polity, 2018.

Hunt, Lynn. *Writing History in the Global Era*. New York: W.W. Norton & Company, 2015. Kindle.

Huntington, Samuel P. "The Clash of Civilizations?" *Foreign Affairs*, Summer 1993. https://www.foreignaffairs.com/articles/united-states/1993-06-01/clash-civilizations.

Huyghe, François-Bernard. "The Kingdom of Silla and the Treasures of Nara." *UNESCO Courier*, July 1991.

Huyghe, François-Bernard. "The Return of the Fulk al-Salamah." *UNESCO Courier*, August/September 1991.

Iannucci, Amilcare, and John Tulk. "From Alterity to Holism: Cinematic Depictions of Marco Polo and His Travels." In *Marco Polo and the Encounter of East and West*, edited by Suzanne Conklin Akbari and Amilcare Iannucci, 201–43. Toronto: University of Toronto Press, 2008.

Iokibe, Makoto. "Introduction: Japanese Diplomacy from Prewar to Postwar." In *The Diplomatic History of Postwar Japan*, edited by Makoto Iokibe, translated by Robert D. Eldridge, loc. 214–454. Oxford: Routledge, 2011. Kindle.

Ingram, Edward. "Great Britain's Great Game: An Introduction." *International History Review* 2, no. 2 (1980): 160–71.

Inozemtsev, Vladislav. "Why Kazakhstan Holds the Keys to the Global Economy." *Independent* (UK), November 10, 2015. http://www.independent.co.uk/voices/why-kazakhstan-holds-the-keys-to-the-global-economy-a6727391.html.

Iriye, Akira. *Cultural Internationalism and World Order*. Baltimore: John Hopkins University Press, 1997.

Ivie, Robert L. "Metaphor and the Rhetorical Invention of Cold War 'Idealists.'" *Communications Monographs* 54, no. 2 (1987): 165–82.

Jacobs, Justin M. *The Compensations of Plunder: How China Lost Its Treasures*. Chicago: University of Chicago Press, 2020. Kindle.

Jacobs, Justin. "Confronting Indiana Jones: Chinese Nationalism, Historical Imperialism and the Criminalisation of Aurel Stein and the Raiders of Dunhuang, 1899–1944." In *China on the Margins*, edited by Sherman Cochran and Paul Pickowicz, 65–90. Ithaca: Cornell University East Asia Program, 2010.

Jacobs, Justin. "Cultural Thieves or Political Liabilities? How Chinese Officials Viewed Foreign Archaeologists in Xinjiang, 1893–1914." *Silk Road* 10 (2012): 117–22.

Jacobs, Justin. "Nationalist China's 'Great Game': Leveraging Foreign Explorers in Xinjiang, 1927–1935." *Journal of Asian Studies* 73, no. 1 (2014): 43–64.

James, S.L. "Swedish Mission Project." Internet Archive. Uploaded September 29, 2009. Video, 1:41:16. https://archive.org/details/swedish-mission-project/sven-hedin-1928-expedition-through-the-gobi.avi.

Japan International Cooperation Agency. "60 Years of Japanese ODA." *JICA's World*, January 2014.

Japanese National Commission for UNESCO, ed. *Research in Japan in History of Eastern and Western Cultural Contacts: Its Development and Present Situation*. Tokyo: Japanese National Commission for UNESCO, 1957.

Jasanoff, Maya. *Edge of Empire: Conquest and Collecting in the East, 1750–1850*. New York: Harper Perennial, 2005.

Jiang Zemin. "Full Text of Jiang's Speech to Saudi Eminent Persons." Speech at Prince's Residence, Riyadh, Saudi Arabia, November 3, 1993. http://en.people.cn/features/Sixnation/txt/19991103A103.html.

Kamola, Issac. *Making the World Global: U.S. Universities and the Production of the Global Imaginary*. Durham: Duke University Press, 2019.

Kaplan, Robert D. *Monsoon: The Indian Ocean and the Future of American Power*. New York: Random House, 2010.

Kaplan, Robert. *The Return of Marco Polo's World: War, Strategy, and American Interests in the Twenty-First Century*. New York: Penguin Random House, 2018.

Kariyawasam, Ambassador Prasad. "Sri Lanka—A Hub in the Indian Ocean." Speech at the East West Center, Honolulu, Hawai'i, February 11, 2016. http://slembassyusa.org/embassy_press_releases/remarks-by-ambassador-prasad-kariyawasam-at-the-east-west-center-hawaii-sri-lanka-a-hub-in-the-indian-ocean/ (site discontinued).

Kastner, Scott, and Margaret Pearson. "China and Global Governance: Opportunistic Multilateralism." *Global Policy* 11, no. 1 (2020): 164–69.

Kennedy, Scott. "Introduction: Learning to Be Insiders." In *Global Governance and China: The Dragon's Learning Curve*, edited by Scott Kennedy, loc. 700–914. London: Routledge, 2018. Kindle.

Kiernan, Matthew. "Silk Road Key to China's Next Move." *Huffington Post*, August 31, 2015. http://www.huffingtonpost.com/matthew-j-kiernan/silk-road-key-to-china-n_b_8068318.html.

Kim Haewon. "A History of the Central Asian Collection at the National Museum of Korea." *The International Journal of Korean Art and Archaeology* 4 (2010): 160–72.

King, John. *Karakoram Highway: The High Road to China*. Melbourne: Lonely Planet, 1989.

Kiy, Evgeniy. "State Hermitage Museum." *Arts Asiatiques* 69 (2014): 173–76.

Klejn, Leo. *Soviet Archaeology: Schools, Trends and History*. Oxford: Oxford University Press, 2012.

Köchler, H. "Civilization as an Instrument of World Order? The Role of the Civilizational Paradigm in the Absence of a Balance of Power." Lecture given at the International Symposium on "Civilizations and World Orders," Istanbul, Turkey, May 13, 2006.

Korybko, Andrew. "What Could India's 'Cotton Route' Look Like?" *Sputnik International*, March 29, 2015. http://sputniknews.com/columnists/20150329/1020170021.html.

Kost, Catrin. "'Yours Ever So Sincerely': Albert von le Coq Seen through his Correspondence with Aurel Stein." In *Sir Aurel Stein, Colleagues and Collections*, edited by Helen Wang, 1–9. London: British Museum, 2012.

Kreutzmann, Hermann. "Geographical Research in Chinese Central Asia: Aims and Ambitions of International Explorers in the 19th and 20th Centuries." *Die Erde* 138, no. 4 (2007): 369–84.

Kuchins, Andrew C. "The Northern Distribution Network and the Modern Silk Road: Planning for Afghanistan's Future." Center for Strategic and International Studies. Last modified December 17, 2009. https://www.csis.org/analysis/northern-distribution-network-and-modern-silk-road.

Küçükyalçin, Erdal. "Ōtani Kozui and His Vision of Asia: From Villa Nirakusō to 'The Rise of Asia' Project." In *Japan on the Silk Road: Encounters and Perspectives of Politics and Culture in Eurasia*, edited by Selçuk Esenbel, 181–98. Leiden: Brill, 2018.

Kumar, Chandra. "The Indian Ocean: Arc of Crisis or Zone of Peace?" *International Affairs* 60, no. 2 (1984): 233–46.

Kurečić, Petar. "The New Great Game: Rivalry of Geostrategies and Geoeconomics in Central Asia." *Hrvatski Geografski Glasnik* 72, no. 1 (2010): 21–48.

Kuus, Merje. *Geopolitics and Expertise: Knowledge and Authority in European Diplomacy*. Chichester: Wiley Blackwell, 2014.

Kuzmina, Elena. *The Prehistory of the Silk Road*. Edited by Victor H. Mair. Philadelphia: University of Pennsylvania, 2008.

Kwa Chong-Guan, ed. *Early Southeast Asia Viewed from India: An Anthology of Articles from the "Journal of the Greater India Society."* Delhi: Manohar, 2013.

Kwon, Young-pil. "The Otani Collection." *Orientations* 20, no. 3 (1989): 53–63.

Lamb, Alastair. *Asia Frontiers: Studies in a Continuing Problem*. London: Pall Mall Press, 1968.

Lane, Michael Barry, and Ronald Lewock, eds. *Rebuilding the Silk Road: Cultural Tourism and Revival of Heritage in Uzbekistan*. Paris: UNDP-UNESCO, 1996.

Larner, John. *Marco Polo and the Discovery of the World*. New Haven: Yale University Press, 1999.

Laruelle, Marlene. "The US Silk Road: Geopolitical Imaginary or the Repackaging of Strategic Interests?" *Eurasian Geography and Economics* 56, no. 4 (2015): 360–75.

Latour, Bruno. "Visualisation and Cognition: Drawing Things Together." In *Knowledge and Society Studies in the Sociology of Culture Past and Present*, edited by H. Kuklick, vol. 6, 1–40. Stamford: JAI Press, 1986.

Lawton, John, ed. *The Integral Study of the Silk Roads: Roads of Dialogue*. Paris: UNESCO, 2008.

Le Fèvre, Georges. *An Eastern Odyssey*. Boston: Little Brown, 1935.

Leibold, James. *Reconfiguring Chinese Nationalism: How the Qing Frontier and Its Indigenes Became Chinese*. New York: Palgrave Macmillan, 2007. Kindle.

Len, Christopher. "Understanding Japan's Central Asian Engagement." In *Japan's Silk Road Diplomacy: Paving the Road Ahead*, edited by Christopher Len, Uyama Tomohiko, and Hirose Tetsuya, 31–46. Washington DC: Central Asia-Caucasus Institute and Silk Road Studies Program, 2008.

Li, Xing, and Wan Wang. "'The Silk Road Economic Belt' and the 'China Dream' Relationship: A Strategy or Tactic." *Sociology Study* 5, no. 3 (2015): 169–75.

Lin, Christina Y. "China, Iran, and North Korea: A Triangular Strategic Alliance." Rubin Center—Research in International Affairs. Last modified March 5, 2010. http://www.rubincenter.org/2010/03/lin-2010-03-05/ (site discontinued).

Lin, Shaun, James Sidaway, and Chih Yuan Woon. "Reordering China, Respacing the World: Belt and Road Initiative (一带一路) as an Emergent Geopolitical Culture." *The Professional Geographer* 71, no. 3 (2019): 507–22.

Liu, Melinda. "Beijing's New High-Speed Rail Line." *Newsweek*, May 9, 2010. https://www.newsweek.com/beijings-new-high-speed-rail-line-70221 (site discontinued).

Liu, Xinru. *The Silk Road in World History*. Oxford: Oxford University Press, 2010.

Lundysheva, Olga, and Anna Turanskaya. "Old Uyghur Fragments in the Serindia Collection: Provenance, Acquisition, Processing." *Written Monuments of the Orient* 6, no. 2.12 (2020): 43–64.

Lyons, Claire, John Papadopoulos, Lindsey Stewart, and Andrew Szegedy-Maszak. *Antiquity and Photography: Early Views of Ancient Mediterranean Sites*. Los Angeles: The J. Paul Getty Museum, 2005.

Maçães, Bruno. *The Dawn of Eurasia: On the Trail of the New World Order*. London: Allen Lane, 2018.

Mackinder, Halford J. *Democratic Ideals and Reality: A Study in the Politics of Reconstruction*. London: H. Holt, 1944. First published 1919.

Mackinder, Halford J. "The Geographical Pivot of History." *Geographical Journal* 23, no. 4 (1904): 421–37.

Mahan, Alfred Thayer. *The Influence of Sea Power upon History; 1660–1783*. Boston: Little, Brown and Co., 1890.

Maillart, Ella. *Oasis Interdites: de Pékin au Cachemire*. Paris: Grasset, 1937.

Majlesi, Afshin. "Tehran Hosts Sino-Iranian Friendship Conference as Ancient Silk Road Backs to Life." *Tehran Times*, October 24, 2016. https://www.tehrantimes.com/news/407630/Tehran-hosts-Sino-Iranian-friendship-conference-as-ancient-Silk.

Majumdar, Boria, and Nalin Mehta. "Hybridity and Subversion: The Olympic Flame in India." In *Bearing Light: Flame Relays and the Struggle for the Olympic Movement*, edited by John J. MacAloon, 170–85. Oxford: Routledge, 2013. Kindle.

Marat, Erica. "Nation Branding in Central Asia: A New Campaign to Present Ideas about the State and the Nation." *Europe-Asia Studies* 61, no. 7 (2009): 1123–36.

Marchand, Suzanne. *German Orientalism in the Age of Empire: Religion, Race, and Scholarship.* Cambridge: Cambridge University Press, 2010.

Martin, Terry. *The Affirmative Action Empire: Nations and Nationalism in the Soviet Union, 1923–1939.* Ithaca: Cornell University Press, 2017. Kindle.

Matsuda Hisao. "The Central Asia in Ancient Times." In *Research in Japan in History of Eastern and Western Cultural Contacts: Its Development and Present Situation*, edited by Japanese National Commission for UNESCO, 39–48. Tokyo: Japanese National Commission for UNESCO, 1957.

Matsuda Hisao. "General Survey: The Development of Researches in the History of the Intercourse between East and West in Japan." In *Research in Japan in History of Eastern and Western Cultural Contacts: Its Development and Present Situation*, edited by Japanese National Commission for UNESCO, 1–18. Tokyo: Japanese National Commission for UNESCO, 1957.

Matsuda Hisao, and Fujieda Akira. "Editor's Notes." In *Research in Japan History of Eastern and Western Cultural Contacts: Its Development and Present Situation*, edited by Japanese National Commission for UNESCO, 3–4. Tokyo: Japanese National Commission for UNESCO, 1957.

Mawdsley, Emma. "South–South Cooperation 3.0? Managing the Consequences of Success in the Decade Ahead." *Oxford Development Studies* 47, no. 3 (2019): 259–74.

Maxwell, Alexander. "Introduction, Bridges and Bulwarks: A Historiographic Overview of East-West Discourses." In *The East-West Discourse: Symbolic Geographic and Its Consequences*, edited by Alexander Maxwell, 1–32. Bern: Peter Land, 2011.

Mayor, Federico. "Preface of the Director-General of UNESCO." In *The Integral Study of the Silk Roads: Roads of Dialogue*, edited by John Lawton, 3. Paris: UNESCO, 2008.

Mazower, Mark. *Governing the World: The History of an Idea.* London: Penguin Press, 2012.

McElvoy, Anne. "The Silver Track to Tashkent." *Times* (London), January 1, 1994.

McMahon, Robert J. "Introduction." In *The Cold War in the Third World*, edited by Robert J. McMahon, 1–10. Oxford: Oxford University Press, 2013. Kindle.

McMahon, Robert J., ed. *The Cold War in the Third World.* Oxford: Oxford University Press, 2013. Kindle.

Medcalfe, Rory. *Contest for the Indo-Pacific: Why China Won't Map the Future.* Melbourne: Schwartz Books Pty. Limited, 2020. Kindle.

Medhurst, Martin J., Robert L. Ivie, Philip Wander, and Robert L. Scott. *Cold War Rhetoric: Strategy, Metaphor, and Ideology.* East Lansing: Michigan State University Press, 1997.

Megoran, Nick. "Revisiting the 'Pivot': The Influence of Halford Mackinder on Analysis of Uzbekistan's International Relations." *Geographical Journal* 170, no. 4 (2004): 347–58.

Meinig, Donald W. "Heartland and Rimland in Eurasian History." *Western Political Quarterly* 9, no. 3 (1956): 553–69.

Mertens, Matthias. "Did Richthofen Really Coin 'The Silk Road'?" *The Silk Road* 17 (2019): 1–9.

Meyer, Karl E., and Shareen Blair Brysac. *Tournament of Shadows: The Great Game and the Race for Empire in Central Asia.* New York: Basic Books, 1999.

Mignolo, Walter. "Globalization and the Geopolitics of Knowledge." *Nepantia: Views from the South* 4 (2003): 97–119.

Millward, James, ed. *James A. Millward* (blog). https://jimmillward.medium.com/we-need-a-new-approach-to-teaching-modern-chinese-history-we-have-lazily-repea ted-false-d24983bd7ef2.

Millward, James. *The Silk Road: A Very Short Introduction.* Oxford: Oxford University Press, 2013. Kindle.

Min-On Concert Association. "Min-On Concert Association—Who We Are." Accessed December 3, 2018. http://www.min-on.org/index.php/about-min-on/who-we-are.

Min-On Concert Association. "Silk Road Series: A Series of 'Musical Voyages along the Silk Road.'" Accessed December 3, 2018. http://www.min-on.org/index.php/cultural-exchange/silk-road-series.

Mitchell, Timothy. *Colonising Egypt.* Berkeley: University of California Press, 1988.

Mitter, Rana. *China's Good War: How World War II Is Shaping a New Nationalism.* Cambridge: Belknap Press, 2020.

Mizoguchi, Koji. "Nation-state, Circularity and Paradox." In *Archaeology, Society and Identity in Modern Japan,* edited by Koji Mizoguchi, 55–120. Cambridge: Cambridge University Press, 2006.

Mohan, Garima. "Great Game in the Indian Ocean." Carnegie India. Last modified June 11, 2018. https://carnegieindia.org/2018/06/11/great-game-in-indian-ocean-pub-76666.

Monnet, Nathalie. "Two Inseparable Names, Dunhuang and Paul Pelliot." *The Institute of Oriental Philosophy Journal* 27 (2017): 57–60.

Mootz, Dennis. "Stamps and Propaganda." *Journal of the History Teachers' Association of NSW* December (2016): 28–35.

Morden, William J. "By Coolie and Caravan across Central Asia." *National Geographic Magazine,* October 1927.

Moreno Garcia, Juan Carlos. "Egyptology and Global History: An Introduction." *Journal of Egyptian History* 13 (2020): 5–10.

Moreno Garcia, Juan Carlos. "Egyptology and Global History: Between Geocultural Power and the Crisis of Humanities." *Journal of Egyptian History* 13 (2020): 29–76.

Morgan, Joyce, and Conrad Walters. *Journeys on the Silk Road.* Guilford: Lyons Press, 2012.

Mori Masao. "The Steppe Route." In *Research in Japan in History of Eastern and Western Cultural Contacts: Its Development and Present Situation,* edited by Japanese National Commission for UNESCO, 19–34. Tokyo: Japanese National Commission for UNESCO, 1957.

Morning Bulletin. "The Silk Road." May 15, 1943, 3.

Morris, Rosalind C., ed. *Photographies East: The Camera and Its Histories in East and Southeast Asia.* Durham: Duke University Press, 2009.

Murray, Edward. "With the Nomads of Central Asia." *National Geographic Magazine,* January 1936.

Myrdal, Jan. *The Silk Road: A Journey from the High Pamirs and Ili through Sinkiang and Kansu.* London: Victor Gollancz, 1980.

Nagasawa Kazutoshi. "Silk Road Studies in Japan: Its History and Present Situation." In *International Seminar for UNESCO Integral Study of the Silk Roads: Roads of Dialogue.* Osaka: UNESCO, 1988. https://fr.unesco.org/silkroad/node/8892.

New York Times. "Hear Radio from Asia: Amateurs Up-State Receive Haardt Expedition's Messages." September 10, 1931.

New York Times. "Scientists to Span Asia in Great Tour." November 21, 1930.

New York Times. "The Screen; At the 55th Street Playhouse." November 18, 1936.

Ngeow Chow-Bing. "COVID-19, Belt and Road Initiative and the Health Silk Road: Implications for Southeast Asia." In *Research Report on ASEAN-China Cooperation in the Fight against COVID-19*, edited by University of Yangon and NACAI Secretariat, 34–39. Yangon: University of Yangon and NACAI Secretariat, 2020. http://www.iis.fudan.edu.cn/_upload/article/files/e0/a2/2242e2114e8a9d43482b7f4ae2b0/7b8e2bac-5c27-4316-a92f-140c52e3c0ee.pdf#page=37.

O'Hara, Sarah. "Great Game or Grubby Game? The Struggle for Control of the Caspian." *Geopolitics* 9, no. 1 (2004): 138–60.

Okakura Kazuko. *The Ideals of the East with Special Reference to the Art of Japan*. Rutland: Charles E. Tuttle Co., 1970. Kindle.

Olenin, Boris. "Sukhum-Kaleh, City of Joy." *Soviet Travel* 3, 1933.

Olstein, Diego. *Thinking History Globally*. London: Palgrave Macmillan, 2015. Kindle.

Öniş, Ziya, and Mustafa Kutlay. "The New Age of Hybridity and Clash of Norms: China, BRICS, and Challenges of Global Governance in a Postliberal International Order." *Alternatives: Global, Local, Political* 45, no. 3 (2020): 123–42.

Orwell, George. *Nineteen Eighty-Four*. London: Harvill Secker, 1949.

Osterhammel, Jürgen. *The Transformation of the World: A Global History of the Nineteenth Century*. Princeton: Princeton University Press, 2014.

Osterhammel, Jürgen. *Unfabling the East: The Enlightenment's Encounter with Asia*. Princeton: Princeton University Press, 2018.

Pai, Hyung Il. *Heritage Management in Korea and Japan: The Politics of Antiquity and Identity*. Seattle: University of Washington Press, 2013.

Pai, Hyung Il. "Resurrecting the Ruins of Japan's Mythical Homelands: Colonial Archaeological Surveys in the Korean Peninsula and Heritage Tourism." In *The Handbook of Post-colonialism and Archaeology*, edited by Jane Lydon and Uzma Z. Rizvi, 93–112. Walnut Creek: Left Coast Press, 2010.

Paine, Lincoln. *The Sea and Civilization: A Maritime History of the World*. London: Atlantic Books, 2014.

Park, Ji Young. "Vestige of an Empire. Treasure of the Nation: Presenting the Ōtani Collection in China, Japan and Korea." In *Toward the Future: Museums and Art History in East Asia*, edited by Suzuki Hiroyuki and Akiyama Akira, 120–29. Tokyo: Japanese Committee for CIHA, Comité International de l'Histoire de l'Art, and the Otsuka Museum of Art, 2020.

Pedro, W. "Mongolia, Kansu, and Sinkiang as Seen by a Member of The Haardt-Citroën Expedition." *Journal of the Royal Asiatic Central Asian Society* 20, no. 2 (1933): 205–19.

Peleggi, Maurizio. *Thailand: The Worldly Kingdom*. London: Reaktion, 2007.

Pelizzari, Maria. *Traces of India: Photography, Architecture, and the Politics of Representation, 1850–1900*. Montreal: Canadian Centre for Architecture and Yale Center for British Art, 2003.

Perez-Garcia, Manuel. *Global History with Chinese Characteristics: Autocratic States along the Silk Road in the Decline of the Spanish and Qing Empires 1680–1796*. Singapore: Palgrave Macmillan, 2021.

Perez-Garcia, Manuel, and Lucio De Sousa, eds. *Global History and New Polycentric Approaches: Europe, Asia and the Americas in a World Network System*. Singapore: Palgrave Macmillan, 2018.

Peyrouse, Sebastien. "The Evolution of Russia's Views on the Belt and Road Initiative." *Asia Policy* 24 (2017): 96–102.

Piccone, Ted. *China's Long Game on Human Rights at the United Nations.* Washington, DC: Brookings Institute, 2018.

Pillai, Chad. "The Great Game in the Indian Ocean: Strategic Partnership Opportunities for the U.S." Center for International Maritime Security. Last modified May 29, 2018. http://cimsec.org/great-game-indian-ocean-strategic-partnership-opportunities-u-s/36590.

Porter, Benjamin. "Near Eastern Archaeology: Imperial Pasts, Postcolonial Presents, and the Possibilities of a Decolonized Future." In *Handbook of Postcolonial Archaeology*, edited by Jane Lydon and Uzma Z. Rizvi, 51–60. Oxford: Routledge, 2016.

Preston Jr, William. "The History of U.S.-UNESCO Relations." In *Hope & Folly: The United States and UNESCO 1945–1985*, edited by William Preston Jr, Edward Herman, and Herbert Schiller, 3–202. Minneapolis: University of Minnesota Press, 1989.

Rai, Adwita. "Silk, Cotton and Cinnamon: Maritime Renaissance of the Indian Ocean." *International Fleet Review (IFR) Series.* New Delhi: National Maritime Foundation, 2016. http://maritimeindia.org/View%20Profile/636437227516774253.pdf (site discontinued).

Rangsimaporn, Paradorn. "Interpretations of Eurasianism: Justifying Russia's Role in East Asia." *Europe-Asia Studies* 58, no. 3 (2006): 371–89.

Raschmann, Simone-Christiane. "The Berlin-Turfan Collection." Staatsbibliothek zu Berlin. Accessed November 30, 2018. https://staatsbibliothek-berlin.de/die-staatsbibliothek/abteilungen/orient/aufgaben-profil/veroeffentlichungen/berlin-turfan-collection/.

Ravina, Mark. *To Stand with the Nations of the World: Japan's Meiji Restoration in World History.* New York: Oxford University Press, 2017. Kindle.

Rezakhani, Khodadad. "The Road That Never Was: The Silk Road and Trans-Eurasian Exchange." *Comparative Studies of South Asia, Africa and the Middle East* 30, no. 3 (2010): 420–33.

Richthofen, Ferdinand von. "The Ancient Silk-Traders' Route across Central Asia." *Geographical Magazine* 5 (1878a): 10–14.

Richthofen, Ferdinand von. "The Ancient Silk-Traders' Route across Central Asia." *Popular Science Monthly: Supplement* nos. 7–12 (1878b): 378–83.

Rolland, Nadège. *China's Eurasian Century? Political and Strategic Implications of the Belt and Road Initiative.* Seattle: National Bureau of Asian Research, 2017.

Roskam, Cole. "Situating Chinese Architecture within 'A Century of Progress': The Chinese Pavilion, the Bendix Golden Temple, and the 1933 Chicago World's Fair." *Journal of the Society of Architectural Historians* 73, no. 3 (2014): 347–71.

Rotter, Andrew J. "Culture, the Cold War, and the Third World." In *The Cold War in the Third World*, edited by Robert J. McMahon, 156–77. New York: Oxford University Press, 2013. Kindle.

Russell-Smith, Lilla. "Hungarian Explorers in Dunhuang." *Journal of the Royal Asiatic Society* 10, no. 3 (2000): 341–62.

Saaler, Sven, and Christopher Szpilman, eds. *Pan-Asianism: A Documentary History Vol 1, 1850–1920.* Lanham: Rowman & Littlefield Publishers, 2011.

Said, Edward. *Orientalism.* Harmondsworth: Penguin Books, 1994.

Salisbury, Harrison E. "Centuries Roll Back in Central Asia to Life as in Genghis Khan's Day." *New York Times,* October 3, 1953.

Salisbury, Harrison E. "Mongolian Communist Line Vies with Genghis Khan's Tradition." *New York Times,* August 5, 1959.

Sarkisova, Oksana. *Screening Soviet Nationalities: Kulturfilms from the Far North to Central Asia*. London: I.B. Tauris, 2017. Kindle.

Schaffer, Teresita, and Howard Schaffer. *India at the Global High Table: The Quest for Regional Primacy and Strategic Autonomy*. Uttar Pradesh: Harper Collins, 2016.

Schoenberger, Karl. "Exposition Celebrating Ancient Route Opens Today: Japan's 'Silk Road Fever' Hits All-Time High." *Los Angeles Times*, April 24, 1988. http://articles.lati mes.com/1988-04-24/news/mn-2704_1_silk-road-series.

Schultz, Kai. "Sri Lanka, Struggling with Debt, Hands a Major Port to China." *New York Times*, December 12, 2017. https://www.nytimes.com/2017/12/12/world/asia/sri-lanka-china-port.html.

Scobell, Andrew. "Whither China's 21st Century Trajectory?" In *The Routledge Handbook of Asian Security Studies*, edited by Sumit Ganguly, Andrew Scobell, and Joseph Liow Chin Long, 11–20. London: Routledge, 2018. Kindle.

Scott, James C. *The Art of Not Being Governed: An Anarchist History of Upland Southeast Asia*. New Haven: Yale University Press, 2009.

Scott-Smith, Giles, and Charlotte A. Lerg, eds. *Campaigning Culture and the Global Cold War: The Journals of the Congress for Cultural Freedom*. London: Palgrave Macmillan, 2017. Kindle.

Sen, Tansen. *Buddhism, Diplomacy and Trade: The Realignment of India-China Relations, 600–1400*. Lanham: Rowman & Littlefield, 2016. Kindle.

Sheng, Andrew. "OBOR and EuroAsia's New Great Game." *China Report* 53, no. 2 (2017): 232–52.

Sherif, Ann. *Japan's Cold War: Media, Literature, and the Law*. New York: Columbia University Press. 2009. Kindle.

Shlapentokh, Dmitry V. "Eurasianism: Past and Present." *Communist and Post-Communist Studies* 30, no. 2 (1997): 129–51.

Shnirelman, Victor A. "To Make a Bridge: Eurasian Discourse in the Post-Soviet World." *Anthropology of East Europe Review* 27, no. 2 (2009): 68–85.

Sidaway, James, Simon Rowedder, Chih Yuan Woon, and Weiqiang Lin. "Introduction: Research Agendas Raised by the Belt and Road Initiative." *EPC: Politics and Space* 38, no. 5 (2020): 795–847.

Silk Road Exposition, ed. "Explanation." In *The Sea Route: The Grand Exhibition of the Silk Road Civilizations*, 150–222. Nara: Nara National Museum, 1988.

Silk Road Exposition, ed. *The Oasis and Steppe Routes: The Grand Exhibition of Silk Road Civilizations*. Nara: Nara National Museum, 1988.

Silk Road Exposition, ed. *The Route of Buddhist Art: The Grand Exhibition of Silk Road Civilizations*. Nara: Nara National Museum, 1998.

Silk Road Futures. "Associations and Networks." Accessed February 19, 2020. https:// www.silkroadfutures.net/associations-and-networks.

Silk Road Futures. "'Sharing a Common Future': National Museum of China Exhibition 2019." Accessed December 2, 2019. https://www.silkroadfutures.net/sharing-a-com mon-future.

Simpich, Frederick. "Manchuria, Promised Land of Asia." *National Geographic Magazine*, October 1929.

Sims, Kearrin, Nicola Banks, Susan Engel, Paul Hodge, Jonathan Makuwira, Naohiro Nakamura, Jonathan Rigg, Albert Salamanca, and Pichamon Yeophantong. "Global Development." In *Routledge Handbook of Global Development*, edited by Kearrin Sims, Nicola Banks, Susan Engel, Paul Hodge, Jonathan Makuwira, Naohiro Nakamura,

Jonathan Rigg, Albert Salamanaca, and Pichamon Yeophatong. London: Routledge. Forthcoming.

Singh, Abhijit. "Sri Lanka's Quest for Strategic Prominence in the Indian Ocean." *Diplomat*, December 9, 2016. https://thediplomat.com/2016/12/sri-lankas-quest-for-strategic-prominence-in-the-indian-ocean.

Sluga, Glenda. *Internationalism in the Age of Nationalism*. Philadelphia: University of Pennsylvania Press, 2013.

Smith, Jeremy C.A. *Debating Civilisations: Interrogating Civilisational Analysis in a Global Age*. Manchester: Manchester University Press, 2017. Kindle.

Snodgrass, Judith. *Presenting Japanese Buddhism to the West: Orientalism, Occidentalism, and the Columbian Exposition*. Chapel Hill: University of North Carolina Press, 2003.

Sontag, Susan. *On Photography*. London: Allen Lane, 1978.

Spykman, Nicholas J. *The Geography of Peace*. New York: Harcourt & Brace, 1944.

Stacey, Kiran. "China Signs 99-Year Lease on Sri Lanka's Hambantota Port." *Financial Times*, December 11, 2017. https://www.ft.com/content/e150ef0c-de37-11e7-a8a4-0a1e63a52f9c.

Starr, S. Frederick. "Introduction." In *The New Silk Roads: Transport and Trade in Greater Central Asia*, edited by S. Frederick Starr, 5–32. Washington, DC: Central Asia-Caucasus Institute, 2007.

Storozum, Michael, and Yuqi Li. "Chinese Archaeology Goes Abroad." *Archaeologies: Journal of the World Archaeological Congress* 16 (2020): 282–309.

Strauch, Ingo. "Priority and Exclusiveness: Russians and Germans at the Northern Silk Road (Materials from the Turfan-Akten)." *Etudes de Lettres* 2–3 (2014): 147–78.

Sudakova, Elena, ed. *See USSR: Intourist Posters and the Marketing of the Soviet Union*. London: GRAD Publishing, 2013.

Sun Yifu. *From Venice to Osaka—A Voyage into Ancient Chinese Civilisation: UNESCO Retraces the Maritime Silk Route*. Beijing: China Pictorial Publishing Press, 1992.

Swenson, Astrid, and Peter Mandler, eds. *From Plunder to Preservation: Britain and the Heritage of the Empire, c. 1800–1940*. Oxford: Oxford University Press, 2013.

Szpilman, Christopher. "Western and Central Asia in the Eyes of the Japanese Radical Right." In *Japan on the Silk Road: Encounters and Perspectives of Politics and Culture in Eurasia*, edited by Selçuk Esenbel, 48–68. Leiden: Brill, 2018.

Tan, See Seng, and Amitav Acharya, eds. *Bandung Revisited: The Legacy of the 1955 Asian-African Conference for International Order*. Singapore: NUS Press, 2008.

Tanaka, Stefan. *Japan's Orient: Rendering Pasts into History*. Berkeley: University of California Press, 1993. Kindle.

Tankha, Brij. "Exploring Asia, Reforming Japan: Ōtani and Itō Chūta." In *Japan on the Silk Road: Encounters and Perspectives of Politics and Culture in Eurasia*, edited by Selçuk Esenbel, 156–80. Leiden: Brill, 2018.

Tao, De-Min. "Shiratori Kurakichi: 1865–1943." In *Encyclopedia of Historians and Historical Writing*, edited by Kelly Boyd, vol. 1, 1090. London: Fitzroy Dearborn Publishers, 1999.

Taskien, Mika-Matti. "On Building a Community of Shared Future for the United Nations: Analysis on China's Performance in the United Nations General Assembly 2013–2018." Master's thesis, University of Helsinki, 2020. https://helda.helsinki.fi/handle/10138/314319.

Thaw, Lawrence Copley, and Margaret S. Thaw. "Along the Old Silk Routes: A Motor Caravan with Air-Conditioned Trailer Retraces Ancient Roads from Paris across Europe and Half of Asia to Delhi." *National Geographic Magazine*, December 1940.

Thorndike Jr, Joseph J. "Geopolitics: The Lurid Career of a Scientific System Which a Briton Invented, the Germans Used and Americans Need to Study." *Life*, December 21, 1942.

Thorsten, Marie. "Silk Road Nostalgia and Imagined Global Community." *Comparative American Studies an International Journal* 3, no. 3 (2005): 301–17.

Thubron, Colin. *The Lost Heart of Asia*. London: Vintage Books, 1994.

Times (London). "Across Asia." March 16, 1931.

Times (London). "All Aboard for Russia." January 9, 1993.

Times (London). "Japan Air Lines." October 3, 1962, 3.

Times (London). "Samarkand to Bukhara." February 20, 1993.

Ting, Joseph. *The Maritime Silk Route: 2000 Years of the South China Sea*. Hong Kong: Urban Council, 1996.

Tiryakian, Edward. "Civilisational Analysis: Renovating the Sociological Tradition." In *Rethinking Civilizational Analysis*, edited by Saïd Amir Arjomand and Edward Tiryakian, 30–47. London: SAGE Publications, 2010.

Travelfilmarchive. "From New Lands to Old, 1938." Uploaded June 24, 2014. YouTube video, 25:15. https://www.youtube.com/watch?v=95BCZ9J2qq0.

Trigger, Bruce. *A History of Archaeological Thought*. Cambridge: Cambridge University Press, 1989.

Tsygankov, Andrei. "Mastering Space in Eurasia: Russia's Geopolitical Thinking after the Soviet Break-Up." *Communist and Post-communist Studies* 36 (2003): 101–27.

Tsygankov, Andrei. "Uses of Eurasia: The Kremlin, the Eurasian Union, and the Izborsky Club." In *Eurasia 2.0: Russian Geopolitics in the Age of New Media*, edited by Mark Bassin and Mikhail Suslov, 63–80. Lanham: Rowman & Littlefield, 2016.

UNESCO. "Hirayama Fellowships." *Integral Study of the Silk Roads: Roads of Dialogue Newsletter*, 1995.

UNESCO. *Integral Study of the Silk Roads: Roads of Dialogue Newsletter*, 1995.

UNESCO. "Project News 1990/1991." *Integral Study of the Silk Roads: Roads of Dialogue Newsletter*, Spring 1989.

UNESCO. "Rediscovering the Silk Roads." *UNESCO Courier*, November 1988.

UNESCO. "Status of Contributions to the Regular Budget as at 17 December 2020." Accessed December 19, 2020. http://www.unesco.org/new/en/member-states/mscontent/status-of-contributions/.

UNESCO. "The International Network for the Silk Roads Programme." Accessed November 12, 2020. https://en.unesco.org/silkroad/international-network-silk-roads-programme.

UNESCO. "Youth Eyes on the Silk Roads Photo Contest." Accessed December 18, 2020. https://unescosilkroadphotocontest.org/.

UNESCO Kazakhstan. "At UNESCO, Kazakhstan's President Nazarbayev Calls for Intercultural Dialogue to Counter Extremism." Accessed July 18, 2018. http://www.unesco.kz/new/en/unesco/news/2998 (site discontinued).

UNESCO Kazakhstan. "UNESCO and 'The Centre for the Rapprochement of Cultures' in Kazakhstan have Defined an Action Plan for the Intercultural Dialogue." Last modified August 5, 2016. http://en.unesco.kz/the-first-scientific-and-methodological-meeting-of-the-council-of-the-state-museum-of-the.

UNESCO and Republic of Korea Funds-in-Trust-Project. *Support for the Preparation for the World Heritage Serial Nomination of the Silk Roads in South Asia.* Paris: UNESCO, 2016. http://unesdoc.unesco.org/images/0024/002460/246096e.pdf.

UNESCO and United Nations. *Dialogue among Civilisations; The Round Table on the Eve of the United Nations Millennium Summit.* Paris: UNESCO, 2001.

United Nations Alliance of Civilizations. "Al-Nasser Remarks at the High Level Symposium on the Synergies along the Silk Road for the 2030 Agenda for Sustainable Development." Last modified March 28, 2016. https://www.unaoc.org/2016/03/al-nas ser-remarks-at-the-high-level-symposium.

United Nations Alliance of Civilizations. "'The Silk Road Concert' Promoting Dialogue among Cultures Kicks-off at Palais des Nations, Co-organized by UNAOC and Fundación Onuart." Last modified October 16, 2017. https://www.unaoc.org/2017/10/ the-silk-road-concert-promoting-dialogue-among-cultures.

UNWTO. "Summary of Silk Road Activities 1993–2011." UNWTO Silk Road Programme. Accessed December 14, 2018. http://.silkroad.unwto.org/sites/all/files/docpdf/summ aryofactivities1993-2011.pdf (site discontinued).

UNWTO. "Technical Cooperation and Silk Road Declarations." Accessed December 7, 2018. https://www.unwto.org/declarations-silk-road.

UNWTO. *The Potential of the Western Silk Road—Working Paper.* Madrid: UNWTO, 2017.

UNWTO. *Western Silk Road Roadmap.* Madrid: UNWTO, 2018.

van Noort, Carolijn. *China's Communication of the Belt and Road Initiative: Silk Road and Infrastructure Narratives.* London: Routledge, 2021.

Vikram, Kumar. "Project Mausam Runs into Rough Weather." *New Indian Express,* January 22, 2017. http://www.newindianexpress.com/thesundaystandard/2017/jan/ 21/project-mausam-runs-into-rough-weather-1562182.html.

Vivekanandan, B. "The Indian Ocean as a Zone of Peace: Problems and Prospects." *Asian Survey* 21, no. 12 (1981): 1237–49.

Wakkumbura, Menik. "SL's Maritime Affairs in Changing Indian Ocean." *Daily Mirror (Sri Lanka),* October 11, 2018. http://www.dailymirror.lk/article/SL-s-Maritime-Affa irs-in-Changing-Indian-Ocean-156710.html.

Wallerstein, Immanuel. *European Universalism: The Rhetoric of Power.* New York: New Press, 2006.

Wallerstein, Immanuel, and Peter Philips. "National and World Identities and the Interstate System." In *Geopolitics and Geoculture: Essays on the Changing World-System,* edited by Immanuel Wallerstein, 139–57. Cambridge: Cambridge University Press, 1991.

Wang Gungwu. *China Reconnects: Joining a Deep-Rooted Past to a New World Order.* Hackensack: World Scientific, 2019.

Wang, Helen, ed. *Sir Aurel Stein, Colleagues and Collections.* London: British Museum, 2012.

Wang, Helen. "Sir Aurel Stein." In *From Persepolis to the Punjab: Exploring Ancient Iran, Afghanistan and Pakistan,* edited by Elizabeth Errington and Vesta Curtis, 227–34. London: British Muse um Press, 2007.

Wastnidge, Edward. *Diplomacy and Reform in Iran: Foreign Policy under Khatami.* London: I.B. Tauris, 2016.

Waugh, Daniel. "The Making of Chinese Central Asia." *Central Asia Survey* 26, no. 2 (2007): 235–50.

Waugh, Daniel. "Richthofen's 'Silk Roads': Towards the Archaeology of a Concept." *Silk Road* 5, no. 1 (2007): 1–10.

Waugh, Daniel. "The Silk Roads in History." *Expedition* 52, no. 3 (2010): 9–22.

Werner, Cynthia. "The New Silk Road: Mediators and Tourism Development in Central Asia." *Ethnology* 42, no. 2 (2003): 141–59.

Wheeler, W.E. "The Control of Land Routes: Russian Railways in Central Asia." *Journal of the Royal Central Asian Society* 21, no. 4 (1934): 585–608.

Whitfield, Susan. *Life along the Silk Road.* Berkeley: University of California Press, 2015.

Whitfield, Susan. "Scholarly Respect in an Age of Political Rivalry." In *Russian Expeditions to Central Asia at the Turn of the 20th Century*, edited by Irina F. Popova, 203–19. St Petersburg: Rossiiskaia Akademia Nauk, Institut vostochnykh rukopisei rossijskoi Akademii nauk, 2008.

Whitfield, Susan. *Silk Roads: Peoples, Cultures, Landscapes.* Berkeley: University of California, 2019.

Whitfield, Susan. "Was There a Silk Road?" *Asian Medicine* 3 (2007): 201–13.

Wilford, John Noble. "New Finds Suggest Even Earlier Trade on Fabled Silk Road." *New York Times*, March 16, 1993. https://www.nytimes.com/1993/03/16/science/new-finds-suggest-even-earlier-trade-on-fabled-silk-road.html#whats-next.

Winter, Tim. "Geocultural Power: China's Belt and Road Initiative." *Geopolitics* (2020), doi.org/10.1080/14650045.2020.1718656.

Winter, Tim. *Geocultural Power: China's Quest to Revive the Silk Roads for the Twenty-First Century.* Chicago: University of Chicago Press, 2019.

Winter, Tim. "Heritage and Nationalism: An Unbreachable Couple?" In *The Palgrave Handbook of Contemporary Heritage Research*, edited by Steve Watson and Emma Waterton, 331–45. London: Palgrave Macmillan, 2015.

Winter, Tim. "Heritage Diplomacy." *International Journal of Heritage Studies* 21, no. 10 (2015): 997–1015.

Wong, Laura. "Relocating East and West: UNESCO's Major Project on the Mutual Appreciation of Eastern and Western Cultural Values." *Journal of World History* 19, no. 3 (2008): 349–74.

Wood, Frances. *The Silk Road: Two Thousand Years in the Heart of Asia.* Berkeley: University of California Press, 2002.

Wu Jianmin. "'One Belt and One Road,' Far-Reaching Initiative." *China-US Focus*, March 26, 2015. http://www.chinausfocus.com/finance-economy/one-belt-and-one-road-far-reaching-initiative/.

Xi Jinping. "Speech by H.E. Xi Jinping President of the People's Republic of China at UNESCO Headquarters." Speech at UNESCO headquarters, Paris, France, March 28, 2014. https://www.fmprc.gov.cn/mfa_eng/wjdt_665385/zyjh_665391/t1142560.shtml.

Xie Laihui. "The Belt and Road Initiative and the Road Connecting Different Civilisations." In *Routledge Handbook of the Belt and Road*, edited by Cai Fang and Peter Nolan, 165–70. London: Routledge, 2019.

Yang Jiechi. "Jointly Undertake the Great Initiatives with Confidence and Mutual Trust." Speech at Boao Forum for Asia Annual Conference, Bo'ao, Hainan, April 10, 2014. http://www.fmprc.gov.cn/mfa_eng/wjdt_665385/zyjh_665391/t1145860.shtml.

Yang, Yang. "Producing Multiple Imaginations of the Silk Road in Xi'an, China's Urban Development." *International Journal of Cultural Policy* 26, no. 6 (2020): 854–66.

Yang, Yi Edward. "China's Strategic Narratives in Global Governance Reform under Xi Jinping." *Journal of Contemporary China* 30, no. 128 (2021): 299–313.

Yanik, Lerna K. "The Metamorphis of Metaphors of Vision: 'Bridging' Turkey's Location, Role and Identity after the End of the Cold War." *Geopolitics* 14, no. 3 (2009): 531–49.

Yellen, Jeremy A. *The Greater East Asia Co-Prosperity Sphere: When Total Empire Met Total War*. Ithaca: Cornell University Press, 2019. Kindle.

Ying, Hu. "'Would That I Were Marco Polo': The Travel Writing of Shan Shili (1856–1943)." In *Traditions of East Asian Travel*, edited by Joshua A. Fogel, 144–66. New York: Berghahn Books, 2006.

Yu Quiyu. *A Bittersweet Journey through Culture*. New York: CN Times Books Inc., 2015. Kindle.

Zhao, Suisheng. "Why China's Vaccine Diplomacy Is Winning." East Asia Forum. Last modified April 29, 2021. https://www.eastasiaforum.org/2021/04/29/why-chinas-vaccine-diplomacy-is-winning/.

Zhu, Yujie, and Christina Maags. *Heritage Politics in China: The Power of the Past*. London: Routledge, 2020.

Zou Dongxin. "PRC Medical Internationalism: From Cold War to COVID-19." ARI Scope. Last modified January 21, 2021. https://ari.nus.edu.sg/ariscope/prc-medical-internationalism-from-cold-war-to-covid-19/.

Zwigenberg, Ran. *Hiroshima: The Origins of Global Memory Culture*. Cambridge: Cambridge University Press, 2014.

Index